Navigating Fieldwork in the Social Sciences

"This book offers moving accounts of risk, vulnerability and the resoundingly human encounter that is fieldwork. Delivered as a generous exercise in reflexive consciousness, it is an education in self-care through story-telling, delivering as it does a searching analysis of the tender, messy, and moving encounters we share while learning with and from others. Fieldwork changes us, and writing of how we are changed takes courage."
—Amanda Kearney, *Co-author of Reflexive Ethnographic Practice and Professor at Flinders University, Australia*

"This book offers lucid and insightful discussions on negotiating the risks, problems and perils of conducting ethnographic research in the social sciences. Covering such diverse populations as sex workers, refugees, street gangs, anarchists, and even Taliban warlords, the authors have produced a must-read for anyone interested in ethnographic fieldwork."
—Mark S. Hamm, *Professor of Criminology and Criminal Justice at Indiana State University, USA*

"This edited collection is about the many risks of field research, including risks that continue long after fieldwork ends. It speaks to the critical importance of field research, but also the need to be aware of the risks that come with it. Ethical fieldwork that does no harm, and is safe for researchers, co-workers and communities starts with honest stories from fieldworkers. This book tells these stories, stories that will emotionally and intellectually challenge readers of all kinds. Read this book!"
—Dorothea Hilhorst, *Professor of Humanitarian Studies, Erasmus University, The Netherlands*

Phillip Wadds • Nicholas Apoifis
Susanne Schmeidl • Kim Spurway
Editors

Navigating Fieldwork in the Social Sciences

Stories of Danger, Risk and Reward

palgrave
macmillan

Editors
Phillip Wadds
School of Social Sciences
UNSW Australia
Sydney, NSW, Australia

Nicholas Apoifis
School of Social Sciences
UNSW Australia
Sydney, NSW, Australia

Susanne Schmeidl
School of Social Sciences
UNSW Australia
Sydney, NSW, Australia

Kim Spurway
Institute for Culture and Society
Western Sydney University
Sydney, NSW, Australia

ISBN 978-3-030-46854-5   ISBN 978-3-030-46855-2 (eBook)
https://doi.org/10.1007/978-3-030-46855-2

© The Editor(s) (if applicable) and The Author(s) 2020

This work is subject to copyright. All rights are solely and exclusively licensed by the Publisher, whether the whole or part of the material is concerned, specifically the rights of translation, reprinting, reuse of illustrations, recitation, broadcasting, reproduction on microfilms or in any other physical way, and transmission or information storage and retrieval, electronic adaptation, computer software, or by similar or dissimilar methodology now known or hereafter developed.

The use of general descriptive names, registered names, trademarks, service marks, etc. in this publication does not imply, even in the absence of a specific statement, that such names are exempt from the relevant protective laws and regulations and therefore free for general use.

The publisher, the authors and the editors are safe to assume that the advice and information in this book are believed to be true and accurate at the date of publication. Neither the publisher nor the authors or the editors give a warranty, expressed or implied, with respect to the material contained herein or for any errors or omissions that may have been made. The publisher remains neutral with regard to jurisdictional claims in published maps and institutional affiliations.

Cover illustration: Sabphoto, Shutterstock

This Palgrave Macmillan imprint is published by the registered company Springer Nature Switzerland AG.
The registered company address is: Gewerbestrasse 11, 6330 Cham, Switzerland

Foreword

As Head of the School of Social Sciences at UNSW Sydney, I have had the great privilege of working alongside every contributor in this book, *Navigating Fieldwork in the Social Sciences: Stories of Danger, Risk and Reward*. I know their work, and the commitment and quality they bring to their research. I also know of the struggles that are so eloquently captured in this unique and innovative edited collection. The first-person narratives presented in this book are powerful accounts demonstrating the ways in which risks in social science research are experienced and conceived throughout the conduct of fieldwork. My own experience of empirical fieldwork is that risk is unavoidable, but it is more than that; it is generative, producing tensions that at the very least demand critical reflection and thoughtfulness about our relationship with those we are researching and who might benefit from our work. Risk is, in many ways, also necessary to the conduct of the types of field research that make a difference.

Like many of the contributors in this book, my journey as a researcher is deeply rooted in my earlier political activism. While this seems an incredibly long time ago now, the lessons learnt have been ongoing and remain salient today. For me, back then, politics was a way of life. It was (and still is) how I made sense of the world, providing me with a purpose and ethical compass.

I grew up with an acute awareness of class and gender inequality. Coming from a working-class background, it was clear to me that the world was divided by socio-economic privilege, or lack thereof. Most Sunday mornings we all sat quietly while my Grandmother listened to Bob Santamaria, the leader of the Democratic Labour Party (DLP) and staunch right-wing Catholic. During my early school years, Australia was involved in a war with Vietnam. While too young to attend Moratorium marches, I could only understand our nonsensical involvement in a civil conflict where we had no interest whatsoever as racist—yet totally consistent with Australia's xenophobic stance towards migration, or I should say *some* migration. So in essence my childhood was shaped by the politics of the time—Germaine Greer's Female Eunuch (which I only understood some years later), the election of Gough Whitlam and a Labor government when I was in primary school, the outrage of his dismissal. I consider myself lucky to have grown up at this time. We questioned all institutions, and social and cultural practices and we held great hopes for change, for a more equal and inclusive society.

It was no surprise to anyone when I started working in my first Women's Refuge at 19 years of age—a committed, self-proclaimed socialist feminist studying a Bachelor of Social Studies. The era of 'new' social movements with the maxim that the *personal was political* was, for me, significant. I still believe this adage to be true; politics are not divorced from our everyday lives, the ways we choose to live. The choices we make cannot and should not be divorced from our political convictions. Back then, feminist struggles were inevitably characterised by risk, whether it be retribution from perpetrators, slurs on individual reputations, loss of employment or risk of arrest during protest action. Many feminists from that time had files with Special Branch and it was known then and we subsequently found out that Federal Police Officers infiltrated feminist groups to report on their actions. Despite these risks, our political actions were transformative and, of course, always personally challenging.

While there was no *one* feminism or singular political focus, there was a definite shared commitment by social actors who saw themselves as part of the 'women's movement' to other struggles. In the 1980s, the spike of HIV infections and deaths of our gay brothers from AIDS-related conditions demanded solidarity and action. We held candlelight vigils, contributed to the Quilt Project, and organised grass roots activism to establish community-run services such as Community Support Network (CSN) and Ankali. Protest marches against advertising campaigns such as the 'Grim Reaper' and activism to pressure government to allow drug treatments to be trialled in Australia and the occasional graffiti campaign were commonplace. While I would never publicly acknowledge membership of Bugger Up or any related graffiti activities (at the time activists could be sacked from their employed positions), it is fair to assume I am competent at community art.

Our unprecedented social actions to end violence against women and children resulted in extraordinary successes, achieving legal and policy reform and service development in areas of domestic violence, sexual assault and child sexual abuse. Consistent with our convictions, political actions were based on privileging the lived experience and wisdom of those affected by gendered violence. Community activists worked hand-in-hand with a new breed of bureaucrat who fast became known as 'femocrats', a term which designated their feminist politics and allegiance with activist groups. At the time there were criticisms that liberal feminism embodied in the femocrat role diluted a more radical agenda of change. However, it is undeniable that femocrats were able to influence the opinions of government by bringing the stories of women and children to the fore. We learnt quickly that credible evidence was required to substantiate the social and political changes we were demanding. Essentially our research field was situated in our political struggles, and our findings authentically reflected women's and children's experiences of gendered violence. While our research methods were scrupulously rigorous, they were most definitely and inextricably bound to our political convictions.

Reading through this collection of local and global field experiences has resonated strongly with the insights gleaned over my many years as a researcher. Each chapter offers guidance to help understand or manage risk in the field. In doing so, they address issues that are usually not spoken of, effectively unmasking the silences that frequently inhabit discussions of methodology and methods. The entirety of this edited collection provides a more honest conversation about risk in fieldwork, in stark contrast to the somewhat ubiquitous sanitised presentation of methods in many research texts inferring all risk can be easily managed or avoided.

While each chapter issues a slightly different challenge for the reader to consider, for me, there were universal themes entwined through the book that all researchers must inevitably tussle with when they enter the field. A passion that I share with the contributors in this collection is that I consider it essential to research in areas that I genuinely care about, that pass what I call the 'so what?' test. Any research I undertake must have a purpose that contributes to political and social change in some way. The research must matter, and relationships with partner participants and other social actors in the field must be both central to the research process and meaningful. Political convictions and research goals can at times be an uneasy pairing, and boundaries between these two roles can be blurred or sometimes non-existent. However, the depth of relationship that evolves for any researcher, where their commitment to a community or political cause matters, has the potential to enrich the research process and outcomes. The strength of relationship between the researcher and field is significance to forging an ethical research process and demands ongoing assessment and management of risk.

It was apparent to me in reading the book that all contributors in this collection have forged deeply meaningful relationships with partners, collaborators, participants, and co-researchers. I recognise this as a privileged position. The centrality of the relationships we forge, or are already a part of, is therefore protective, and the constant critical reflection that all contributors describe in various ways effectively functions to identify and manage potential risks. Yet with it comes a vulnerability (or dare I suggest risk) of having to manage expectations of the research process and project outcomes by our partners/co-researchers or a need to think strategically about how to position findings so that they constructively address our partner's goals.

Indeed, I have often agonised over the most productive way to present findings, and, at times, have struggled with mediating different needs and political perspectives both within partner groups and between partners and funders. I have learnt the importance of working with all parties from the commencement of the project to ensure a joint understanding of goals and a shared political vision. These are very real tensions, laid bare throughout this book. The contributors are patently aware of the responsibility to present their findings in ways and in forums that do no harm to their partners or political purpose. This involves scrupulous attention to maintaining the confidentiality of partners and participants, choosing carefully what data is presented and in what ways, and ensuring the narrative of their research authentically captures what they observed, the data they collected, and protects, or at least honours, the political intentions of field actors. This type of consideration must be empathic and recognise that all participants are taking a risk in sharing their stories, be it either physical or to their sense of self.

The most obvious risk that I have not commented on which all chapters deal with to varying extents is the actual physical risks of undertaking fieldwork—particularly evident in the chapters where contributors were undertaking field research in contexts of civil strife and war or where criminal activities were the focus of the research. The physical risks to the researcher, participants, partners, and to others in the field space are real and potentially lethal. Demonstrated respect for cultural customs and traditions, listening to the advice of local stakeholders, and being able to pull back research goals and aims where necessary are but a few of the strategies nominated. More to the point, as many of the contributors noted, if anything could be traced back to your international contacts, the research could became a literal 'kiss of death'. The chapters contain elegant strategies and solutions to reduce such risks and in particular it was clear that contributors were deeply respectful of their partners' capacity to make informed choices about their own risk, and for many, they were living and managing these risks in their everyday lives in any case.

For all field researchers there is a growing concern about University ethics requirements. Increasingly, University ethics processes have become more formalised which, in some senses, makes it much more difficult to undertake social science research in the field. Formulaic and instrumental ethics protocols seek to eliminate risk by changing the nature of the proposed research or altering research questions to make them 'safe'. I propose it is time for field researchers to push back and demand genuine engagement from Ethics Committees regarding potential risks—not to eliminate all risk from field work but to productively manage these risks. The alternative is to accept the limitations imposed by current Ethics regimes which would effectively limit the questions we can ask, exclude certain field contexts, and ensure the stories of marginalised and oppressed groups remain untold.

Put simply, this edited collection is a compelling *must read* for any researcher considering field research. Once read it is difficult not to conceptualise risk as a necessary and productive part of any research project. Each chapter beautifully describes the researcher's passion, the strength of their commitment to their relationships with partners and key stakeholders, and carefully crafted ethical processes. This work exemplifies that risk and ethically informed field research can and should go hand in hand.

Sydney, NSW, AustraliaJan Breckenridge

Acknowledgements

We acknowledge Aboriginal and Torres Strait Islander peoples as the first custodians of the lands and waters where we live and work. These are Stolen lands. We pay our respects to Elders past and present.

Always was, always will be.

We thank our collaborators for their contributions to this book and for all those who have been a part of our time in the field.

We thank the School of Social Sciences, UNSW, for providing funding for this project, and our amazing colleagues who we have had the privilege to work alongside.

We thank Professor Jan Breckenridge for her generous foreword.

We also thank our research assistant Timothy Edmeades, for his energy, diligence and professionalism.

Finally, we thank our families and partners. We could not have done this without you.

Now, we sleep.

Marching on together, you'll never walk alone.

Contents

1 Collecting Stories 1
  Nicholas Apoifis, Phillip Wadds, Susanne Schmeidl, and Kim Spurway

2 Sex in the Academy/Sex in the Field: Bodies of Ethics in Activist Research 13
  Zahra Zsuzsanna Stardust

3 Sitting with the Mess 39
  Caroline Lenette

4 Fear and Loathing in the Cross: Researching the Policing of Nightlife in Sydney 61
  Phillip Wadds

5 Doing Critical Drugs Research: From Deconstructing to Encountering Risk in the Field 85
  George Dertadian

6 'I Hope Little Worms Die in Your Arse': Fieldwork, Anarchists, Fascists and Academic Snitches 107
  Nicholas Apoifis

7   Doing Elite Interviews in Feminist Research: Confessions
    of a Born-Again Observationist   129
    Louise Chappell

8   Risking the Self: Vulnerability and Its Uses in Research   147
    Tanya Jakimow

9   Enter the Dragon: Coming of Age as Blond, White,
    Female Researcher in Fragile Contexts   163
    Susanne Schmeidl

10 'If You Want to Know About Evil, Ask the Devil':
    Research in Post-conflict Countries   189
    Kim Spurway

11 **Sharing Stories**   215
    *Phillip Wadds, Nicholas Apoifis, Susanne Schmeidl, and
    Kim Spurway*

Index   221

Notes on Contributors

Nicholas Apoifis is Senior Lecturer in Politics and International Relations at UNSW Sydney. He works with the application and development of settler-colonial theories, social movement theories and radical qualitative research practices. His 2017 manuscript, *Anarchy in Athens*, was based on unprecedented access to one of the world's most militant anarchist movements and involved highly engaged ethnographic fieldwork, referred to as militant ethnography. An aspect of this methodological approach has Apoifis disseminating his research insights and findings amongst international activist networks and anti-fascist and anti-authoritarian collectives.

Louise Chappell is the Director of the Australian Human Rights Institute and a Scientia Professor in the Faculty of Law, UNSW Sydney. Chappell has spent her career undertaking feminist research to understand how gender operates through various institutional arenas—parliaments, courts, building sites and other places—and has published widely in these areas. As a qualitative researcher, she is curious to try new methods, all the while recognising the limitations of these approaches and the ethical binds they can create. Chappell has two award-winning monographs, *Gendering Government: Feminist Engagement with the State in Australia and Canada* (2002) and *The Politics of Gender Justice at the International Criminal Court: Legacies and Legitimacy* (2016).

George Dertadian is a Lecturer in Criminology in the School of Social Sciences, UNSW Sydney. He is a social researcher interested in alcohol and other drugs, the sociology of crime and health, and social and cultural theory. Dertadian is author of *A Fine Line: Painkillers and Pleasure in the Age of Anxiety* (2019), which is the first full-length critical scholarly work to conceptualise the practice of the non-medical use of pharmaceutical pain medications. He has conducted several projects on the non-medical use of pharmaceuticals, focusing in particular on young people's use of opioids. Dertadian has also conducted research on the marginalisation of people who use and inject drugs, as well as the drug use of non-marginalised groups. He has conducted projects in field contexts such as the inner-city suburb of Kings Cross, in partnership with Sydney's Medically Supervised Injecting Centre and via online platforms. More recently, Dertadian has been a strong advocate for the expansion of supervised injecting facilities in Sydney.

Tanya Jakimow is Associate Professor of Anthropology at College of Asia and the Pacific, Australian National University. She is an Australian Research Council Future Fellow, working on a project examining women's political labour and pathways to politics in Medan, Indonesia, and Dehradun, India. She collaborates with scholars and practitioners in Indonesia, India and Australia, aiming to make theoretical contributions to the anthropology of politics (in particular, gender and politics) and to enhance understandings about the enduring problem of women's political under-representation.

Caroline Lenette is Associate Professor in the School of Social Sciences at UNSW Sydney and Deputy Director of the Australian Human Rights Institute. She is an arts-based researcher and teaches courses on qualitative research methods, research impact and ethics. Lenette has collaborated with resettled refugee-background women, people seeking asylum, youth advocates and artists on many participatory research projects in Australia. She has published widely on using creative methods like digital storytelling, participatory video, photography and music to explore the links between art, health and well-being, ethics and policy. She co-produces knowledge and co-writes with co-researchers with lived experiences to challenge and decolonise established research norms. She received a 2017 European Union–Durham University Co-fund International Senior Research Fellowship and a 2014 Endeavour Executive Fellowship. Lenette is editor-in-chief of the magazine *Human Rights Defender* and author of *Arts-Based Methods in Refugee Research: Creating Sanctuary* (2019).

Susanne Schmeidl is Senior Lecturer in Global Development at UNSW Sydney. A scholar-practitioner, she has nearly three decades of experience working at university, think tanks, non-governmental organizations and the United Nations. Her research journey started during a one-year social work field placement in a Mexico City slum, and she later facilitated a peace brigade in Nicaragua. Schmeidl co-designed the Conflict Early Warning and Response Mechanism for the Intergovernmental Authority on Development in the Horn of Africa. Since 2000 her primary research focus has been Afghanistan, where she lived over a decade working with two local organisations she co-founded. Schmeidl sees herself as a transdisciplinary peace and forced migration scholar, focusing on participatory action-research, aiming to understand the world while also changing it a peace at a time. She is the Current Perspectives Editor of the *Australian Journal of Human Rights* and sits on the Boards of Peacifica and the Research for Development Impact Network.

Kim Spurway works as a research associate at the Institute for Culture and Society at Western Sydney University. Her love of research started while she was managing nationwide research projects in post-conflict countries. She worked on these kinds of surveys for another ten years or so. She was paid by international non-governmental organisations (INGOs) to manage surveys in places like Vietnam, Lebanon, Iraq, the Democratic Republic of the Congo and Chad. Since returning to Australia, she has mostly focused on narrative research syntheses. Spurway has now returned to focus group discussions (yarning circles) and interviews in her current projects. In addition to humanitarian emergencies and natural disasters, she also works on projects about disability, indigeneity and queerness. Spurway is writing an auto-ethnography based on her years working in the humanitarian mine action and development sectors.

Zahra Zsuzsanna Stardust is a sex worker, lawyer, artist and academic whose work is concerned with intersections between criminal law, sexuality, labour and justice. Her doctoral research examines feminist pornographies, regulatory fantasies and resistance politics and draws upon her experience as a porn performer. She has worked in human rights and social justice projects for over fifteen years with community organisations, NGOs and United Nations bodies in areas of sex worker rights, LGBTIQ health and HIV prevention. Her films have screened at festivals across Europe and North America and she is on the editorial board of the academic journal *Porn Studies*. She is a former Penthouse Pet and Hustler Honey and was the 2014 Feminist Porn Awards Heartthrob of the Year. Her writing has been published by Palgrave, Routledge and Cambridge University Press.

Phillip Wadds is Senior Lecturer in Criminology at UNSW Sydney. He has spent the last decade undertaking ethnographic and field-based research examining various features of nightlife in Sydney with an enduring focus on its policing and regulation. More recently, he has been appointed to a number of local government advisory panels tasked with developing new nightlife policy. Each of these experiences has provided unique and first-hand insight into the dramatic and ongoing recent changes in Sydney's night-time economy. His monograph *Policing Nightlife: Security, Transgression and Urban Order* was published with Routledge in 2020 and examines the inherent challenges of policing unruly bodies in urban nightlife settings, as well as the work cultures of both public and private police engaged in this space.

1

Collecting Stories

Nicholas Apoifis, Phillip Wadds, Susanne Schmeidl, and Kim Spurway

It was late in the trimester. A few of us were sitting on our university's library lawn drinking coffee, chatting about the world. One of our colleagues, an experienced fieldworker, approached, bustling anxiously. They looked stressed, their fast-paced walk shackled by a burden that needed to be released. They had been looking for us. They had no time for niceties. There were no greetings. When a story begins without pleasantries, you know to shut up and listen.

Their book was due at the publishers in two days, and they were panicking. They laid out their reasons, their fears. They were writing about

---

N. Apoifis (✉) • P. Wadds • S. Schmeidl
School of Social Sciences, University of New South Wales,
Sydney, NSW, Australia
e-mail: n.apoifis@unsw.edu.au; p.wadds@unsw.edu.au;
s.schmeidl@unsw.edu.au

K. Spurway
Institute for Culture and Society, Western Sydney University,
Sydney, NSW, Australia
e-mail: k.spurway@westernsydney.edu.au

© The Author(s) 2020
P. Wadds et al. (eds.), *Navigating Fieldwork in the Social Sciences*,
https://doi.org/10.1007/978-3-030-46855-2_1

some heavy violence, a rough and tumble world they had worked so hard to get access to. It had nearly broken them. But they had prevailed, sort of. They now had these deep and confronting stories about life on the streets in some place, somewhere, emancipating a whole collection of visceral lived experiences. Another facet of our human complexities to be brought to a new audience. But this was a brutal space to be writing about—where recriminations were vicious and swift. And their work, their book, was full of intensely personal encounters, with identities that needed to be protected. Had they de-identified enough? What if someone could work out who the characters were? What if someone gets beaten up, or worse, dies because of this book? For the next two hours, we heard their concerns. We listened. And, in return, we offered insights from our own work, our own research, our own time in the field. Because we understood, we empathised, and we sympathised with their plight. Because we knew what they knew: fieldwork never ends. The risk is ongoing, well after your body has left the space.

This edited collection came to life in that moment. It was born from a desire to share stories about fieldwork, stories that transcend disciplines and the rigidity, formality, and constraint of journal articles. We wanted fieldworkers to have a new body of work to mine, to learn from, and to enact in the field.

We didn't give our colleague advice. We didn't tell them what they should do. We gave them our stories, so that they could make their own decisions. And that is our hope with this book. This is a collection of first-person narratives that explore the physical, emotional, and psychological manifestations, and consequences, of risk and fieldwork; where risk *and* fieldwork are variably embodied, experienced, and conceived.

The authors of these chapters are all academics who benefit from privilege in myriad ways. But a personal privilege, a luxury we all share, is that we get to have these amazing conversations about fieldwork with our colleagues; in the corridors, in meetings, and at the pub. We have discussions across disciplines, across demarcated fields of study, sharing familiar and unfamiliar methodologies, locations, and research paradigms. All of the contributors to this book have also, at one stage, shared a physical space, a geographical location of employment, the University of New South Wales, Sydney. And through a web of interactions, fleeting moments here, longer moments there, we have shared our fieldwork experiences. This edited collection animates these discussions. It captures fragments of these conversations but reconstitutes them in a particular form; as candid, vulnerable, and inviting narratives.

Why Risk?

We know that undertaking field research can be a risky and dangerous enterprise. A long list of ethnographies from sociology, anthropology, development studies, peace studies and, more recently, criminology corroborate this claim (for example, see Apoifis 2017; Bourgois 1995; Ferrell 1996; Ferrell and Hamm 1998; Hobbs 1988; Hobbs et al. 2003; Jacobs 1998; Knott 2019; Lee-Treweek and Linkogle 2000; Lyng 1990; Sanchez-Jankowski 1990; Scheper-Hughes 1992; Shesterinina 2019; Wadds 2020; Whyte 1943; Westmarland 2001; Winlow 2001). Conducting and producing field research presents particular risks that require careful navigation. In these spaces, the line between safety and danger can be crossed in quick time, often with little warning.

These risks manifest in diverse and novel ways. They can be physical and psychological, ephemeral and enduring. They can impact the researchers, participants, collaborators, and interviewees. They can affect our families, our work life, our reputations, and our employment. Indeed, they can condition the very foundation of our processes of knowledge production.

Field research is also intrusive. It is transformative. It can alter lives and communities. When done well, it enables the telling of powerful and important stories. It can give public voice to those who are deliberately marginalised. It can speak truth to power. When done poorly, however, it can be extractive and destructive, entrenching oppression and subjugation. Fieldwork, in any context, is no small-stakes game.

But What Is Risk, and How Is It Conceived?

The social sciences demand definitions. 'Risk' needs to be put into a box: disciplinarily siloed, categorised, and necessarily restricted. Controversially perhaps, as editors, we have deliberately resisted such protocols. We don't define 'risk' (and we certainly don't define 'the field'). The purpose of this collection is to transcend these boundaries that limit our conceptualisation and engagement with risk *and* fieldwork. We encouraged our contributors to play with the idea of risk, to bring to the fore their unique and diverse understandings of what risk means to them. In doing so, we believe readers will be better equipped to deal with the intricacies and uncertainty of everything that field research entails.

Collated, curated, and presented in this form, these diverse and idiosyncratic narratives from across the social sciences showcase first-hand stories of danger, risk, and reward. Not simply an edited book about risk in the field, this collection offers an arsenal of practical examples where fieldworkers have attempted to negotiate these complexities.

And we need these stories.

Given the nature of our work, given the fact that we are dealing with systems of power, people, and places that are in constant flux, we need to continually adapt. We need to be perpetually learning. And it is through the sharing of stories—these vivid and immersive narratives—that we can begin to prepare for the risks that are ubiquitous to all fieldworkers. That is one of the purposes of this edited collection.

But we have to be honest. There is another reason. This is a resistance piece. We cannot speak about risk without speaking about ethics. And we cannot speak about ethics without speaking about the existential threat to embodied qualitative research coming from university ethics committees. This is serious business for us. We are worried. Our research is increasingly misunderstood and constrained by onerous and overbearing institutional demands. We are under attack. And we return to explore these sentiments in the epilogue.

With all of that in mind, we knew we wanted an edited collection from an inter-disciplinary group of researchers who had conducted fieldwork in a diverse range of intense research settings. We knew we wanted to ask them about risk. We knew we wanted them to move beyond clinical and clichéd responses. We wanted to challenge them to more deeply reflect on the risks they had faced, that they continue to face. And so, we chose to interview field researchers. After all, this is what we do.

Getting the Stories

For each chapter, two of the editors spoke at length with each of the chapter authors about their own fieldwork. The idea behind this was to have field researchers interviewing field researchers. We needed the authors to open up, to relax into the space, and to make themselves vulnerable. So we deployed our craft.

As interviewers, we used our shared knowledge, our familiarity and empathy with the contributors to build rapport. We listened to their stories. We chatted like old friends, and when needed, we pushed; we pushed to draw out the richness of these encounters, to uncover practices often normalised and made unexceptional through years of experience. This not only gave an energy to each interview, it fostered deeper reflections and more poignant responses.

Each interview went for between one and two hours. We spoke about risk in multiple forms. We asked about 'personal risk', like risks associated with physical harm, and the psychological toll and moral strain associated with researching particular groups or topics.

We discussed the diffusion of risks to others: our partners, our participants, our collaborators, and those peripherally connected to research projects. We talked about the complexity of working across cultures and languages and in spaces where customs are unfamiliar. We spoke about the challenges of working with translators, with large teams of research assistants, with financial 'sponsors' and donors, and within highly politicised contexts where different actors are *after* your data.

We asked about risk related to data collection and dissemination—risks to the production of knowledge. We asked about the impact of ethics processes, data ownership, funding concerns, post-colonial tensions, and potentially exploitative and gendered practices. We sought to draw out nuanced discussions about forms of power and privilege that often manifest in the formal and informal structures surrounding research.

Finally, we asked our contributors about their personal strategies for mitigating and managing these risks. We wanted to hear about the practices deployed to navigate the myriad challenges presented in the field.

These were the 'themes' covered during our interviews, but how much was said about each depended on the experiences of those we were speaking to. We weren't formal or rigid in moving through the same interview schedule. We wanted to encourage diverse and unique interpretations and expressions of risk. Working in the field is never the same. It is shaped by so many factors: age, gender, sexuality, employment, body size, language, ethnicity, and cultural competence. Our contributors represent this diversity, and they reflect on the way it shaped their time in the field. At the end of each interview, we sent the transcript to each author, to fine-tune and rearrange as they saw fit. These were their stories, and are the basis of each chapter in this book.

Presenting the Stories

We gave all the contributors one clear instruction: present the chapter in a conversational form.

We wanted to replicate the way we had heard these stories as we passed each other in the corridors or debriefed over beers at end-of-month drinks: as first-person accounts rich in nuance and colour. The chapters are presented in a accounts form, with gentle interjections from the interviewers used as signposts to signal a transition in direction or tact. In doing so, we position this body of work within a tradition that embraces the narrative style as a means of presenting unique stories (Frank 1998, 2001; Game et al. 2013; Goldberg 1988; Terkels 1992).

When given the opportunity to present in this style, some authors wrote colloquially, while others wrote more academically, mirroring the way they spoke in the interviews. We want readers to get a sense of tone and idiosyncrasies splashed across discrete chapters. We want *you* to feel when the pace of the chapter quickens or slows, the tempo a marker conveying emotions and sentiments. We want you to experience their bouts of doubt and confidence. Through the repetition of words—and matter of factness of tone—you may get a sense of the certainties and uncertainties in the moments they are describing. We want you to see their reflections played out on the page, the constant, incessant, and unending questioning of practices, of ethics, of purpose. We want you to sense their moments of confidence and clarity, and, in doing so, in reading these words, glimpse the erratic nature of fieldwork, its dynamism, ambiguities, and challenges.

These narratives invite you into a space. Standing alongside the authors, you bear witness to events, smells, and sounds. You get a sense of the physicality of these encounters. You are welcomed into moments, to vicariously experience the complexities of field research. We ask you to attend, to imagine, to transport yourselves into these places, spaces, and situations. We encourage you to read these chapters deeply.

Presented like this, the narrative form moves us away from more traditional, or perhaps at least more common, approaches in the social sciences, where we cut up interview quotes into bite-sized pieces. Where we truncate and direct meaning through the selective editing of spoken or written word. To qualify, we are not saying there is anything wrong with dissecting text; quite literally every one of the authors has presented writing in that way throughout our careers, but for this work we wanted to let that part of our training go. We wanted to move away from the search for 'underlying codes' or strict themes. We didn't want chopped-up quotes. Because when we cut up quotes, we tend to convey a clarity that just isn't there in the work. We mask the messiness of particular moments. We lose the poetry of voice, the tensions, trials, and tribulations. After all, this is the richness of the story, the necessary depth that encourages you as a reader to play with text in ways that resonate with you.

Ultimately, we are offering a body of literature that is yours to adapt. It is a handbook of insights for you to draw from.

The Structure

The ordering of chapters is based on the location of research undertaken, starting with local Australian research, and moving to fieldwork done around the world. This is a compilation of stories from research conducted in Afghanistan, Chad, DR Congo, Greece, the Horn of Africa, Iraq, Laos, Lebanon, Palestine, India, Indonesia, Mexico, the Netherlands, Vietnam, and Australia.

In Chap. 2, Zahra Stardust speaks of her experiences while undertaking auto-ethnographic fieldwork with sex workers, porn producers, and performers, both in Australia and internationally. From parental complaints to public outcry, community forums to fisting workshops, Zahra's chapter takes a personal journey into her pioneering, theoretically informed, activist research.

In Chap. 3, Caroline Lenette explores several challenging situations encountered over the last ten years in collaborative projects with refugee-background co-researchers in Australia. Using examples ranging from gender politics and academic writing norms, to juggling insider/outsider labels and self-care as diverse sources of risks, the chapter offers candid reflections on wrestling with difficulties that can have a major impact on research outcomes.

In Chap. 4, Phillip Wadds details the lessons he has learnt from over a decade of field-based research in nightlife settings in Australia. He speaks candidly about the many challenges of undertaking research in field settings defined by inherent volatility, and highlights encounters involving severe violence, participant paranoia, and unfortunate cases of mistaken identity.

In Chap. 5, George Dertadian tells stories of frightening and uncomfortable scenarios he found himself in when doing critically-oriented drugs research in Sydney, Australia. He explores the risks faced by those committed to helping people who inject drugs, and who experience considerable harms associated with social marginalisation and criminalisation.

In Chap. 6, Nicholas Apoifis offers his honest reflections, insights, and concerns about the co-production and dissemination of activist wisdoms from his ethnographic fieldwork with anarchist and anti-authoritarian social movements in Athens, Greece. He highlights the intense demands of working with people at the frontline of the very real struggle against fascism, capitalism, and the state.

In Chap. 7, Louise Chappell considers the challenges of doing feminist research and 'elite level' interviews at the International Criminal Court. She shares her experiences of learning how to be a 'feminist critical friend' and highlights the limitations of interviews as a form of data when engaging with people in positions of power.

In Chap. 8, Tanya Jakimow writes of her field research interrogating new forms of decentralised governance and community-driven development in Medan, Indonesia, and in Dehradun, India. She discusses how long-term relationships between researcher and research participant are characterised by constant negotiation and moral risk. Tanya compels us to consider the importance and influence of vulnerability on both the self and others when conducting highly engaged ethnographic fieldwork.

In Chap. 9, Susanne Schmeidl speaks of her two decades of researching conflict and peacebuilding with grassroots organisations in Afghanistan, Mexico, and elsewhere. In particular, she writes of the risks to Afghan co-researchers, how to negotiate with insurgents and private security companies, and the risk associated with interviewing warlords and members of the Taliban. She tells stories of navigating a highly politicised and gendered environment where the lines between socio-political research and military intelligence are blurred.

In Chap. 10, Kim Spurway gives voice to her experience of undertaking fieldwork in insecure, high risk, post conflict settings in Africa, Asia, and the Middle East. She shares stories about being pushed out of her comfort zone while researching post-conflict landmine identification and removal in the 'Global South'.

And finally, in the epilogue, we wrap up the edited collection by pulling back the curtain and unveiling what we learnt while bringing this book together. We go 'behind-the-scenes' to highlight the struggles, extended conversations, and flurry of emails from contributors that reinforce the fact that risk and fieldwork have an enduring relationship that continues to require careful navigation long after we have left our research sites behind.

References

Apoifis, N. (2017). *Anarchy in Athens: An Ethnography of Militancy, Emotions and Violence*. Manchester: Manchester University Press.

Bourgois, P. (1995). *Search of Respect: Selling Crack in El Barrio*. Cambridge: Cambridge University Press.

Ferrell, J. (1996). *Crimes of Style: Urban Graffiti and the Politics of Criminality*. Boston: North Eastern University Press.

Ferrell, J., & Hamm, M. S. (1998). *Ethnography at the Edge: Crime, Deviance, and Field Research*. Boston: North Eastern University Press.

Frank, A. (1998). Just Listening: Narrative and Deep Illness. *Families, Systems & Health, 16*(3), 197–212.

Frank, A. (2001). Can We Research Suffering? *Qualitative Health Research, 11*(3), 353–362.

Game, A., Metcalfe, A., & Marlin, D. (2013). *On Bondi Beach*. Melbourne: Arcadia Press.

Goldberg, N. (1988). *Writing Down the Bones*. Boston: Shambala Press.

Hobbs, D. (1988). *Doing the Business: Entrepreneurship, the Working Class, and Detectives in the East End of London*. Oxford: Clarendon Press.

Hobbs, D., Hadfield, P., Lister, S., & Winlow, S. (2003). *Bouncers: Violence and Governance in the Night-Time Economy*. Oxford: Oxford University Press.

Jacobs, B. (1998). Researching Crack Dealers: Dilemmas and Contradictions. In J. Ferrell & M. Hamm (Eds.), *Ethnography at the Edge*. Boston: Northeastern University Press.

Knott, E. (2019). Beyond the Field: Ethics After Fieldwork in Politically Dynamic Contexts. *Perspectives on Politics, 17*(1), 140–153.

Lee-Treweek, G., & Linkogle, S. (Eds.). (2000). *Danger in the Field: Risk and Ethics in Social Research*. London: Routledge.

Lyng, S. (1990). Edgework: A Social Psychological Analysis of Voluntary Risk Taking. *American Journal of Sociology, 95*, 851–886.

Sanchez-Jankowski, M. (1990). *Islands in the Street: Gangs in American Urban Society*. Berkeley: University of California Press.

Scheper-Hughes, N. (1992). *Death Without Weeping: The Violence of Everyday Life in Brazil*. Berkeley: University of California Press.

Shesterinina, A. (2019). Ethics, Empathy, and Fear in Research on Violent Conflict. *Journal of Peace Research, 56*(2), 190–202.

Terkels, S. (1992). *Race: How Blacks and Whites Think and Feel About the American Obsession*. New York: New Press.

Wadds, P. (2020). *Policing Nightlife: Security, Transgression and Urban Order.* Oxon: Routledge.

Westmarland, L. (2001). Blowing the Whistle on Police Violence: Gender, Ethnography and Ethics. *British Journal of Criminology, 41*(3), 523–535.

Whyte, W. F. (1943). *Street Corner Society: The Social Structure of an Italian Slum.* Chicago: University of Chicago Press.

Winlow, S. (2001). *Badfellas: Crime, Tradition and New Masculinities.* Oxford: Berg.

2

Sex in the Academy/Sex in the Field: Bodies of Ethics in Activist Research

Zahra Zsuzsanna Stardust

I am a sex worker first and a researcher second. Or a writer second—I love writing. The research is really a means to document stories around me. My research is informed by my lived experience as a queer femme sex worker. I've been working in the industry for about 15 years in various capacities—as a stripper, adult model, full-service sex worker and porn performer. My background is unique as I have also worked as a lawyer, policy analyst and academic, so my research is interdisciplinary—it spans across gender studies, media studies, law, criminology, policy and sociology. My key interests are the intersections between sexuality, labour and criminalisation. Right now, I am collaborating on projects relating to sexual consent law reform, BDSM (Bondage/Discipline/Dominance/Submission/Sadism/Masochism) and the law, sex worker theory, feminist pornography as a social movement, and the gap between public health and criminal law approaches to HIV (*Human Immunodeficiency Virus*).

Z. Z. Stardust (✉)
School of Social Sciences, University of New South Wales,
Sydney, NSW, Australia
e-mail: z.stardust@unsw.edu.au

Sex work and sexual subcultures have been part of my life throughout my undergraduate and postgraduate degrees, and later in professional jobs. I was at Sydney University Law School, Australia, by day and working shifts in Kings Cross by night.[1] I was involved in human rights and social justice work throughout that time, including with the United Nations in Australia and internationally, working on gendered violence, discrimination and reproductive health. When I began my master's degree in Gender and Cultural Studies, I was interested in feminist activism and labour rights issues (like sham contracts and unenforceable penalties that were being issued in the clubs I worked at), so I began interviewing my peers and conducting an auto-ethnography of erotic performance—striptease, burlesque and queer performance art, which was thriving at that time in Sydney. Speaking with industry elders and pioneers was a really formative experience for me because the university texts I had read up until that point were dominated by second-wave feminism and so I was struggling with my own internalised stigma. Then I read Jill Nagle's *Whores and Other Feminists* (1997) and realised that we had our own sex worker feminism with its own histories, values and traditions. It totally changed my life.

Whilst I was sex working and studying, I ran for federal, state and local government as a candidate for the Australian Sex Party, for House of Representatives, New South Wales (NSW) Senate and Lord Mayor of Sydney. I advocated for LGBTIQA+ (lesbian, gay, bisexual, transgender, intersex, queer, asexual) rights, extension of medically supervised injecting rooms, decriminalisation of abortion, and to end religious exemptions to anti-discrimination law. During that time, I worked in the community sector as a policy advisor and international spokesperson for Scarlet Alliance, Australian Sex Workers Association, writing submissions and giving evidence at parliamentary inquiries on sex work law reform. After that I worked as the Manager of Policy, Strategy and Research for ACON, formerly the Aids Council of NSW, working with legislators and policy-makers on LGBTIQA+ health and wellbeing and HIV treatment and prevention. I was on the Board of the Gay and Lesbian Rights Lobby

---

[1] Kings Cross is an inner-city suburb and red-light capital of Sydney known for its sexual economies.

for a while at that time, and also volunteered with the Women's Justice Network assisting women exiting custody with social reintegration.

By the time I started my PhD research at the University of New South Wales I was working as a pornography performer. I saw a vibrant movement emerging around me for queer and feminist approaches to pornography and I really wanted to document it. I was aware that there was an onerous criminal framework around the production, sale and screening of pornography in Australia, and I was interested in what performers and producers had to say about it. These subcultures had their own ethical codes and self-governance processes which were far more sophisticated than the heavy-handed approach of politicians. I wanted to provide a space for sex workers to speak back to the law, to expose the divergent gap between how sex work is regulated and practiced.

What Does the 'Field' Mean to You? What Approaches Do You Use?

I did auto-ethnography. I really love it as a medium for linking personal experiences to broader cultural, structural and global themes. I think it is quite poetic and beautiful. I have read some auto-ethnography that is literary art. It really has capacity to move people, to invite readers into new world-views, to prompt them to make meaning out of everyday life. It's a form of reflexive storytelling that lingers and untangles and finds threads that might not otherwise exist. I think it is unique and necessary for those reasons.

The concept of 'the field' doesn't really resonate for me as an insider researcher. I understand that social sciences are vexed with questions of gaining access to various 'hard to reach' populations and subcultures, but I see that as a legacy of a colonialist, voyeuristic history. In my research there was no pretence that I was a neutral observer. There was no 'field'. There was just my life. Our lives. I didn't do anything differently; I just documented what was already happening around me. That's one benefit of insider research—when you are an active participant in those spaces, you are much more attuned to particular issues facing your communities.

Instead of trying to gain access, I think researchers should be thinking about how to build partnerships to support research emerging from within communities.

I knew most of my participants because I had been immersed in those spaces for many, many years, whether we were filming scenes together or working at our local sex work organisation or attending rallies together. Sexuality studies generally is a field where scholars and practitioners overlap—key figures like Michel Foucault and Gayle Rubin both drew from their personal experiences in queer subcultures. But also in porn communities, sex workers, sexological body workers, sex educators and artists are all collaborating. Thinking back to Annie Sprinkle's Public Cervix Announcement where she invited people to view her cervix through a speculum (Sprinkle 1998) or Betty Dodson's group masturbation 'Bodysex' workshops in her apartment (Weiss 2018) or Carol Queen's instructional home videos in anal sex (Fatale Media, Inc. 1998), there has been a real overlap between sexual cultures and the academy. Often qualitative researchers are expected to disavow sex or intimacy in the field, but some scholars argue that desire and attraction already influence fieldwork in an unconscious way (Martin and Haller 2018). Others argue that that fieldwork research into sexual interactions, networks and encounters (in particular, to understand social codes and conventions of cruising, hook-up cultures and anonymous sex) can be both useful and possible whilst maintaining professional ethics (Langarita Adiego 2017).

In my research, I offered up excerpts from behind-the-scenes—small peepholes into my life on set, at festivals and in forums. I called my method 'auto-pornographic ethnography', which was in part an extension of Kristen C. Blinne's approach in her writing on masturbation, which she describes as 'auto-erotic ethnography' (2012). Her work is inspired by Ken Plummer's (1995) work on the power of telling sexual stories and Audre Lorde's work on the erotic potential (1997). But I also wove in Paul Preciado's reference to the 'autopornographic body' (2013, p. 38), a phrase he uses to describe people who produce their sexual selves in an online commercial sex market. I wanted to explore how the pornographic self is manufactured, how we fashion and produce ourselves online. Creating porn for me was, in fact, quite ordinary, and I wanted to invite the reader in to experience it with me, in the hope that it would lead to different ways of understanding the labour of pornography, and in particular precarious, sexual labour in a gig economy.

And What Kinds of Spaces Did You Do Your Fieldwork In? What's It Like for You There?

Well, throughout the project I was running my own website and creating films for the international circuit. I performed with alternative Australian erotica companies, independent producers, feminist producers and individual sex workers. We created products that were sold on websites and DVDs, licenced to overseas companies and screened at film festivals. I worked both in Australia and internationally, including performing in 30 films and shooting scenes with performers from Sydney, Melbourne, Canberra, San Francisco, Los Angeles and London. I won awards for both porn performance and production—that was quite special, one of them was Feminist Porn Awards Heartthrob of the Year—and I screened films at festivals across North America and Europe. Various community groups in Australia fundraised to fly some queer porn performers and directors out here, such as Jiz Lee, Courtney Trouble, Madison Young and Tristan Taormino. I was really lucky to shoot with Jiz and Courtney while they were in Australia, to participate in Tristan's workshops and to host Madison Young in my home. I also collaborated on art projects related to pornography, including photo essays for queer women's health promotion, a durational window display for the Australian sex worker artist troupe Debby Doesn't Do it For Free, artist panels and sex education workshops. It was all stuff that was just going on in my life at that time.

A real highlight was attending the Feminist Porn Awards in Toronto in 2014. Australian producers were gaining profile and notoriety for our work, which had been sparked by the work of feminist producers such as Ms. Naughty and Anna Brownfield. The Feminist Porn Conference was on concurrently at the University of Toronto where performers, producers, academics and tech geeks all came together to talk about the politics of production, consumption and regulation. It was super surreal because people came together to screen and celebrate porn in public spaces in ways that you just can't in Australia. So on one night, there was a queue half way down the street of people lining up to the Hot Docs cinema to come and watch our porn. We were able to have all these critical conversations about content over popcorn and during the Q&A, which you can't always do in Australia because of the criminal laws. We even had a BBC journalist sit in and take notes on a threesome scene that I did with James Darling and Wolf Hudson (Nasaw 2014).

In Europe it was similar. When we were in Amsterdam, Gala Vanting and I ran a g-spot ejaculation workshop at a leather bar that actually received funding from a local Pride committee group (Stardust 2018). I screened some of my films at an independent cinema there for a night called Queer Porn Down Under. At the Berlin Porn Film Festival, I cofacilitated a fisting and ejaculation workshop with three other porn performers from France, the United States and Australia, Wendy Delorme, Sadie Lune and Gala Vanting, that involved live sex demonstrations. We used queer pornography as educative material, screening extracts from films, and using pleasure-based anatomical drawings that had been developed by sexologists and porn producers, the kind that don't ordinarily appear in medical textbooks. During the live demonstration, people could walk around us, interact with us, ask us questions. It was an incredibly special experience and it also emphasised to me how backward Australia's regulatory framework was.

This was all part of my ethnography, and it supplemented my qualitative interviews, legal analysis and archival review. I had mixed methods. I did 35 qualitative interviews with producers and performers and as well as industry and classification stakeholders. And I went down to the Eros Association Archives at Flinders University in Adelaide, which holds a whole lot of porn correspondence in a special collection you need permission to access, and the Australian Lesbian and Gay Archives in Melbourne, which have a really awesome collection of queer print materials like Slit Magazine and Wicked Women, which really paved the way for the film and digital pornographies we see now.

When I was designing the interview questions, I took as a starting point a documentary that had been screened at Berlin about independent pornography in Australia, which was made by a local partnership here called Sensate Films. I wanted to make sure that people actually involved in porn performance and production were setting the research agenda. From there I had a consultation process with Scarlet Alliance as the peak national body representing sex workers, and Eros Association, who had been the key industry lobbyists for sex industry businesses, as well as representatives from an Australian feminist porn panel held at the Perv Queerotic Film Festival, to ensure that the questions I was asking were relevant to the communities that I was studying and that they would inform a meaningful research agenda that would contribute a useful resource for activism.

Were There Legal Risks That Came with the Ethnography or Interviews?

Well, luckily I was researching production ethics rather than doing a content analysis, so that meant I avoided a lot of typical issues that plague porn researchers in terms of navigating university technology usage policies when you want to access porn online. But in my research, the risk of self-incrimination was obviously present. It is legal to produce and sell pornography in Australia in some limited places and via particular avenues, but so much of the law is also grey and selectively policed, especially now that people are producing online content. In 2009, Abby Winters, a Melbourne-based producer of girl-girl pornography was raided and charged, and in 2013, a manager of an adult store on Oxford Street in Sydney was incarcerated for three months for selling unclassified DVDs (Stardust 2014). In my interviews, producers reported having their hard drives confiscated at airports (even though they contained legal material), police raiding adult retail stores during election time, or not being able to advertise or screen their films. And so I didn't want my participants to admit to filming in a particular location or particular content that could potentially incriminate them if my research was ever subpoenaed.

So I put a number of precautions in place for the interviews. I borrowed some strategies from my supervisor Kath Albury, who had conducted research with young people into 'sexting' (Albury et al. 2013). In her research there was a risk that young people could potentially admit to producing and disseminating child pornography when they spoke about creating their own images and sharing with their peers. She had used techniques like asking people to speak in third person and interrupting people if they began to disclose details. I gave interviewees the questions in advance and gave people options of being identified by a pseudonym or business name. After the interviews I asked them to edit the transcripts so they could have better control over what data was on record, and also gave them an opportunity to elect to review draft publications. I then deleted all the audio so only the edited transcripts remain on record. I made sure the contact forms were kept separately to consent forms. If I did it again, I wouldn't use consent forms at all, I would just verbally record consent.

Rather than being a detailed history, I wanted the interviews to be about people speaking back to the law, because porn performers, producers and performers are rarely invited in for consultation on pornography law reform. It means that the popular and policy debates have stagnated around freedom and protection, speech and danger. And yet my participants were raising all these other issues about workplace health and safety, industrial rights, representation, access, monopolisation, distribution of wealth, which were being completely eclipsed by the dominant, tedious debates about pornography in media. And meanwhile, industry is developing their own ethical practices which governments should be listening to if they actually want effective, evidence-based policy.

What Kind of Things Were You Worried About Going into the Research? What Came to Fruition and Was It Expected or Unexpected?

Well, researching sex can be risky business, because sex work is treated differently than other occupations and attracts unjustified scrutiny. During my research I wrote an article for *The Conversation* on International Women's Day about porn tube monopolies and the importance of ensuring the profits are democratised and make their way down to independent producers, directors and performers, rather than being concentrated among private tech platforms. And somebody wrote an article in response that said that my piece would have been a marvel of Marxist analysis had the subject matter not been so 'putrid'. She was outraged that I was funded by an Australian Postgraduate Award and said that if I did get a PhD, 'so much worse for women, so much worse for Australia'.

So those kinds of things are always present, the risk of them is always present. The study of it is one thing, the teaching of it is another, the doing of it is something else. Academics like Brian McNair (2009) have spoken about their experiences teaching pornography, and the kind of hostile reception that they've received. Feona Attwood has suggested it's probably only a good idea to teach pornography if you already have tenure (2010, p. 178). Constance Penley, who is a porn professor at University of California Santa Barbara, had her porn studies course outline subpoenaed during the obscenity trial of John Stagliano (Penley 2015). So there are risks for researchers who are not even sex workers, and then if you come out as a porn consumer there's another stigma associated with that. Alan McKee (2017) has written about the Othering of porn consumers in legal, social and public policy debate. And then, for sex workers who are actually doing research ourselves, often there's a pressure for us to come out as 'former sex workers' to distance ourselves from work. Or there's assumptions that we will be biased, that we're too close to the subject matter. There have been a number of porn stars who've gone to speak at universities to share their experiences (Maxxine and Hidalgo 2015), although in some cases they have had their events cancelled, protested or faced backlash (Comella 2015, p. 283; Lee 2015, p. 272).

Has Anything Like That Happened to You?

A few years ago, when I was teaching a gateway criminology course at a Go8 university,[2] a student's father complained that I was a porn performer. He emailed the Dean of the Law Faculty who then emailed the Dean of Arts and Social Sciences with screen shots from my personal

---

[2] The Group of Eight (Go8) comprises Australia's leading research-intensive universities comprising some of the largest and the oldest universities in Australia.

Facebook page. Apparently, the father was outraged that the university would hire someone who was also a porn star. I was told the university was getting legal advice about whether it was ok for them to hire an academic who was also a sex worker. The complaint had nothing to do with my teaching, I had above average student evaluations, it was just someone's father who had a bee in his bonnet. But for me, early in my career, I had this moment where I thought, wow, I am never going to belong here, I was disillusioned to think that maybe I did. And a friend of mine, who was also a sex worker writing her PhD, said 'Zahra, none of that is your stuff, that is someone else's stuff. Don't let your internalised stigma get the better of you'. So I guess it had been there for some time in the back of my mind, an additional layer to the imposter syndrome. That we don't belong. That any moment someone might 'Google' me and find naked photos on the Internet. That I would never be able to work in criminal law or human rights because I was not a 'serious' candidate. I know better now how to exist more authentically and unapologetically in the system (that took a lot of work), but the experience of being a sex worker in the academy is quite a unique experience. Jennifer Heineman (2016) wrote her whole PhD thesis about how it can involve fragmenting out our bodily experiences and professional lives.

In another example, Lynn Comella, who is an Associate Professor of Gender and Sexuality Studies from the University of Nevada, came to Australia and we did a seminar together called 'The Future of Pornography'. We were speaking together at Max Black, which is a women-friendly adult boutique store in Newtown, and I suggested to her should we film our conversation and maybe put it on YouTube. Because that's always been something that's been very valuable to me, to be able to watch academic or industry conversations online, so they're accessible to people who couldn't attend in person. But Lynn was worried about the risks for her as an academic in the US, particularly in a Trump era. At that time, porn star Stormy Daniels had just been arrested in an Orlando nightclub after she had sued the President. And that kind of risk of repercussion is always there, it was something that came up constantly in my interviews: 'all it takes is one complaint', and then everything gets derailed.

Did You Feel Like There Was Institutional Support, and What Gets You Through That?

I wasn't sure at first whether there would be institutional support, and I wasn't sure who was safe to talk to about it. I really panicked; it was during my first fixed-term teaching role. Even now, I am a casual, sessional teaching staff, and I work across two buildings on campus on shared hot desks. In one space, I work down the hallway from someone who is very public about campaigning for the abolition of sex work and the criminalisation of clients. In the other, I work on the same floor as academics with pictures and quotes from notorious anti-sex work advocates Catharine McKinnon and Andrea Dworkin on their doors. Just last week, one colleague announced to me out loud in the hallway, 'I've just been watching your porn'. Sex worker friends of mine in the academy have faced sexualisation and sexual harassment from supervisors and have been vulnerable to sexual assault (Dr Anonymous 2020). People don't understand that sex workers have boundaries, or private lives, or that we selectively disclose. We are often treated like a public utility, open for dissection and available for invasive and inappropriate comments.

I think that is the fear for a lot of sex worker students. Students contact me all the time to disclose their sex work and ask for advice on whether they should continue their studies and how to navigate the academy. In disciplines like nursing or law or psychology, for example, where there are admissions and ethics boards that determine whether a person is fit to practice, sex workers are petrified of doing a whole degree and then finding out that they are not seen as eligible people who should be working in those professions. Many sex workers study social work; it is a natural extension of their skills as listeners and counsellors. But that subject is notorious for having saviours and rescuers who only see sex workers as victims and where sex work is seen as a 'risk factor'. It makes it difficult for sex workers to participate and engage in class discussions where their entire lived experience is dismissed. I know so many who have dropped out. My advice has largely been to find allies among the staff and students, to find out who would be there for you and stand up for you, and to create a bubble of support around you in order to survive in the institution.

How Do You Deal with the Emotional Outcomes? How Do You Balance Those Multiple Roles as Sex Worker, Activist and Researcher?

I think self-care has always been a big issue for sex workers because sex workers have issues with burn-out generally. It comes up a lot, not just because of the stigma or discrimination but because of the constant emotional and educative labour sex workers do for free just to occupy space. Sex workers have been developing self-care strategies and peer networks for a very long time. I have really relied on talking to peers to debrief and digest my experiences. There is only so much other academics can provide if they're not immersed in the industry or community itself. It can be a lonely business, being in the middle.

It can be a delicate task juggling multiple roles. I had to really learn how to separate out my voices. It was a massive learning journey. One supervisor often told me that my writing was too polemic, or that I needed to re-think who I was writing for, or that I needed to differentiate my academic voice from my policy voice. That was an interesting exercise—how to write strategically. Because it was an important part of my methodology that I brought it back to the community, that it wasn't just siloed to the ivory tower. You know, for any activist researcher it's important that your work can be accessible and disseminated. And given the current academic climate of publish or perish, where we are increasingly required to produce, produce, produce, and have these quantitative metrics that value and measure our productivity, it also is always important to remember, as Laura Pulido says (2008), that journal articles do not constitute a contribution back to the community. Like, whom is the research for? So I kept writing news pieces, policy submissions, for industry magazines and websites. I helped other sex workers to write their first submissions to government inquiries, proof read their work, found academic references and journal articles that were hidden behind pay walls and shared them. I have a lot of coffees with undergrad sex worker students just to talk about life and work and whorephobia. So all of that is important solidarity work.

You Have So Many Things to Juggle! Do You Ever Sleep?

Not really. I used to have a strategy where I didn't sleep on Monday nights because I could get an extra day out of the week. I did that for a couple of years, then I got completely run-down. I had to work on my own boundaries and self-care. But in this work, you don't have the luxury of switching off. And I think that's something that comes with also feeling under attack with your research—that you need to put rebuttals in place and build a buffer around yourself and have an encyclopedia of statistics in your brain ready just in case. Feeling the need to prove your worth as a sex worker but also because of the dominant influence that anti-sex work social commentators have on policy, media and government. And the ways in which you front up to that constantly in your day-to-day life in conversations with friends or family or on the street or on the news.

I did an interview recently with Julie Bindel, a UK journalist who is regularly invited to speak on national news programs and who promotes criminalising the purchase of sex. I really think it is an abrogation of their responsibility to pitch these issues as a two-sided debate. There is so much evidence now that decriminalisation of sex work is good for occupational health and safety, minimises risk of STI (sexually transmissible infection) and HIV transmission, and facilitates better access to justice. Sex workers all over the world are advocating for decriminalisation. And yet, it is constantly pitched in the media as an adversarial debate, as if those sides ought to be given the same sort of credibility and weight. And so, the issues become polarised, it totally reduces the nuance and complexity of the discussion, we lose any common ground we might have had, and evidence is represented as simply one of many opinions.

So, going on national TV is infuriating and exhausting, but it's necessary unpaid labour that we do to try and make our lives more liveable. On the one hand, you don't want to credit the wild hyperbole with a response. On the other, if no one is there to offer a counterargument, it could prompt a parliamentary inquiry the following day, and lead to even worse outcomes for the community. Are we complicit if we do nothing, and the narrative leads to greater risks and poorer material conditions for sex workers? I came back from that interview to a lot of messages from sex workers saying, 'take some self-care, take some time out'. I think there's a responsibility to do those things when you have the capacity to. But yeah, I went home and took a couple of Nurofen for my migraine and went to sleep.

What Is the Role of a Researcher, Given Your Concerns About How Knowledge Is Produced and Whose Voices Are Represented?

I think researchers need to think of ourselves less as experts and more as cogs within broader movements. Sex workers are already experts on their own lives. Researchers have access to information that we need to share widely among community. Some sex worker academics bring printouts of their research along to local forums so they can be accessed by individuals who don't have institutional journal subscriptions. Even while we are trying to publish open access, that kind of old school hard copy distribution is important. There are so many sex workers right now using their lived experience and specialised knowledge to conduct some awesome postgraduate research projects around Australia. Too many of us are white and cisgender. The real frontline work is happening in local sex worker organisations. Many of those people may never access academic institutions. That's why practice-led research is so important. And it is why academic forums and research journals should always proactively invite and make space to foreground the voices of practitioners and communities. Researchers ought to have a capacity-building function in that way, because research would not exist without participants.

Researchers also have an important referral function—we should be putting media in touch with local sex worker organisations, who can provide on-the-ground representation because of their extensive networks, steering committees, working parties and membership. I think we have a responsibility to use media opportunities wisely. I learnt the hard way not to trust media. Too often journalists want puff pieces or tragedy porn, and we have to redirect them. Most sex workers I know go through a lengthy screening process for journalists before they agree to engage with them, at least to find out the angle and who else they have interviewed. I almost always give interviews via email now because of the number of times I've been misquoted. Another sex worker Janelle Fawkes taught me to pay attention to the type of media you're doing, whether it is radio or print or television. If you are live on air, they can't easily stop you talking, so you can just let loose. But if you are being pre-recorded, you have to speak in sound bites so your messages aren't distorted in editing. It's a good idea to supply your own images or you will end up with stereotypical stock photos of headless women in fishnet stockings. But I think a real take-home lesson is that if you're approached by media as a researcher, you should always touch base with local sex worker organisations first and make sure that the comments you want to provide are aligned.

It's important to remember that I am operating within this space with a significant degree of privilege, as someone who will be treated as if my decisions are agentic. With insider research it's easy to fall into the trap of having a credibility fallacy. You know, just because we were all sex workers doesn't mean that we necessarily have shared experiences. We are all attuned to the regulatory risks of porn production in very different ways. Some states in Australia still make it an offence to do any kind of sex work if you are living with HIV, for example. For others, there could be risks of deportation for working in breach of visa conditions. In my interviews, gay male producers spoke very differently about their production ethics than queer feminist women. What constituted ethical porn production meant something much more specific for people with disability with particular access needs. Trans- and gender-diverse performers were also navigating stereotypes, fetishisation and pejorative marketing language, with compounded privacy implications of being out. So when we talk about 'nothing about us without us' in sex worker organising and among porn performers specifically, we are not a monolithic group—we are really a heterogeneous alliance of people of different identities, experiences and projects, classing ourselves together as a political alliance for a particular joint struggle. So we need to prioritise listening to people with the least privilege, whose lives are the most impacted by poor laws and policies.

What Are Some of the Challenges of Insider Research in Porn Studies, Being Part of the Communities You Are Studying?

Well, there are some important discussions happening at the moment around the ways in which feminist, ethical and queer porn producers—and in particular cisgender white women—are experiencing positive media reception and are taking up a lot of advocacy space that could be directed to address more pressing and urgent structural issues, such as racialised policing and carceral approaches. Many of us involved in pornography, although we experience specific risks related to image-based abuse, doxing, hacking or discrimination because of our visibility, are largely protected from the criminal 'justice' machinery that is directed towards some sex workers in our communities, particularly migrant, Aboriginal and street present workers. In her PhD thesis, Crystal Jackson (2013) argues that 'it is clear that the feminist sex wars never went away, they just re- focused from pornography to sex trafficking' (p. 188). In my research, sex workers were often very critical of how producers were marketing their content, especially in their language about green, organic or fair-trade pornography, or in their conflation of legality with ethics. Just because something is illegal does not make it unethical. And sometimes that language can create new hierarchies about what constitutes 'good pornography' and who deserves legal protection. We've seen from the gay and lesbian rights movement that when you only have privileged people at the top directing where the movement is going, it becomes very assimilatory and hand in hand with a capitalist state. So it is important that we keep coming back to a politics from below that is driven by people who experience the most shame and the most stigma, the most marginalisation.

In the writing up of my project, I made a deliberate decision to prioritise the voices of performers above producers. Sometimes this was complex, because often performers were also producers, either starring in their own content, or collaborating with other performers, or shooting others for their own sites or short films. But sometimes this distinction was clear-cut where websites were run by non-performers and they had received serious criticism from sex worker communities. This was an important step for me in foregrounding the needs and experiences of workers rather than the marketing campaigns of businesses. I didn't want it to be a soap box for people to self-promote their business. I wanted performers to hold those representations into account.

As a Lawyer and a Sex Worker, You Have Had Different Kinds of Contact with the Criminal Justice System, How Has That Affected Your Research and Your Fieldwork?

Obviously, sex workers experience massive barriers to accessing justice, and crimes against sex workers have not been taken seriously by police, prosecutors or judiciary. I've been working on a project for Scarlet Alliance and the UNSW Centre for Social Research in Health where we are measuring sex work stigma across Australia using both qualitative focus groups and a quantitative survey instrument and we have a lot of data about appalling experiences sex workers have had in the criminal legal system. On many occasions police and courts fail sex workers who experience sexual assault at work, because sex workers are seen as being in a state of perpetual consent by virtue of our work.

Sex worker organisations like Vixen Collective in Victoria have been doing some important training sessions with police on this issue. There are also some really significant changes happening right now via law reform commissions in multiple states as we move towards a model of communicative consent. Sex workers have really been leading conversations about boundaries and consent law reform. I am writing a piece with Hilary Caldwell, who wrote her PhD research about women who buy sex in Australia, about how sex workers have used sexual consent laws to convict clients who have obtained sex by fraudulent misrepresentations. I have been volunteering at the Inner City Legal Centre's Sex Worker Legal Service in Kings Cross, Sydney, which has assisted a number of sex workers where clients have reversed their transactions after the session or manufactured a false receipt of payment.

One important thing for me when doing my doctoral research was to ensure that, in a context in which sex work research is regularly cherry-picked, I build in some directives about how the research should not be used. So, just because there may be low compliance with the legal framework doesn't mean that we need more law enforcement. Just because some people disrespect the law doesn't mean we need more police. I wanted to critique the law and selective policing, but I didn't want it to be used to create laws or policies that place sex workers at further risk.

That was quite tricky for me during the writing process. I wanted to critique my own industry, whilst still recognising the agency and self-determination of people working within it, the importance of queer subcultures and feminist artistic representation and the significance of alternative pornographies to audiences in affirming and validating people's bodies and sexualities and desires. There were things I wanted to illuminate about the direction of the movement, in terms of being influenced by a politics of respectability. And I wanted to call those in, to suggest there were places we were going awry and to provide some conversations from within the movement as to where we might go next. But also, because it is a stigmatised industry, I didn't want it to be used by anti-sex work advocates to prove that there's 'no such thing as feminist porn' or to be co-opted and used as justification to shut down the entire industry, which is always the risk when we talk honestly about sex work. So, I had to write carefully. I tried to do a kind of loving critique.

How Did You Learn About All These Strategies That You Have Implemented?

Oh, I learnt everything through sex work and sex worker organisations, for sure, and I am still learning. I already had a good sense of the benchmarks for ethical research precisely because of my involvement in sex worker advocacy. Those standards have been driven by sex workers, not by university ethics committees. And they are still changing, which is important. There are lively discussions among sex worker communities all over the world at the moment about what constitutes best practice research, and each time they are becoming increasingly refined. Those are what guided me and held me to account. I then supplemented this with reference to practical handbooks on ethical research with marginalised communities (Pitts and Smith 2007), in particular lessons from people who use drugs about their experiences with research (O'Brien and Madden 2007) and reflections by queer researchers about what queer methodologies might look like (Gorman-Murray et al. 2011).

Sex worker organisations have released demands with criteria for researchers to engage with before they will agree to work with them. Some of those things include critical reflection by researchers about their own involvement, ensuring that sex workers are paid for their time and expertise and clear benefits for sex worker communities. But the key part is the insistence that sex workers are involved in every step of the process, from research conception and design through to data collection, drafting and dissemination, because things can go wrong at any of those steps.

For that reason, sex worker organisations are often loath to partner with research organisations unless they've really been vouched for and proven themselves. In most cases, they won't partner with them at all. They might sit on an advisory panel, or they might consult on the methods. But they rarely endorse projects that they have no control over. That has been an important distinction, because in the community, sex workers are paying attention to what technical type of relationship exists. Migrant sex workers like Nada DeCat are leading this discussion and demanding accountability from both sex worker organisations and researchers (2019). If a project promotes its sex worker advisory panel as a measure of its ethics, then that comes with a whole other level of accountability. Sex workers will want to know, well how come the project received so many million dollars, and yet participants are only to be paid this amount? Why haven't you held information sessions to keep the community informed about the progress of the research? Why have you collected data in this way when our communities advised against it? A whole lot of ethical issues arise when sex worker organisations agree to work with non-peer researchers who don't understand the community expectations of doing sex work research.

There is a sentiment among sex workers that academics just want to do 'edgy' research, that they want to dip their toes in a sex-saturated culture but they don't want to be contaminated by the associated stigma. They want to improve their CV. And there's a real awareness that academics are often in a more fortunate condition, in some form of paid employment or with book contracts and that they are using sex workers as a kind of tragedy porn. Of course, academia now is increasingly casualised and the process of publishing is notoriously exploitative. I mean, almost everything I have ever written—including journal articles and book chapters—has been for free, in my own time and at my own cost. In my experience sex workers are more likely to pay each other than academics or publishers are to pay contributors, because we recognise the value of the labour. But obviously, in being afforded a platform and voice in the first place, there's a real exposing of privilege, and of social capital—my own included—in terms of who is writing the stories about sex work and whose voices get heard. It's particularly stark if researchers won't then necessarily stand up for sex workers or come to rallies or write policy submissions.

Elena Jeffreys, who is a former president of Scarlet Alliance and who wrote her PhD on sex worker political autonomy in the current funding environment, did a presentation at UNSW a few years ago where she had reviewed NSW-based academics writing about sex work to see whether they had also written policy submissions for law reform (Jeffreys 2016). This was in the context where the NSW government was proposing to introduce brothel police and a licensing regime for sex work and sex workers were running advocacy campaigns to prevent it. And she made a critique of this kind of armchair academia, where researchers don't have the same vested interests as people within the communities they are researching. They have less to lose. They are not going to be arrested. And that's something that's really real for sex workers. So it was a call to academics to put their money where their mouth is. If you're going to write about it, prepare to turn up on the streets and defend it.

So I had a pretty solid base framework for this before I started this research. I was living in a community with really heightened debates about the politics of non-peer researchers. I didn't really learn from books, I learnt from community.

It's Clear That Your Research Is Underpinned and Guided by a Body of Ethics That Is Not Located in the Formal, Bureaucratic Ethics Process. You Have Also Mentioned a Number of Key Figures That You Have Learnt from Along the Way. Why Is This So Important, Do You Think?

Well that body of ethics has developed in part because the existing research on sex work was so problematic. And so sex workers mobilised and intervened, the same way other marginalised populations have, to demand standards for researchers who wanted to engage with us. It developed out of necessity in that sense. But also, because sex worker rights movements have a very strong anti-hierarchical and anti-oppressive politics, we are always in discussion about power, access, risk, and this is a natural extension of that.

In terms of names, I think in sex worker movements, we have a history of crediting the people in the movement who fought before us. That doesn't appear so much in white feminist movements but it's a very notable part of Black feminist traditions, and it is there to some extent in queer histories as well, although not to the same degree. It's a recognition that we haven't arrived here independently. We owe what we know to those who have come before us. In Australia much of our sex work research was pioneered by the late Roberta Perkins. That tracing back of the fore-founders of the movement and particular pioneers and projects is what keeps us connected to a global movement and keeps those legacies alive and active.

What Do You Wish Somebody Had Told You Before You Started Doing the Research That You've Done? And What Would You Like to See More Of?

I think we all have to keep asking—who are we speaking to? There has been a shift away from treating sex work as a kind of individual deviance and towards looking at its structural conditions and regulation, and I am glad for that. What I'd like to see more of are studies that expose the values, practices and tactics of anti-sex work advocates, police, judiciary and law-makers—projects that research up rather than research down. Jay Levy and Pye Jakobsson (2013) have done some of this in Sweden where they've examined how Swedish abolitionism operates as a kind of patriarchal control. I think that's really useful research.

When I first started my doctoral project, I was driven by a policy perspective. I wanted to tell governments how they should regulate pornography: just decriminalise sex work, expand the X18+ category in Australia's National Classification Code, decriminalise production, exhibition and screening so that we can run vibrant porn film festivals like in Europe, make arts grants and subsidies available to people to create sexually explicit film and media, develop comprehensive sex education programmes with better information about gender diversity and relationship skills, that kind of thing. And I went in thinking that, in the spirit of applied social research, that would be a useful output for advocacy.

But as I progressed, I started to realise how preoccupation with law and policy reform had really dimmed the visions of our movement. My data was telling me that internal debates about reform were creating or exposing hierarchies within the movement itself. So my research changed direction significantly to think about how social movements generate and sustain themselves, how they speak back at regulatory frameworks and how their demands are also shaped by them. And while I'll continue to write submissions to government inquiries on porn law reform, sometimes talking to the state is simply a waste of our time. And the more useful move is the production of peer resources that keep us safe, skilled and connected, talking to one another in the movement so we can mobilise together.

I think one of the biggest issues in sex worker research and advocacy is that it is often reactive. We are reacting to governments or media or anti-sex work commentators, sometimes to bizarre, spurious or irrelevant claims that are quite deliberately intended to drain our resources and energy. So we end up in this constant process of having to justify ourselves: I choose my work, I love my work, my work is my identity, and we arrive at this respectability politics that is an appeal for acceptance and recognition and inclusion in the state's mechanisms instead of a fundamental challenge to systems of labour and our relationship to sex. It's such a fraught space, it creates so many problems. The conversations we are having about pornography—in the frameworks of speech and censorship—are so narrow in their parameters. But worse, it means that we are not setting our own research agendas. It means that we are still responding on the terms set by the state. It means that we spend less time doing the world making, imaging alternatives, prefiguring our own ethical standards, giving mutual aid, building different worlds. I think that's the place where we ought to be directing our energies and resources.

The thing is sex work is often positioned as a risky activity in itself. But in sexuality research, the sex is not the risk. The issues that repeatedly arise relate to participant value, community control, reflexive voice, unlearning privilege and owning up to mistakes. It's about creating space, capacity development, managing burn out, maintaining accountability, and navigating a hostile political climate. Those risks are constant, but being alert to them is necessary, and as they say in feminist porn, it's about the process not just the product.

References

Albury, K., Crawford, K., Byron, P., & Mathews, B. P. (2013). *Young People and Sexting in Australia: Ethics, Representation and the Law*. Sydney: ARC Centre for Creative Industries and Innovation/Journalism and Media Research Centre, UNSW.

Attwood, F. (2010). Dirty Work: Researching Women and Sexual Representation. In R. Gill & R. Ryan-Flood (Eds.), *Secrecy and Silence in the Research Process: Feminist Reflections* (1st ed., p. 177). London: Routledge.

Blinne, K. C. (2012). Auto (Erotic) Ethnography. *Sexualities, 15*(8), 953–977.

Comella, L. (2015). Navigating Campus Controversy: An Interview with Adult Performer Conner Habib. *Porn Studies, 2*(2-3), 283–285.

DeCat, N. Z. (2019, March 28). The Racism of Decriminalisation. *Tits and Sass*. http://titsandsass.com/the-racism-of-decriminalization/

Dr Anonymous. (2020). Researchers at Risk: The Precarious Positions of Researchers Conducting Dangerous Enquiries. In P. Danaher & D. Mulligan (Eds.), *Still Anonymous: Stigma, Silencing and Sex Work*. Palgrave Macmillan.

Fatale Media Inc., & Kinney, N. (1998). Dir. Rednour, S. *Bend Over Boyfriend*.

Gorman-Murray, A. W., Johnston, L., & Waitt, G. R. (2011). Queer (ing) Communication in Research Relationships: A Conversation About Subjectivities, Methodologies and Ethics. In K. Browne & C. J. Nash (Eds.), *Queer Methods and Methodologies* (pp. 111–126). England and USA: Ashgate.

Heineman, J. (2016). *Schoolgirls: Embodiment Practices Among Current and Former Sex Workers in Academia.* UNLV Theses, Dissertations, Professional Papers, and Capstones. 2866. https://digitalscholarship.unlv.edu/thesesdissertations/2866

Jackson, C. (2013). *Sex Worker Rights Organising as Social Movement Unionism: Responding to the Criminalisation of Work.* UNLV Theses, Dissertations, Professional Papers, and Capstones. 1844.

Jeffreys, E. (2016). Research for No Reason: Academically Present, Politically Vacant. Social Research Conference on HIV, Viral Hepatitis and Related Diseases. University of New South Wales.

Langarita Adiego, J. A. (2017). On Sex in Fieldwork: Notes on the Methodology Involved in the Ethnographic Study of Anonymous Sex. *Sexualities*, 1363460717716581.

Lee, J. (2015). They Came to See the [Queer] Porn Star Talk. *Porn Studies*, 2(2-3), 272–274.

Levy, J., & Jakobsson, P. (2013). Abolitionist Feminism as Patriarchal Control: Swedish Understandings of Prostitution and Trafficking. *Dialectical Anthropology, 37*(2), 333–340.

Lorde, A. (1997). Uses of the Erotic: The Erotic as Power. In K. Conboy, N. Medina, & S. Stanbury (Eds.), *Writing on the Body: Female Embodiment and Feminist Theory* (pp. 227–282). New York: Columbia University Press.

Martin, R. J., & Haller, D. (Eds.). (2018). *Sex: Ethnographic Encounters.* New York: Bloomsbury Publishing.

Maxxine, C., & Hidalgo, D. A. (2015). A Performer and a Professor: Two Friends and Colleagues Talk Porn… in College. *Porn Studies, 2*(2-3), 279–282.

McKee, A. (2017). The Pornography Consumer as "Other". In *The Routledge Companion to Media, Sex, and Sexuality.* London: Routledge.

McNair, B. (2009). Teaching Porn. *Sexualities, 12*(5), 558–567.

Nagle, J. (Ed.). (1997). *Whores and Other Feminists.* New York/London: Routledge.

Nasaw, D. (2014, May 9). In Toronto with the World's Feminist Pornographers. *BBC News Magazine.* https://www.bbc.com/news/magazine-27192724

O'Brien, M. L., & Madden, A. (2007). Knowledge, Relationships and Identity in Research on Drug Use. In *Researching the Margins* (pp. 45–65). London: Palgrave Macmillan.

Penley, C. (2015). Collision in a Courtroom. In *Images, Ethics, Technology* (pp. 70–100). New York: Routledge.

Pitts, M., & Smith, A. (Eds.). (2007). *Researching the Margins: Strategies for Ethical and Rigorous Research with Marginalised Communities.* Springer.

Plummer, K. (1995). *Telling Sexual Stories: Power, Change and Social Worlds.* London: Routledge.

Preciado, P. B. (2013). *Testo Junkie: Sex, Drugs, and Biopolitics in the Pharmacopornographic Era.* New York: The Feminist Press at CUNY.

Pulido, L. (2008). FAQs: Frequently (Un) Asked Questions About Being a Scholar Activist. In *Engaging contradictions: Theory, Politics, and Methods of Activist Scholarship* (pp. 341–366). Berkeley: University of California Press.

Sprinkle, A. (1998). *Annie Sprinkle: Post-Porn Modernist: My 25 Years as a Multi-Media Whore.* San Francisco: Cleis Press.

Stardust, Z. (2014). 'Fisting Is Not Permitted': Criminal Intimacies, Queer Sexualities and Feminist Porn in the Australian Legal Context. *Porn Studies, 1*(3), 242–259.

Stardust, Z. (2018). Lessons in Sex: Porn Performers and Sex Education. *Archer Magazine, 9,* pp. 80–87.

Weiss, S. (2018, March 6). I Went to a Masturbation Workshop in Search of My Best Orgasm Yet. *Harpers Bazaar.* https://www.harpersbazaar.com/culture/features/a15893157/betty-dodson-masturbation-workshop-orgasms/

3

Sitting with the Mess

Caroline Lenette

I've been doing creative co-research with people from refugee backgrounds for over ten years. I've collaborated mostly with resettled women and their families, and people who have been in detention in Australia. I use arts-based methods like digital storytelling, photography, community music, participatory video or walking interviews, so I enjoy approaches that are less static. I'm not just interested in sitting down and asking questions. My main interest is in new forms of storytelling, the kind of storytelling that comes from or is led by participants. That's why I use the term co-researchers, and I build research relationships where knowledge is co-produced. As much as possible, I align my approach with what co-researchers want to get out of the research. This form of research involves very close collaborations.

Needless to say, it's not unusual that things get messy.

C. Lenette (✉)
School of Social Sciences & Australian Human Rights Institute,
University of New South Wales, Sydney, NSW, Australia
e-mail: c.lenette@unsw.edu.au

How Do I Manage Blurred Boundaries?

There is one incident I remember clearly, that was particularly risky for me. When I was doing my PhD, I was a 'green' researcher and I had very limited understanding of what participatory research meant. I had a naïve understanding, actually, of what I should be doing and how I should develop and maintain relationships with my co-researchers.

At the time, I was doing research with young women and I had become quite close to one of them. She got married and she was doing great in her studies. I received a phone call from her one night and she said, "I fear for my life, my husband says he wants to kill me". The first thing I said was, "Stay where you are, I'm coming to get you". That was my immediate response. At that moment, it didn't matter that she was a research participant; she was a young woman who feared for her life. She needed someone to help, and she rang me.

I went to pick her up and she came to my place. She didn't want to talk about it, and she just wanted to be by herself. That was all fine with me. But later on that night, I thought to myself, "What have I done?" I lived 15 minutes away from her (and her husband's) place and I thought, "What if he knows where I live? What if he decides to come here? What do I do then?" So it was after the fact that I thought, "Maybe I should have thought this through?" She didn't want to go to the police and just wanted to feel safe, and I was the person she called upon to get that feeling of safety. I felt a huge sense of responsibility.

She slept over and the next morning she said, "I want to go back now", and I drove her back to her place. I spent the whole day, then the whole week, wondering how she was and whether she was safe. It was actually quite distressing for me to think, "I don't know if she's safe". She didn't respond to my text messages, and I didn't want to ring her so that my calls wouldn't raise suspicion. I became more conscious about my name being on her phone and whether her husband might check to see who she'd called.

I've thought about this incident a number of times over the years, and whether I would do things differently. I probably wouldn't. If I ever get a phone call like this again, I would probably do the same, but with a little bit more of a strategy. For example, I would say, "Yes, I will come to pick you up" if someone felt they were in danger. But then, I'd be firmer about discussing the need to go to the police together or finding out the contact details for a family violence service to get immediate assistance. I didn't know any such details at the time. So I didn't know how to manage the mess.

I've talked about this incident as a research participant (see Sunderland et al.'s work on moral distress among community-based researchers, 2010) because for me, it is one of the most critical examples of thinking about boundaries in research. When we (academic researchers) come across human beings who are going through really difficult circumstances—irrespective of whether or not they are research participants—we can become the person they call upon.

Nothing happened to me after that, but I've kept thinking about other ways of getting someone in her situation to safety. What I found the hardest was wondering what happened when she went back home. She didn't want to talk to me about the situation anymore. I understood and respected that; she needed to keep going, and she may have felt embarrassed that I knew about this part of her life. But I was left alone to deal with those feelings of concern and uncertainty. I reached out to colleagues to debrief, and that was helpful.

That incident has led me to think more carefully about risks in participatory research, particularly as a young woman in the field. So much rests on maintaining strong relationships with co-researchers (see Lenette et al. 2019) that I sometimes go in head first without thinking, "What's the plan? What's the plan after that?"

I know that she reached out to me precisely because I was an outsider. She trusted me because I was not part of her community and didn't represent the gender expectations that contributed to her situation. We get too hung up on boundaries. I'm not sure we're always open to the possibilities of redefining our role in the field in messy situations, instead of drawing artificial boundaries that might be unhelpful or even hurt others.

How Do I Deal with Trauma in Research?

Whenever people ask me, "What do you do?" and I say, "Refugee research", the usual reaction is, "Oh, it must be dreadful". Actually, I've never felt dreadful about the research conversations I've had. Even though people assume that there must be a lot of traumatic and sad stories, we've mostly enjoyed the creative processes we've undertaken together. I find that my co-researchers are *relieved* that they don't have to talk about trauma and that we're talking about hopes for the future, what women do for their children and their aspirations in education, work and language acquisition.

My feeling is that co-researchers are actually looking for a research space to talk about something else, like cultural memories of belonging, that perhaps they're not asked about in other forms of research that focus too much on trauma.

When ethics committees ask, "What are the risks? And what are you going to do to mitigate those risks?" I think I have a different understanding of risk. For example, just because someone cries and gets distressed during an interview doesn't mean you shouldn't interview them. Just because it's hard to talk about something, doesn't mean that we shouldn't or that we shouldn't pick that as a topic of research. We can't anticipate everything either. We just don't know what might happen. But it's about making sure that we have a plan to decide what to do next, or to discuss with others about how to proceed.

The approach that I take is trauma-informed (Lenette 2019). Being trauma-informed means showing sensitivity, empathy and understanding to the possibility that trauma may be part of co-researchers' lived experiences. I know that by virtue of being humanitarian entrants or asylum seekers, co-researchers might have gone through some pretty awful situations. But that's not what we talk about. The topics we've explored together have never been directly about the trauma or traumatic experiences. We talk about their lives in Australia and what makes someone, or somewhere, feel like home, what contributes to their wellbeing, or aspirations for the future. I let my co-researchers guide me. They might want to bring in stories of trauma, in their own terms and in their own time.

When we use trauma-informed practices, we "collaborate in a way that neither triggers past trauma nor exclude trauma narratives if and when these emerge" (Lenette 2019, p. 16).

Inevitably, difficult memories do come up. For instance, I was with a group of South Sudanese women in Sydney, and we were listening to music from their homeland on YouTube. Most of it was joyful and they were dancing and singing, and they seemed to really enjoy it. Then a song came up that was about caring for children, and one woman said, "I remember I had to care for someone's kids because they died, and then one day I didn't know where my son was". It was mentioned in passing and then she moved on and said, "But it was a happy time, when I found my son again; it was such a relief". No one dwelled on that story; it was just mentioned as a fact of life.

My co-researchers can be talking about traffic one minute and then share about having lost a child, then chat about what they're going to cook tonight—it's an interesting process that means that we don't really dwell on trauma stories, and move on to something else, and I follow their lead on how they deal with the 'mess' and simply take note of what is said.

So, often, distressing things are mentioned in passing, but these stories are not the focus of our dialogue. Because it's a form of research led by co-researchers, I never prompt someone to share, just to satisfy my curiosity. If they've made choices about what stories they want to share, I take that on board and respect that, and I'm grateful that they're sharing part of their experiences. I'm there to receive these stories. If they wanted to tell me more, they would.

Having said that, I have also created research spaces to talk about difficulties or feelings of despair, like for example, with people seeking asylum who are in that state of limbo and have no idea what's going to happen to them. There's a whole body of literature that discusses the benefits of talking about trauma in research, but often, because of institutional ethics requirements, we don't get a chance to reflect on the benefits of having a safe space to express that trauma. But if this does occur in the research encounter, people might want to have a bit of chat about it, and then move on. It's about picking up on body language and cues and being respectful about the story shared and not prompt just for the sake of it. There's often relief that we're going to talk about and enjoy, say, music and singing together, and not try to find answers to their situations.

Some of the topics they want to talk about, like not being able to get a job in Australia, actually generate more distress in our conversations than remembering having gone through war. Women, for example, will often say that they came here for their children and their children's future, but they're stuck and spend hours at home for years and do 'nothing', apply for jobs that don't require any skills and still don't get them. That's really hard for people to come to terms with. It's distressing to be misunderstood on public transport because they can't speak English really well, and it creates a sense of not being safe in this country. There's like a collective experience of hope after resettling to Australia, and at times it feels like the difficulties and the mental health issues that can follow—and that sense of despair—can be harder to manage and talk about, than having lost someone in the past.

Sometimes, trauma is hidden in unexpected stories, so it's interesting to consider what ethics committees judge as potentially traumatic content or situations. That paper-based process doesn't necessarily prepare us for what awaits in the field. This is something I find especially important to consider when supervising research assistants. Traumatic content can come through field notes, and so conversations about what it's like to receive these stories in the field are super important. Research assistants might be struggling to figure out the best way to respond or process that information, because they don't want to appear as incompetent, so we should keep a close eye on vicarious trauma.

I've learnt many things in the field through trial and error, and some things I've learnt the hard way, so I don't want to stop new and emerging researchers from having their own experiences. And those experiences might be hard and researchers might be unprepared for them or not know what to do. But I think that there's a bit of a parallel when you're raising children: should you stop them from experiencing things in case they get hurt? And does that then mean that they won't experience anything and won't learn anything.

How Do I Recruit Participants?

It can be really tricky to think about recruiting co-researchers in an academic context, where there are timeframe and funding implications. Ideally, I aim to work with what we call 'hard to reach' co-researchers, the most marginalised of the marginalised, as a refugee-background co-researcher once said. But in reality, it's quite difficult to do that. There might not be enough money to pay interpreters for different language groups, and so already, I have to make choices about picking maybe one language group or two at the most. In other cases, I can't work with co-researchers who are not comfortable using English (or French, my first language) in our conversations.

Co-researchers who are confident and can express themselves well in English are usually the first ones to volunteer for research projects, and so what ends up happening is that, if I get a bit of money, I'll go back to them and say, are you interested to work on this project? I've created a cycle of going back to the same people because they quickly understand what the research process is about and there's trust already. And they do research well. They're generous and articulate. They know that there are deadlines and they respond to emails. So, if I've only got a little bit of time, I'll go to the people who can jump on board quickly.

There's nothing wrong with that per se in terms of getting great perspectives on a topic, but it doesn't resolve the bigger issue of having opportunities to work with people whose perspectives also matter, but who might require more time and information, perhaps in different languages, before they can agree to become co-researchers. I'm thinking more and more about this tension, and I've written about how we can try to address this problem together with refugee-background co-researchers (Lenette et al. in-press) because we always need to reflect on what we could do better, even when projects go really well.

For those who might need more information before participating, like women who have been at home for 15 years and haven't been able to work, study, or learn English, that's an added level of difficulty. We usually have to go through community organisations and community leaders (and maintain good relationships with them), and give women a clear sense of why they should come to, for example, an information session about doing research in collaboration with me or with our team in the first place. Informed consent is an on-going process and requires more than signing on the dotted line on a template that the institution designed.

Even in the context of explaining research projects to potential participants, using interpreters can be problematic, whether we go with accredited interpreters or bilingual community workers who sometimes happen to be relatives of other people in the room. Gatekeeping or withholding information can become a big issue, especially when I work with women and we can't find an interpreter who's also a woman or from the same language group. Trying to engage isolated women in research can be quite difficult, but I find that once a group of people knows me and I go back to them and I ask them to recommend other people, that works really well.

Needless to say, some people don't want to be part of research projects because of previous (bad) experiences with academics, people who misrepresented their stories, or researchers they never saw again, or heard back from again, once they had their questions answered. I understand that this might be the starting point for many people who think twice before saying 'yes' to research participation. In those cases, it's even more important to explain what participatory research means, what the tangible outcomes might be, or co-researchers' role in leading the research process.

What Insider/Outsider Identities Do I Bring to Research?

I often think about my insider/outsider role. I mentioned before that being an outsider meant that co-researchers might be more open to telling me things that they wouldn't necessarily tell someone from their community or with a similar cultural background. That's because there are close to no risks to them that their opinions might spread like wildfire among people they know, their families and friends (but again, that might not be possible if there's an interpreter from their community involved). So there's a sense of safety that research conversations can offer, which is excellent. That's especially important for women, if they share difficulties or talk about gender issues that might be taboo; they might be more comfortable revealing these stories to outsiders who are keen to know more.

I'm also conscious that because I have brown skin, that affects how I'm perceived and welcomed in the community. Even though I'm not from a refugee background (outsider), for some co-researchers, there's a sense of commonality, because I'm not white, I wasn't born in Australia and my migrant experience is recent (insider). Much of the literature on doing cross-cultural work, and doing it well, assumes that researchers are white. Many are, but there's very little out there on the implications of being a researcher who doesn't fit into the dominant cultural group but does cross-cultural work. Just because I'm a migrant woman, and I understand, on a personal level, the difficulties of building a new life in a new country, that doesn't mean that I am free from prejudices or assumptions. I can still get it wrong in the field. We should all be reflexive in our research practice.

I bring another outsider identity to the field as an academic. Sometimes, there's a degree of formality that co-researchers associate with talking to an academic or a university lecturer, even though my style is very informal. Before they get to know me well, they might draw on previous experiences of working with academics (in Australia and overseas) and assume that being formal is the right way to go. That's something I try to challenge straightaway, because it affects the nature of our interactions. Making sure we're both comfortable with the research relationship is important to me.

An insider identity I sometimes draw on is that of being a mother. When I'm working with mothers and children on weekends, there are times when I get to take my daughter into the field (she's 11 and independent). It's a rich and unique experience for her. But I have to think about implications in terms of risks to researchers' family members—in my case, what she could see or hear. I usually choose days when there are creative activities, when I know that women will bring their children. So if I bring my child, that's not a problem at all, and the women are happy seeing her there, they love it. They feed her, dress her up, and do her hair.

Co-researchers then see me differently, as a carer, a mother, not just a researcher or an academic. That's another part of my identity that becomes almost like an asset, to be welcomed into the group, so other mothers look at me and think, well, maybe she knows a thing or two about mothering. I earn their trust at a different level. Fieldwork is a gendered space (see Bell et al. 1993), and I don't have to hide parts of my identity to do research well.

What Are the Risks of (Mis)representing?

When I write about my research, the framing really comes down to what key messages I want to share. Writing a journal article, for example, is when I can report on and share rich and complex research findings and raise new questions.

But we still tend to extract key words and sentences from our data that best illustrate the things that we want to say, rather than presenting the whole story—how would you do that anyway, presenting a whole transcript, so to speak? We have to think about the journal's imposed word count, find balance in the structure. We have to write something that others will want or find easy to read. So we can become extractive. We 'tidy up' what's meant to be messy. That's the norm.

I try to find ways of sharing findings using what I call 'whole' narratives or narrative threads to challenge that tendency. I had to think about finding a different strategy to report on qualitative findings a few years ago when I had the chance to work with a young woman who lived (and still lives) in a refugee camp in an African country. We met in Geneva, at a United Nations High Commissioner for Refugees [UNHCR] gathering in 2016. She was an excellent speaker. I wanted to ask her questions about her experiences as a youth advocate at the UNHCR and she accepted to be part of my research. This is a young woman whose everyday is a refugee camp, and there she was, in expensive Geneva for a youth consultation, and there I was, asking her questions about what it was like, so that I could meet my research objectives and justify the funding I received to attend.

For her to be able to answer my question fully, about what it meant to her to represent young people and speak at the UNHCR, she had to tell me her whole story. She couldn't just answer that question in a few minutes. I would not have understood the significance of this time in her life. She wrote her whole story for me. And it was only in the last paragraph that she talked about her experiences at the UNHCR. She needed to share her experience as a whole.

That was a huge lesson for me, because I wanted to find out about her time at the UNHCR and I hadn't planned on asking broader questions. Sure, people can tell me a few things about who they are and the journey they've travelled, but there is a research focus that ultimately guides encounters, that directs the conversation in a particular way. But for this young woman, it was important that I understood everything about her life: when and where she was born, details about her family, the first time her family was displaced, her anguish while she was growing up, all the things that mattered to her. It was incredible. She was happy for me to share her story widely, so I felt the weight of this responsibility, not to simplify, pick and choose what suited me.

I tried to write about her in the form of a reflection for a youth magazine, which was really difficult because I wanted to do justice to everything she had shared with me. I had to try several times to hit the mark. I was tempted to represent her story in different ways, not really like she'd shared it. I had to find an editor who understood this approach and would let me write a 'whole' narrative or narrative threads to get closer to representing her experiences.

There are very few (academic) outlets that will allow us to write such long narratives to contextualise co-researchers' lived experiences so that we don't run the risk of misrepresenting.

I feel the weight of that responsibility every time I'm tempted or have to choose quotes to illustrate certain points in my writing. We make very deliberate choices as to why we chose this particular quote and not another. Sometimes, to save space, we take out a sentence in the middle of a paragraph to make it shorter. By using (...), we pretty much indicate that this part was not as important.

Often, reviewers' suggestions will be to shorten direct quotes. The decontextualised nature of some of those quotes, especially when they're about things that the world doesn't understand very well, can cause damage.

So the process of writing becomes a matter of questioning. Why am I choosing these particular words? Are they pretty much reflecting my idea about what I wanted to know in the first place? It's difficult to know for sure whether I'm writing well and doing justice to co-researchers' narratives, and I can't say that I've done it well all the time.

There are times when I've chosen co-researchers' 'best looking' sentences because they 'hit the mark' and were expressed well—that meant less work for me. But when I think about a reader who might not know all the rich or contradictory information that comes before and after that sentence, and I might know about the background and why they're saying things in a particular way, there's a real risk of presenting a 'here's-something-I-prepared-earlier' perspective, and this is what readers need to believe because it's in a paper.

I really struggle with the dominant format of academic writing that forces us to do things like this. I don't like the times when reviewers have said, "Oh, this is too long. You need to get rid of a few quotes", as if the words of co-researchers have no weight in the paper. And I've pushed back and said, "No, I don't think I'm getting rid of them, the quotes are the most important part of the paper, and that's why they're long and that's why they're big paragraphs", so that someone who's reading these quotes gets a sense of the person who's 'speaking'.

I think it's our responsibility to challenge that norm in academic writing in particular that privileges the tell-me-quickly-what-I-need-to-know. And that can be really dangerous, because in the telling quickly what one needs to know, you can only get a partial understanding. I know that it is not ever possible to give or get a 'whole' understanding, but I'm trying to, in different ways; or I'm striving towards that goal, I guess.

Same with conferences, you get 10 or 15 minutes: tell people everything you want to say in 15 minutes. I don't know how to be respectful to people's stories in that format. It's still very colonialist. I use the work of Alison Phipps (2019) on decolonisation to unlearn these ways of sharing, and recreate new ways of being.

The thing is, I'm aware I'm contributing to this industry/to the academy through my publications (that largely stick to traditional formats), but I'm trying to respectfully challenge these ways by pushing back on some of the feedback that asks to reduce contextual information and co-researchers' words. I take other things out, but these stories, they need to be told. In that particular way. In that particular order, so that it makes sense to someone who doesn't know the person who told their story, to do justice to the time they've taken to talk to me, and to share all of those details. Who am I to pick and choose one sentence here or there? I struggle with that. I try to imagine what it would be like if I was the person being asked to share at times really personal details, about my lived experiences, and then if I only saw one random sentence published. How is that respectful? What does it actually achieve?

So we have to question ourselves about our purpose when we want to publish about situations, experiences and relationships that were quite complex in a neat format. Even when a paper gets accepted, and as we proof-read, we have to read it through someone else's eyes to decide whether we've written well, without misrepresenting or harming.

And that's why I enjoy co-writing with co-researchers, because if I'm writing about someone's lived experiences and they're also reading the drafts, and commenting on them and adding to them, I get that bit of reassurance that they're happy with the narrative that goes in, that it reflects more or less what they wanted to say, more or less their experiences.

But when I'm writing by myself about someone else's experiences, I always have this fear and this anxiety as to whether I'm doing justice to their narratives, or whether I'm creating a stereotype. Am I creating a caricature or confirming prejudices about a particular community?

That's why I'm really mindful about how to document sensitive issues like violence—that doesn't mean I don't want to see these issues addressed if they exist, but I try to think carefully about the way I present that information to someone who has five seconds to look through a paper. What would that actually achieve?

What Stories Do I Choose to Tell?

I recently had a fieldwork experience that didn't go so well, where a male community leader was actively gatekeeping access to women in his community, women who didn't speak English very well. Even though we (the research team) went through a collaborative process and asked for permission and explained the project, and he agreed to help, the situation became problematic because we held workshops for women and he wanted to be there all the time. He said he understood the purpose of having women-only activities but wanted to listen to the conversations, and interpret for us, even though we had an interpreter present.

The team didn't quite know how to manage the situation without damaging relationships and our professional reputation. We knew his presence changed the dynamics. Because we were working within a tight timeframe, we did not identify this problem as a major concern. We had another male community leader as an ally, and we did not think to raise the issue with him early on. We only discussed the gatekeeping issue informally at the end of, say, a conversation about workshop logistics. In hindsight, we should have definitely developed a culturally appropriate strategy to address it, because that might have prevented a number of misunderstandings that eventually emerged.

One collaborator (a woman) did ask the gatekeeper not to attend the workshops, and he was offended, and there was a long process of asking for and being granted forgiveness. There were minor repercussions on the project itself, but we spent a lot of hours discussing this situation afterwards. This incident took its toll on us, as we felt guilty that we hadn't managed it very well. And we feared that the project might not continue to receive community support. Fortunately, his and other community leaders' support remained, after the process of asking for forgiveness.

That raised a really tricky issue for me, about whether (and how) I should write about this incident (which I still feel I can't outline fully), and about gender norms, patriarchy, lack of respect, as it was probably the most energy-sucking part of the project. I worry about identifying him and perpetuating stereotypes about that community. Even now that the co-authored academic paper on this project has been published, and

I'm really proud of it, I still worry that he will read it (or this chapter) or hear about reports on the project, and be unhappy about how we framed our writing. I know that we can't always please all stakeholders, but I don't feel I'd be able to approach him for support on another project if I wanted to work with women from this background and area again.

There are many other situations where we have to make (sometimes) difficult choices about what to include and exclude, thinking about the repercussions of publishing certain kinds of information. I've heard this from many colleagues who do participatory research (Lenette et al. 2019) but also from others. There isn't a clear answer that comes up when people are asked: is it unethical to withhold information that comes up in interviews, for example?

When women start talking to me about how gender norms are different in Australia, they might go down the pathway of talking about difficult topics like FGM (female genital mutilation), or domestic violence, and forced marriages. Because I usually work with very small groups of women, there is no way that I can talk about that in my writing. I have to think carefully about the cost or the risk of talking about these topics in a publication or at a workshop where people don't have the contextual information to make sense of these stories. We have to think about all possible repercussions for co-researchers and academic researchers, of revealing information out of context. There's still a tendency to view refugee-background women as 'oppressed', as women who need to abandon the sociocultural norms of their communities to 'embrace Australian values'. So I need to manage the information they've shared—anything that might reinforce those stereotypes—in sensitive ways.

We must also think more about the impact that sensitive, provocative, or graphic content can have on audiences. While it's great to write about or create videos with stories that might be difficult to hear, or organise a theatre project on trauma, or show images that are confronting, we don't think often enough about how audiences receive and process those stories. We don't always give audiences the necessary tools to avoid confusion, compassion fatigue or indifference. We might be failing our responsibilities as researchers, if we don't pay more careful attention to that issue. Audiences are not just an afterthought to projects, and we should think about how we want to achieve shifting their thinking in meaningful ways from the beginning.

What Are My Strategies for Self-Care and Support?

We sometimes lose sight of the importance of self-care, especially in challenging projects, when we think about our roles and responsibilities as researchers. People who choose to do participatory research or research that involves close collaborations are usually women (Lenette et al. 2019). There's a whole body of literature on feminist ethics of care in research; it seems like women are more likely to feel a 'duty' to do this kind of research that requires more time and more energy, more presence, more emotions, and that's actually harder. And sometimes, we'll get it wrong, and we can't be too hard on ourselves.

Researcher self-care is super important. There's a research culture that gives the impression to younger/new researchers especially, that it's almost like their duty to feel distressed, that if you're not distressed enough, you're not doing research the right way. You're not going deep enough. It's almost a quasi-requirement (Sunderland et al. 2010): if you're not feeling the stories fully and sharing the pain, perhaps you're not a good researcher.

I really try to challenge that when I mentor researchers, because I think that way of thinking can be soul-destroying. Close collaborations can be really difficult to navigate for someone who might think, "Well, if I don't spend five hours with this co-researcher, it means I haven't done my work properly. If I don't bow to all their requests, I might damage the relationship". That's why it's so important to have great women mentors, who can give advice on how to deconstruct assumptions like these, and offer practical strategies to overcome those risks.

It's also important to model self-care for new and emerging researchers. I have really long conversations with research assistants about expectations before projects begin, their understanding of what the research outcomes should be, and about being able to identify fairly early on if a situation seems uncomfortable or risky to them and how to step out of it.

We dialogue on that anxiety about causing offence so that it doesn't become stronger than preserving their own wellbeing, it comes first.

I've had discussions with other researchers about situations where perhaps, we should not do interviews by ourselves. For example, in rural, remote areas, that can be a particular risk if something happens in someone's home and you have to drive back two hours to take care of yourself or seek help, that's a problem.

Clarity about research tasks and activities is one thing, but open discussions on potential risks and how to minimise them are equally important. I have a 'system'/agreement with research assistants: if they go into someone's home for interviewing, they send me a text message beforehand and one after, just to let me know that they're done, but also as a way to alert me if there is a particular issue they want to raise straight away.

That's a way of saying, "I trust in your abilities, but just so you know, I'm also there on call if you need to talk about it afterwards". This is an example of a safety measure to make sure we're not sending people out there in the field and they feel, "Well, I'm by myself and nobody will know what happens or when I go home". I think it's an important responsibility.

I encourage research assistants to write notes about the content but also how they felt about the process, so everything that they felt, everything they observed and their interpretations. And then, when we read their notes together, and if I can see that there are some things that maybe need to be unpacked, we have a dialogue about it, and discuss strategies to address messy situations that might come up in other interviews.

For a new or inexperienced researcher who doesn't have a good support network, they can find themselves pretty much alone. It's luck of the draw. If I have a great support person, I'm lucky. But if someone doesn't have that—you're kind of by yourself to deal with new situations and ethics.

But that's the key message I tell colleagues and research assistants; you're not alone with whatever you've experienced, there's support to debrief and to work through emotions. Recognise the situations when you need to ask for help, then seek help. It's not a weakness; it's a strength to ask for help.

Everyone, even experienced researchers, can become vulnerable in research practice.

The care that we provide to one another in research teams doesn't necessarily have to come straight after a difficult interview, or even during fieldwork or the writing stage. Sometimes, it might be needed well after everything is done and dusted, and we've moved on to something else, that's when difficulties can come up. Mentoring or support can be difficult to offer when we're working on several short-term projects or on too many things at the same time.

But it's our responsibility to make sure that everyone who was involved is fine—everyone: interpreters, note takers, transcribers, research assistants, artists, and if you're making a film, the crew, especially people who are recording sound because they're listening to the stories very closely.

What Is the Role of Institutional Ethics?

It's clear that the ethics committee's role is to reduce the likelihood of risk for research participants, not necessarily for researchers. But I wouldn't go down the pathway of advocating for ethics committees to have a say about researcher wellbeing. I think they're already not in a position to know the models that are used in the field, especially co-research and the role of participants in that model, let alone if we open a can of worms about our roles as researchers in situations that can be messy and tricky and sometimes risky.

I've changed my tune on that. There was a time when I advocated strongly for ethics committees to do more to support researchers. I thought it was their responsibility. I thought, "Well, they should care about us because researcher wellbeing is really important and researcher safety is really important, and our work depends on it". Now that I can see how much ethics committees 'overreach' into how we implement research projects, I definitely don't want them to touch on researcher wellbeing.

I've only thought about that more carefully when someone challenged me and said, "Do you realise what you're asking for? You're asking for people on ethics committees, who already have no idea about the type of research you do, to actually assess the risks to you as a person?" So now I'm a little bit wiser about that. I'm much more inclined to think about ways to build networks with similar-minded researchers outside of formal processes, to support one another and share strategies.

Institutions are so worried about risks to the university's reputation that they would police what we do in the field too closely—I think it would place us in really tricky situations. Besides, if a research assistant encounters a difficult situation, they're going to ring me; they're not going to ring the ethics committee. Ethics committees have made themselves quite inaccessible to resolving day-to-day, everyday situational ethical dilemmas.

There are some pretty good and pretty bad supervisors and project leaders out there. I wouldn't always trust them with looking after a new researcher or their colleagues' wellbeing. We can't assume that, if we have these structures in places, then surely someone is going to be safe in the field and receive the support they need. It doesn't always happen this way. And I don't know that institutions have other formal structures to support researcher wellbeing that well, and that's a problem.

How Do I Apply Ethics in the Real World?

When I teach about ethics and ethical dilemmas, I use this great case study where someone is interviewing a woman about a health issue and then the participant discloses the sexual abuse of her daughter by the father (Guillemin and Gillam 2004). And I often present this as an ethical dilemma to my class and I say, "What would you do?"

Very often, the 'textbook' responses quickly come out, for example, we'd switch off the recorder and stop the interview; we'd refer her to a support service and we'd give her a pamphlet. I challenge them with new questions to think about it more broadly: "You do understand that you're sitting in this woman's kitchen; she's just told you that she's found out her daughter is being sexually abused by her dad. Is your first response going to be 'I'll switch off the recorder and here's a pamphlet'. Is this what you'll do? You're a human being alone with another human being who's telling you probably the most difficult thing they've ever shared with someone, what would you really do?"

We don't necessarily come up with one, definite answer in our discussions, but it's important for students and future researchers to realise that, very often, we're not prepared for when the difficult information comes out. It makes us all realise or remember that it's not all black or white in the field. That things do and will get messy and we don't always have the right tools to manage straightaway. That it's important to ask for help when there's a dead-end.

I tell my students to question why they want to go down a particular route: what is the purpose? What are you trying to achieve? This is not only important when we're writing a project proposal and an ethics application, but even more so during data collection and analysis (and dissemination): I question and question again, so that I don't fall into this trap of thinking, "I know why I'm doing this – I've done this before", especially when there's new information that I become aware of. I have to question my approach all the time: whose agenda is driving the questioning, and who benefits? What's the cost-benefit of each decision? What are the risks to me and to others?

How Do We Trust Ourselves?

I think people need to rely much more on their gut feeling. If you feel that your wellbeing is being compromised, whether you're right or wrong, you step out of the situation. Whether or not there was an actual risk, that's irrelevant to me. It's about what one feels when you're out in the field, and you think, "Nope, this is not what I anticipated, I don't want to do this", and to feel empowered and confident to make that decision without worrying about "Oh, I'm going to have to reschedule that interview"—that doesn't matter. It's about listening to your gut feeling that something is not quite right. And not being embarrassed to talk about it and not being shy about sharing details.

Even the most experienced researchers come across really tricky situations sometimes, where we don't know what to do. Coming across risky situations is almost like an apprenticeship for new and emerging researchers, within reason of course. We're not going to throw anyone into really difficult situations with no support. But it's about developing the capacity to note what was uncomfortable, what was risky, what was not quite right and to be able to talk about it afterwards, and to talk about what we can learn and strategies to be prepared for future situations like this.

I think that gut instinct, that feeling that something's not quite right, is not really recognised as a tool for research, an important one. But emotions are central to research. The emotion that is triggered in situations like these shapes individual understandings of what risks mean, but we're not taught what to do with it, other than recording feelings in fieldwork notes. That's important, but by itself can also be superficial or unhelpful.

What Do I Recommend? Sitting with the Mess

I said earlier that I have a different understanding of risk, but I've never attempted to define it until this interview. When I think about risks in the field, I think mostly about risky situations for researchers, especially women, about circumstances where it might be physically unsafe or emotionally draining. I think of risks to our social wellbeing, to wellbeing in general of whoever is involved in the research relationships. I also think about risks of not completing projects or getting meaningful outcomes, of seeing efforts go down the drain. I think about our decisions that might mean that co-researchers are worse off or feel dissatisfied about research processes and outcomes.

I'm writing more and more about mess in research and how we are taught to be so 'neat' and 'clean' about our research processes and outcomes, that when the mess 'happens', we have no idea what to do with it. We fear it. Sometimes, fieldwork situations can become completely messy, and I don't have a clue what to do about it. I worry about the project, about my reputation, about my co-researchers.

But when things become messy, it's probably the time when we can learn the most. It's the time when we have to be brave enough to sit with the mess, and be patient. That's where the rich outcomes emerge.

References

Bell, D., Caplan, P., & Karim, W. Z. (1993). *Gendered Fields: Women, Men and Ethnography*. London/New York: Routledge.

Guillemin, M., & Gillam, L. (2004). Ethics, Reflexivity, and "Ethically Important Moments" in Research. *Qualitative Inquiry, 10*(2), 261–280.

Lenette, C. (2019). *Arts-Based Methods in Refugee Research: Creating Sanctuary*. Singapore: Springer.

Lenette, C., Stavropoulou, N., Nunn, C., Kong, S. T., Cook, T., Coddington, K., & Banks, S. (2019). Brushed Under the Carpet: Examining the Complexities of Participatory Research. *Research for All, 3*(2), 161–179.

Lenette, C., Blomfield, I., Yuol, A., Bordbar, A., & Akbari, H. (in-press). Self-Representation in Participatory Video Research: Ethics and Lessons Learnt. *Art/Research International.*

Phipps, A. (2019). *Decolonising Multilingualism: Struggles to Decreate* (Writing Without Borders). Bristol: Multilingual Matters.

Sunderland, N., Catalano, T., Kendall, E., McAuliffe, D., & Chenoweth, L. (2010). Exploring the Concept of Moral Distress with Community-Based Researchers: An Australian Study. *Journal of Social Service Research, 37*(1), 73–85. https://doi.org/10.1080/01488376.2011.524526.

4

Fear and Loathing in the Cross: Researching the Policing of Nightlife in Sydney

Phillip Wadds

So, Tell Us a Bit About Your Fieldwork and the Research You Have Done?

I've been doing field research into drinking, drug use, violence and policing in nightlife settings for over a decade now. This has ranged from ethnographic and immersive fieldwork to street intercept surveys and more structured observations across a number of related projects. I'm going to focus on my doctoral and early post-doctoral research here as it was the most intense and sustained period of fieldwork I have undertaken, and really did involve years of weekend night work in places like Kings Cross (the Cross) in Sydney's inner-city. For reference, Kings Cross is Sydney's notorious red-light nightlife district located just outside the Central Business District

---

P. Wadds (✉)
School of Social Sciences, University of New South Wales, Sydney, NSW, Australia
e-mail: p.wadds@unsw.edu.au

© The Author(s) 2020
P. Wadds et al. (eds.), *Navigating Fieldwork in the Social Sciences*,
https://doi.org/10.1007/978-3-030-46855-2_4

(CBD) which has historically had a high density of large nightclubs, bars and strip clubs. It has also been long linked to organised crime and incredible levels of police and government corruption in New South Wales (for overview see Wood 1997; Wadds 2020). My PhD research was primarily concerned with the working relationships between private security and public (state) police in the night-time economy, their views towards nightlife and each other, and the way in which their occupational cultures influenced their work and the lived experiences of those going out at night. I have also done projects on violence and other harms linked with drinking and drug use which involved different fieldwork experiences and methods.

I started work on this research in 2008 when Sydney had a very different nightlife landscape. This was prior to the introduction of the controversial 'lockout laws',[1] so places like the Cross were distinctly different places than they are now. Sydney nightlife was heaving—streets in the Cross were bustling with revellers, so much so that you would often need to walk on the road to get down the main strip. It had an edge. Policing and regulation were different as well. Police were engaging in lots of high-visibility, high-intensity operations as part of a 'war on alcohol-related violence' (see Wadds 2015), and so there was a lot of contestation and tension between revellers, security and street cops. My doctoral fieldwork involved thirty-six nights of observation in key nightlife precincts on (mainly) weekend nights, with sessions usually going for between six and ten hours, and thirty in-depth interviews with police and security staff working in Sydney's night-time economy.

Towards the end of my PhD, and in the first few years after graduating, I also managed a few major projects that involved the supervision of large teams of research assistants conducting street-intercept surveys and covert venue observations in nightlife districts. We were asking those out in the city about their drinking and drug use, alongside other aspects of their night out including if they had seen or experienced any harm or violence. The surveys took between five and ten minutes and ended with the participant completing a breathalyser to test their blood alcohol concentration. We did about 3000 interviews in Sydney across the two projects and

---

[1] The regulatory interventions introduced in designated zones of inner-city Sydney in 2014 which included a 1:30 a.m. 'lock out' (a one-way door policy) and 3 a.m. cessation of service alongside a wide range of other trading restrictions for licensed venues.

another 7000 across the country in different nightlife areas of capital cities and regional towns. They were massive projects.

Given Your Research, What Are Some of the Difficulties or Complexities That Come with Your Work?

In researching police and security operating in urban nightlife, it would be naïve to think that physical risk and violence would not feature in the course of fieldwork. Risk is ubiquitous in these spaces. That's the reason a lot of people go out, you know, to have fun, transgress, take risks (see Presdee 2000; Hackley et al. 2015; Lee et al. 2020; Wadds 2020). And the line between safety and danger can be crossed really quickly, often without warning. Dealing with that volatility and unpredictability is a test.

I was constantly dealing with intoxicated people. Every night. I was also trying to access guarded information from groups who it can be difficult to build rapport with from the outside (i.e. door staff and police). I had to be comfortable with hearing about violence, some of which was justified (if there can be such a thing), but lots of which wasn't. Then there was everything else that came with the turf, the gross misogyny and racism, the incredible bravado and masculine performances, and the casual sexual harassment and objectification. I had to sit through it. You are there to document it all. And that's not to say it is *all* like that, but that's a part of the world I was researching. Reacting in the 'wrong' way could undermine relationships, limit access or the type of information different people would provide. It was a challenge that required constant and careful navigation and wasn't without stress.

And I don't think you ever get trained for the types of experiences you have in the field. That's a major challenge. A lot of what you experience in the field is stuff you are facing for the first time. I certainly didn't feel overly prepared in that sense when I first started fieldwork. I'd done an Honours year where I conducted interviews and focus groups with 'at risk' Muslim youth who were involved in a peer-mentoring-based anti-radicalisation program in South-West Sydney. So, I guess I had had some exposure to working with 'difficult' groups, not difficult in the sense that they are themselves difficult, but difficult in terms of building rapport, trust and relationships that is so critical to getting access to the type of information that you want to get access to. But I certainly hadn't done field observations and any kind of ethnographic work before.

It is also physically taxing. My observations were all late at night. I would start at between 8 and 10 p.m. and would regularly go through to 4 or 6 a.m in the morning. I often waited until the end of shifts to do interviews with security staff. That sometimes meant doing an interview at four o'clock or six o'clock in the morning after being out all night. That was the rhythm they worked to, so that was the rhythm I worked to. It may seem like a little thing, and just something you do, but it takes a toll. I got in really bad sleep habits. I would often get home and want to type up notes. After that I would just crash. When you do that often enough, your body adjusts and then you struggle to sleep to a regular pattern. And it can affect everything else you need to do on the day-to-day—things with your family, your friends, your partner.

So, First Day in the Field! What Does It Entail?

My first day was really tough. It was probably the most intense experience of all the fieldwork I have done. So, to set the scene—I had just got my ethics clearance and I wasn't planning on recording field notes this night, I was just going into the Cross to do a bit of scoping to see which spots might be good to get an 'in' with door staff. Anyway, I've gone in with some friends—around 11:30 p.m.—and it's a really busy weekend night. We walked the strip for about an hour and decided to spend some time in this bar that's pretty (in)famous, linked to the local underworld. I've got to be careful about how I tell some of these stories as many of the people involved are still working in and around these spaces and I don't want to get them (or me) into trouble. So, we went into this venue at around 12:30 a.m. It was lively: really loud music, dark, atmospheric— the type of venue where you wake up with ringing in your ears the next morning (another side-effect of this type of research that you need to manage) and a sore throat from having to shout conversation all night. The venue was packed.

This night was significant because I'd been going out (a lot) for years and had never really seen that much severe violence. Sure, you'd see scuffles (pushing), lots of heated verbal exchanges, an occasional fight, but I had never seen really serious violence in person. And on this night that all changed. So, I was sitting there, and there was a bit of commotion—you know pretty routine stuff as it was getting later in the night. Everyone sits up. It was probably 2 or 3 a.m., and a woman in the bar was drunk and had said something to somebody in another group. It kicked off a bit—back and forth—until security intervened and told the woman she had to leave. I vividly remember the size of the security guard who stepped in. This guy must have been 6'4" or 5" (195 cm), a big Polynesian guy with long hair at the back, tattoos on his arms, his black 'uniform' on—such an imposing character.

Anyway, the woman was clearly very intoxicated and acting a bit erratically. The security guard grabbed her by the arm and started walking her out. Again, all pretty standard practice at this stage. As the guard was walking her out, she was lashing out at him, you know, trying to get free of his grip, writhing around, and all of a sudden, about five metres from the exit, he just turns around and whacks her in the face. It was sickening. I had never seen somebody collapse like that before; she just folded at the knees and went down. It was absolutely brutal.

All of a sudden, the place erupted.

She was with a smallish group who immediately got involved and it quickly turned into this big melee. Venue security were piling in, more people were drawn into it, onlookers were shouting or trying to get out of the way, all while a few people were trying to get to the now unconscious woman who was in a really bad way. The guard at the centre of it all was clearly trying to get out of there, but others from the group were trying to reach him. I remember watching him and a few others from the security team just standing there, absorbing people, throwing them down as they got within reach. It was a really severe fight.

When I reflect back on it, I think it only lasted for a few minutes, maybe not even that long, but it was just this flashpoint moment that got so out of control so quickly. And that was my first night of fieldwork. It was a baptism of fire. As I said before, I had been going out a lot—almost every Friday and Saturday night for five or six years—so I knew the city and the Cross well. I had seen the usual conflict and lower-level violence, but this was severe, really intense.[2]

It was also really telling. It woke me up a bit and became a key case study into aspects of police and security cultures and their relationships with others in nightlife settings. There was a real antagonism between patrons and police in the follow up—police were frustrated in interactions with those who were providing statements, but, more than that, they seemed to come to the scene with a pre-existing hostility that only exacerbated their animosity towards patrons. There were a lot of really angry, shocked and scared people around, and that left a palpable tension and hostile energy in the space. People were jacked-up. Security had receded into the venue and the guard at the centre of it all vanished altogether. In my own experience giving a report to police, I was treated with suspicion and disdain by a senior police officer, and when I called out this treatment he was openly hostile until two female officers intervened.

I learnt very quickly that both police and security had cultures of protection from 'outsiders', people they perceive as a threat. Of course I had read about all of this before I arrived in the field, but this experience drove home how challenging access was going to be for me and how hard I was going to have to work to build relationships and rapport with these groups so that they would be comfortable to talk to me about their work. There have been a few other episodes since, but nothing has really stuck with me as much as this.

---

[2] Nothing happened to the private security guards as far as I am aware. I followed up on the case and stayed in touch with some of those involved in the years since. I found out later that the woman assaulted had her jaw fractured in three places and required multiple surgeries.

What Impact Did That Have on You Emotionally?

It was tough. I didn't feel threatened that night. I made sure I wasn't in the thick of it when it kicked off, but seeing that type of violence was really confronting, as was speaking with others about the violence that was part of their daily work. There were other times over this project when I was fearful, where I was threatened. I was shirt-fronted one night following a major misunderstanding with some really *munted*[3] Irish guys, but that first night was by far the most extreme thing I saw during my fieldwork.

In terms of the impact, it was definitely something that tainted my view for the next few weeks. I was angry that nothing happened to the guard, and at the police intervention afterwards. I was affected, for sure, and it would have been easy to let those initial impressions continue, to become hostile. But that would have been the worst thing I could have done, it would have really limited my research, my access. I wanted to do fieldwork to gain a detailed understanding of the people policing these spaces, their life experiences, the way they viewed their work and nightlife in general. I wanted to move beyond stereotypical depictions of 'bouncers' and cops. I wanted to understand their violence, their performances, their interactions with others. It would have been too simplistic to say this was the way it was, that they were all thugs that overreact. Of course that happens, I am not the first to document that, but not everyone was the same. I met plenty of doormen who were averse to violence, who would go out of their way to help people who were struggling, who had had too much to drink. I also got a deep insight into the violence and abuse that police and security face on a near daily basis. Both these groups are doing dirty work and, while paid, it's usually thankless.

I am a critical policing scholar, if I am going to criticise practices, institutions, organisations or people for the work they do, or harms they cause, I need to know as much about them as possible, and I think the fieldwork I did provided me with an amazing level of insight into culture

---

[3] This is slang for heavily drunk and/or drug-affected.

in practice that wouldn't have been possible through other methods. Yes, that first night was a sickening episode of really unnecessary violence, but I wanted to know why, I wanted to know more about the experience of working in that environment that might have led to such a situation.

It is important to also note that that was not my general experience of security working in the city. There is no question that violence is a routine part of their work, but that *is* their work. They are paid to control unruly bodies, to deal with situations and issues that no one else wants to. It's shit work a lot of the time, but I met some good people, and I keep in touch with many of the guards I interviewed. I also met some vile humans who inspired loathing and who I had to battle to get through an interview or meeting with. I suppose the point I am trying to make is that it isn't always black and white with these groups and, for me, it was only through spending lots of time documenting my observations that I really understood this.

So How Did You Gain Access? What Did You Do?

With great difficulty. It was a slow process, but I had a few plans in place to try and build relationships and recruit doormen.[4] My main strategy was simply spending time in bars and clubs, getting to know people, speaking with bar staff. At the start, it was just observations and trying to build relationships that might help, trying to show that I was 'alright' and trustworthy. If an opportunity arose, I would try to get a phone number, or chat with someone over a cigarette on their break or at knock-off drinks at the end of a shift (if I managed to get an invite).

An important part of all of this was trying to fit in. I guess I was lucky in that respect. I did fit in, and I had enough cultural capital to use to gain access. I think that's a massive part of any fieldwork (see also Winlow

---

[4] I will focus on them, because access to the police was very different and involved a far more routine and formal process of institutional approval, albeit one with its own politics and challenges (see Wadds 2020). I should also add a note about the use of the term 'doormen'. Try as I did, when it came to security staff, all my participants were men. While there is research about the role of women in the industry elsewhere (Erickson et al. 2000; Hobbs et al. 2007), in the areas I was researching, there were very few if any women working doors.

et al. 2001). There is only a really small window in which I think I could have done this research, so in many ways I was incredibly fortunate to be doing it in my mid-20s. I didn't stand out; I was an insider in terms of the city and the scene (not the work). I was young enough to not look out of place in a nightclub at four in the morning. That said, I still did stupid things. There were things I took for granted. Like on one of the few times I did solo observations inside a venue. How, with all my knowledge of the space, did I not think about how suss it would be for a single young guy to be sitting by himself in the back corner of a bar slowly sipping a drink and just watching? I must have looked like the ultimate lurker. I had people asking me for drugs, bar staff offering me free soft drink (assuming I was a cop). I learnt very quickly that you can't be too static when you are alone. If you sit down, get your phone out, and don't spend too much time just looking around. Get up, move around, prop against a wall. Always have a drink.

Having a fieldwork buddy or someone you meet up with is also a great way to look less overt in the space. Being alone is pretty strange in pubs and clubs. Not many people go out by themselves. So I often met up with friends or other people I knew who were already in the space. People I knew. People I trusted. It helped me relax in the space and feel a lot less awkward. I didn't have to move around as much, and so it was easier to do my observations.

In building relationships, I also played on other things, like my love of sport. It was a really good conversation starter. A lot of the door staff in Sydney are Polynesian. Sit down in front of an All-Blacks game and you would always get asked the score by a security guard who was half-watching the screen, half-watching the venue. Talking rugby was a powerful language and got me access on more than one occasion. It's all snowballing from there. Once you get 'in' with a group, you just try to get them to like you, to trust you, to let you into their world.

And you might have to play a bit of role sometimes.

But that familiarity and banter can also get you into trouble. In your focus on getting access and building relationships with people you want to speak with, you can forget about everyone else in the space and how they perceive your interactions. That story about the shirt-fronting is a perfect example. I was at a sports bar in the Cross with a friend, someone who I often met up with during observations. Anyway, it was a place where I often started the night. I knew some of the door staff at this place and you could talk to the guards more freely there because it was a bit more relaxed, just people sitting around watching sport or playing pool. Those early conversations were really important because security out front scoped the street and would tell you if anything was happening, what the vibe on the strip was like. I suppose it was part of my risk management strategy in some respects, although I certainly didn't see it that way at the time—you might get a tip about where to avoid as you moved around the area. Anyway, so this night, there were a load of Irish backpackers in this place, playing pool and watching a big boxing bout that was on. Between the boxing fight and a big Premier League football game, the venue was busier than usual.

We ended up playing a doubles game of pool, something I did a lot during observations. It was another good way to be in the space and do your observations without standing out. Anyway, so me and my friend were playing pool against these two Irish guys. They were really drunk. And this was probably a bit after midnight—probably around 12:30 to 1 a.m. I'd been out for four hours or so already. And my friend had a group of mates (and this is all important) who were also out. We were going to meet up with them when I finished at around 2 a.m. and have a few drinks. Anyway, so we're playing pool. There was a lot of banter going on and we were winning the game of pool. And the Irish guys weren't very happy about that. We were getting towards the end of the game, well on our way to victory. Then my friend scratched. And so it started. The issue was around the rules of pool in Australia, particularly the two-shot penalty. In Sydney, at bars, we don't usually play two shots. Let's just say there wasn't much reasoning on their side and it escalated.

So, there was a bit of back and forth and eventually it calmed down, we conceded the two shots, played on and won the game. Everyone relaxed. We went off and sat in a different part of the room. They went off and did their thing. Anyway, as I said, I knew security in this place, and I was talking to them a little later on. The Irish guys were still there. They clearly saw me talking to security, but they were also really drunk and had been playing up a bit. Within about ten or so minutes they were getting kicked out of the bar. I didn't really think much of it. At that hour that wasn't unusual, and given their earlier behaviour it wasn't a shock.

Not quite so simple.

It would later emerge that they thought I got them kicked out—they thought I was speaking with security *about them*. They'd obviously held on to the incident at the pool table more than we had. So, it's getting close to the time we were going to leave. We left the bar. My mate called his group of friends. They were just down the road, probably less than a hundred metres away. Anyway, we start walking to meet them and about 20 metres away from the venue I see the Irish guys. They'd been waiting around outside for thirty or forty minutes. Another one of those moments where I'm like "oh, fuck, here we go".

And so it starts: "you fuckers got us kicked out", "fuck you"—really aggressive from the start. They walked over towards us. I notice one of their group was heavily drug affected—he was pacing like some people on stimulants do. And he was kind of lurking around the back of their group. These guys weren't particularly big, I felt like we could probably manage the situation if they would listen to us, and we weren't that far from the venue so I knew security could probably still see us if things kicked off. Whether or not they would come and help I wasn't as sure about. But it got into a pretty heated exchange—one of the guys grabbed onto my collar —he ripped my shirt—and it kind of developed. I was really trying to calm the situation, but that's not easy when someone has you by the throat. They weren't having a bar of it. Out of the corner of my eye, I kept looking at their drug-affected friend; he was doing really weird stuff. It was disconcerting. He was swinging back and forth on a street sign and shaping like he was going to get involved. I was stressing. Anyway, I kept trying to talk them down, but was increasingly fearing this was going to come to blows. Luckily one of the guys from the group my buddy had called had come out of the venue to see where we were and spotted us. He grabbed the rest of the group and bailed us out. Once we had the numbers, it settled quickly, but the legacy of that was with me for the rest of the night: that adrenaline kick, the ripped shirt, some marks on my neck. Adding insult to injury, I was blocked from getting into the next pub because of my shirt.

I suppose that is one of the risks when you want to get access: you can become blind to other things in the space.

You Mentioned Other Access Techniques? Also, Did You Tell the People You Were Engaging with About What You Were Doing?

One of the other ways I got access was a little more routine. I would cold-call security companies and ask them to participate. It didn't work very well. I think I probably only got two or three interviews that way, the rest were through field contacts. I was lucky that I did know some people who worked doors before I went into the field, I played sport with a few of them when I was younger, and they helped a lot. I also knew an older publican who introduced me to some retired 'bouncers'. These characters (and they were just that) told the most incredible stories about years gone by in the Cross which were great and gave me material which was really helpful in building relationships with others. It's amazing how powerful storytelling is among both police and security. I can guarantee that the knowledge gained from these stories got me at least three or four interviews.

As for telling people about my research, my observations were mainly covert. Of course, there always comes a point where you need to tell some people what you are doing—that you are researching nightlife, security, the Cross. Usually this was when you were trying to get an interview. Sometimes this was the point where contacts became suspicious or disinterested, so that groundwork of relationship building was critical. And I did the groundwork. For me, it was important to have a few gatekeepers who could vouch for me—bar managers or doormen with reputations who helped a lot with interviewees and contacts. This was all a pretty precarious game. I also had to be careful about who I was seen with in bars or out on the strip. If I was seen hanging out at a particular bar, with a particular security team, or interacting with the police, that might impact who I could speak with later on or how I would be received.

It was also a risk for my contacts. In the security world in the city, particularly in the Cross, they're all deeply familiar with what's going on in their areas. A lot of people in the industry are worried about other players. Some groups don't like each other. As I said before, there is a connection between *some* door staff and organised crime in the Cross, and the fear of reprisal from them is powerful. There are a few key people in the Cross who run a lot of security, and they have deep influence over others. They enforce unwritten codes. One of those codes is that you don't implicate others, you keep your head down and your mouth shut. There are very real physical and career threats for people if they step out of line, if they betray trust or do anything that might be perceived as such. This was a major challenge for me in my work, with both police *and* security.

You Mentioned Role Playing, Can You Tell Me a Little More About That? What Do You Mean?

I think you're often performing a bit of a role to get into those situations when you are meeting people you don't know. For me, it wasn't necessarily playing a foreign role, but more about maybe holding back in responding to something, or not calling something out that you may really struggle with hearing. I can give an example. Knock-off drinks at pubs used to be one of the best times for me to meet contacts and get access to a world that was usually really closed off. A security team would sit around and exchange stories about their night. This was absolute research gold. I could sit at the table, prompt discussion with one or two people and just sit there and gain this amazing insight into door work cultures: the bravado, the performance, the way they celebrated things that happened, but also finding out more about them as people. But these discussions were sometimes repulsive—talk of different women in the venue, the war stories about fights—much of which was infused with racism, sexism, misogyny and homophobia. You know, like "did you see that chick with the huge tits? Man, I would love to [insert any number of sexual fantasies]" or violent stories about "poofs" and "fags". It varied from uncomfortable to sickening.

How Do You Respond? Did You Call This Out?

No, I never called it out. And that's tough when you would in other parts of your life. Because that's part of the work—you're capturing that culture, right? Me calling it out then shifts that. It would risk the core of my research. It would be counter-productive to the knowledge that I was seeking. Do you want just a surface level understanding of these groups? Or do you sit with the discomfort to get a deeper insight? There is definitely a moral strain there. Because I'm sitting there going 'fucking hell'—he's talking about targeting someone for a bashing. Now you don't know if it's true or for show, but I had seen some of these guys working, and knew they were violent, so you're sitting there asking yourself if this is real.

It would've also put me at incredible physical risk—say goodbye to your face or worse.

So no, I didn't call it out. It's uncomfortable and you are often really torn because it is such rich insight, but also disgusting. You're sitting there, and you don't want that to become normalised—you feel dirty—and you play a role in that right? I want to get information out of this group. I have to sit there listening. It happened in interviews too, with both police and security, where you would be talking to someone and ask them a question about violence, or something, and they would come up with a response that shocked or challenged you. Like overt racism—someone using really vile language when talking about different ethnic groups. It was tough to grapple with, and when I reflect back on this work, I think it took more of a toll on me than any of the physical stuff did.

When it comes down to it, I had to push it all down. I had to prioritise the research; it was the only way to deal with that tension, that inner-conflict—because that access, that insight, is ultimately at the core of what I was looking for.

What About Other Risks?

Physical risk was probably the most present in my research, for both me and those who I was speaking with. I was often worried about how their interaction with me would impact on them. I always tried to do my interviews in quiet places, away from other people and ideally away from areas where you might bump into other people who knew your contact (i.e. not in pubs after shifts, etc.). But again, I think I was a bit naïve in the early days with this. I always wanted to voice record interviews, so I was trying to find places like libraries that everyone else in my PhD group were using for their interviews. I mean, what was I thinking?! "Hey, you have just finished a ten-hour shift, it's 6 a.m. in the morning, do you want to meet me at the library?" It's so ridiculous when you think about it, but I was new to this and I wanted to do things by the book, like everyone else. It's something that I think university ethics processes can really impose on field researchers, particularly when you are early in your career. I remember attending an ethics workshop as part of my 'researcher training' and being told that failure to comply with university ethics protocols could result in you getting kicked-out of the PhD program. It was huge pressure for a young researcher. The main problem: my research wasn't like everyone else's. I wasn't speaking to government workers about policy development or museum curators about cultural heritage. I was speaking with 'bouncers' and cops.

There were a few times that my naïvety got me in trouble, and one incident was particularly bad. It was sometime between five and six o'clock in the morning, the sun was coming up, I had been out all night and I had breakfast with this guard following his shift—he'd finished at about 4:30 a.m. I had a pretty good relationship with this guy, and he was quite a big player in Kings Cross, so I was stoked—of course I'm going to wait around until like six o'clock in the morning to do this interview despite being absolutely exhausted. Problem was, he didn't want to do it at the café and nothing else was open. He lived not far from the strip and so said we could go back to 'his flat'. As I said, I knew this guy reasonably well, we had mutual connections through sport, I felt pretty comfortable with him and I really wanted this interview, so I went back to 'his' place.

So, it turns out that 'his flat' was a bit of a crash-pad for a few of his 'mates' who also worked security in the Cross—they'd go there, have a sleep, and then go back out, home, or whatever. Anyway, we had gone back to this place, and there was no one else there. So far, so good. I had asked the guy if I could record it beforehand and he had agreed. We were right at the end of this interview, and it had probably gone for an hour, and then this guy comes in—and I immediately knew who he was—FUCK! He sees my voice recorder and goes "what the fuck is this?" This guy was a notorious hard man in the Cross at the time and someone very well known for violence. I felt like all the blood must have left my face. And I'm pretty sure it did.

So, there I am, looking like Casper the shit-scared Ghost, and I have no idea how to manage this situation, you know, you're not prepared for that. I'm sitting there going 'how do I explain this?!' How do I explain I'm doing research into nightlife and policing in a way that's he's not going to have a problem with? Luckily the guy I was speaking with was strong in vouching for me—saying "no, no, he's a good guy, he's writing a book about the Cross", all this kind of stuff. Thank God, it didn't get heated, but I could tell by the tone in his voice that he was suspicious. It was fair enough too, people he was affiliated with had been under criminal investigation for decades.

I think beyond everything it was the voice recorder that was the issue. If it wasn't there on the table, there would have been no issue. I ended up having to delete the recording and that seemed to placate him. My contact was also dropping names, saying that I knew X and Y, and that I played sport with X. That seemed to put the issue to bed, but I was still in their space—I'm in their house. I was desperate to get out of there. I had read all the history about the Cross. I knew about the people bashed to death, the 'hits', the people going 'missing' or some other horrific scenario. As much as you try, that is the stuff that's running through your head when something like this happens. I've seen this guy depicted on TV! Get. Me. Out. Of. Here.

It was only when I calmed down afterwards, following a long train ride home (it was only 30 minutes but felt like an eternity) that I really realised the implications that this could have for my contact. I checked in with him regularly for the next little bit, and he said it was all good, but it did rattle me. If I hadn't had those contacts, if I was interviewing a random guy that I didn't know very well, who knows how that would have ended.

After that, I was very reluctant to use a voice recorder; in fact, I only did it in interviews that I did with more formal participants, those that were arranged through official phone calls to security firms, not anything I organised in the field. Luckily, I had already done a fair few interviews by then, but still, it was another hard lesson to learn.

So, the Formal Ethics Requirements Can Cause Issues?

Definitely. There were challenges with ethics throughout a lot of my research. Just like using a voice recorder, it's ridiculous to expect things like written consent in lots of field settings. You work so hard to build relationships with groups that are really tough to gain trust with, and then when it comes to the point where you want to interview them, you pull out this formal three-page legal document. No. I mean how absurd for me to be carrying around paper-based forms to sign when I am doing research with people who are often engaged in criminal activity and are super wary of outsiders—like what was I thinking?! It's completely senseless. But a research ethics committee will often say no to verbal consent, that it must be written. They often have no idea of the risk that could produce in the field, for both the researcher and those participating in research. Like what would it look like to a suspicious onlooker if they saw a 'bouncer' signing a formal-looking legal document and speaking at length with some random guy they had never met. They would probably think I was a cop. That could have serious implications for my contacts. This is serious business.

I feel like when you are new to field research, you don't always have a developed understanding of institutional ethics—I know I certainly didn't—and because of that you don't always know that there are other ways to achieve the same goals. Fundamentally, for me, it came down to what an ethics of practice looked like. Like what are the really critical aspects of ethics—do no harm, research with a clear purpose, informed consent, respecting those you are working with, keeping promises, maintaining anonymity and confidentiality. I think a lack of training and experience can leave junior researchers with a sense that institutional protocols are set in stone and that the particular ways of meeting prescribed standards are not debatable or flexible in certain instances. I know I didn't have the confidence to push back on some of these 'requirements' early on in my career, so the first time I went to interview someone for my PhD, I pulled out the three-page information sheet and consent form for my interviewee to sign. It didn't go down well. It put them on edge, and I think it was part of the reason they also didn't let me voice record the interview. And that was with someone who was in management with a security company, not working doors.

Again, this was all a great learning experience. As I said before, it highlights the unpredictability of field research. You have to be ready; you have to have thought through different scenarios, you have to plan, and probably most importantly, you have to adjust. What's the alternative? Do you say "OK, I can't do the interview"? Of course not. You adapt. This is not to say that consent isn't absolutely critical to research, of course it is; but there are other ways of getting it that are less confronting to those you are speaking to. What are the key things you need to tell them about? What your study is about, what does participation look like, what you are going to do with their words, that they will be anonymous and you will de-identify, that they can see the transcript and edit it, that they can withdraw consent at any time. The outcome is the same, you get informed consent but the path to it is different.

That unpredictability was really a major feature of my fieldwork, and really did play out in multiple ways, some risky, some less so, but always underlined the importance of planning and knowing the space you are in.

What Other Issues Did You Come Up Against?

Interestingly, another big challenge for me was that I was doing this research in my own city. This was a space that I was already deeply familiar with. I knew where things happened, who hung-out where, who owned which nightclub. And that brought with it its own benefits, risks and issues. One of the challenges for me with doing research in my home city was that so much of my 'field' was really familiar. As I said earlier, I used to go out a lot in the city. I worked in the CBD during my undergrad and I spent most weekends of my early to mid-20s going to pubs and nightclubs in and around the city. The familiarity with the space was great preparation, but I also felt I might have been complacent and missed out key details of the spaces that I was in—like the really basic things that you would otherwise take for granted in your day to day.

Things like the omnipresent signage signalling a mix of warning and allure for incoming patrons when you get off the train ("don't take drugs", "make sure you look out for your friends", "don't have unprotected sex" etc.); the unique and often completely nonsensical design of Sydney streets that could leave others in precarious positions if they got lost; or the routine interactions between security, police and patrons that others may be unfamiliar with and so pick up extra details. This may sound bizarre, but I have reflected on this a lot. I think in the end it was a major bonus to know my city well, but there were definitely ways in which it shaped my experience, none more so than not really wanting to go into the city for years after my research because going out, previously a key part of my social life, had morphed into work through association with this research.

What About Risks to Others You Have Done Research with, Maybe from Some of Your Other Projects?

There is no question that meeting up with other people in the space exposes them to risk. These are inherently 'risky' spaces, I suppose. Everyone I met up with was already really familiar with nightlife, and we had been going out together in these spaces for years. I think an important point is that they were there already. I wasn't bringing them along. Does it make it more risky that they are with you? I suppose it can. The incident with the Irish guys certainly did. It's something I had to adjust to. I had to do better. And I was more conscious about how my interactions might be perceived by others in the space. I planned a bit better.

My other research brought a really different set of concerns, mainly because it wasn't just me and a buddy anymore; it was big teams of research assistants who had different levels of experience in nightlife scenes. But you also learn from all the other experiences you have had. You bring that knowledge into your next projects and get better at managing certain risks.

So, as part of that work, I was coordinating a few teams of research assistants conducting street-intercept surveys and covert venue observations between 10 p.m. and 2 to 4 a.m. in nightlife districts in Sydney, but also in regional NSW, places like Newcastle, Bathurst and Orange. We were asking those out in these places about their drinking, drug use, and other aspects of their night out, if they had seen or experienced any harm or violence, and how they were planning to get home. The surveys took between five and ten minutes and ended with the participant completing a breathalyser to test their blood alcohol concentration. We did about 1700 interviews in Sydney and around 7000 across the country for one project (see Miller et al. 2013) and 1300 for another project (see Lubman et al. 2013). They were massive projects and brought new risks.

As I said, I found I could manage my own risk when I was out, but it was much more challenging to manage the unpredictability of nightlife when you have such big teams. Luckily nothing ever happened. One major part of our plan to manage the team was to run a briefing and debriefing every session and have lots of protocols in place for what to do if anything happened. We also ran safety training sessions for everyone on the project to make sure they were aware of plans should anything go wrong. Part of our strategy was to have our teams together in groups of six, and one of those six was designated as the breathalyser person. It was their job to keep everyone in sight and keep an eye out for the wellbeing of their team. It was stressful at times, particularly on some of the really big nights in the city that we worked, like after major events or festivals when everyone would converge on the city and it could get a little edgy. These nights generally also had a lot more intoxication, and so again it came down to knowing where different groups might go in the city. I knew what type of patron particular venues attracted and tried to avoid those where I thought there might be a higher chance of aggression or other issues.

What About When You Are Writing Up Your Fieldwork?

Yeah, I am very conscious about how I write up my work, you have to be. I can often get paranoid, and so grappling with how to write up some of my research has been a real battle. I find it quite a draining process. I have spent hours stressing about whether something I have written will be identifiable, if it will get someone in trouble, if it will get me in trouble, especially now that I am a bit older, less unencumbered. I have a young family now which can add to the stress.

There's a lot of 'in group' sharing that happens within both security and the police. That increases my wariness about what elements of stories will identify certain people. I also have to be careful with my interview transcripts. Will a story be identifiable to others who were there or heard about it? Will there be blow-back for my interviewees? I mean, realistically, I don't think too many of these guys are going to go and read my thesis or articles—I'm not kidding myself—but you lose control once something is published. That is terrifying. It's something that has kept me awake at night on more than one occasion. This could be someone's career, someone's safety—possibly mine too.

So How Do You Deal with That?

To start, I avoid using real names or names of places outside of general areas if it is needed. I always edit down stories asking myself if I need to present certain details. It even shaped my thinking about this chapter—what stories am I going to tell? I stick with ones I have told before, with the same level of detail. This editing is part of an on-going process of mental work to keep my work within 'safe' boundaries while remaining true to the research and the material people have given me.

I also regularly call or speak with my colleagues—researchers who have done similar work. I bounce ideas and discuss concerns with them, asking them what they have done in similar circumstances, or what they recommend. It is ultimately your call what you do, but I have found these conversations invaluable, not only because of the content of discussions, but because getting a different perspective can really help you think through all the different potentialities. They also allow you to vent some of that stress, which, for me, has been a massive help.

So, What Would You Tell a Student or Someone Else Going Out to Do Fieldwork?

It's tough. I guess a big part of my 'training' has come from making mistakes. We all make mistakes. This happens in the field. Sometimes you only have a split second to make a big decision—do I push the envelope to get an interview I have been desperate for? Do I hang around somewhere when my gut is telling me to leave, or if things are kicking off? Making the wrong call can place you in a precarious position; it can place you or your collaborators at risk.

So, what do you do, what do I tell my students?

Learn from other people's experiences of fieldwork. Read. Speak with people who have been in the field. Not because you yourself will face those same issues, but because reading stories or hearing about different challenges can equip you with the tools to navigate the unpredictability of different scenarios that may come up for you. We need field research to be done. In fact, I think it is more important now than it has ever been, and it's under threat. University ethics committees are making it very hard to do—much qualitative research is derided in the era of 'hard' science, but we need to critically balance and juxtapose simple narratives that are sometimes produced and reproduced by reliance on statistics and quantitative research alone. We need to capture the lived experience of people affected by different regimes of power. We need to understand the complexity of our social domain. If you are going to go out into the field, commit to it—know there are risks, have plans, have contingencies. To navigate the thousand different possibilities, the different scenarios, the 'shit, I'm fucked' moments, you need to be deeply familiar with culture, customs, language and the places you are going to, their histories, their people. If I hadn't been as familiar as I was with the spaces I was doing research in, well, things could have gone very wrong for me.

Always be mindful of the impact that your research can have on others, particularly your participants. Look beyond self-interest, the amazing publication, the incredible, shocking, edgy quote that impresses at conferences, but which potentially jeopardises your field contacts. Push back on things at an institutional level that you know aren't right, that unnecessarily limit your work in the field. We need to resist the institutional compulsion to eliminate all risk from research. That will be the death of fieldwork, and it is too important to let go without a fight.

References

Erickson, B. H., Albanese, P., & Drakulic, S. (2000). Gender on a Jagged Edge: The Security Industry, Its Clients, and the Reproduction and Revision of Gender. *Work and Occupations, 27*(3), 294–318.

Hackley, C., Bengry-Howell, A., Griffin, C., & Szmigin, I. (2015). Transgressive Drinking Practices and the Subversion of Proscriptive Alcohol Policy Messages. *Journal of Business Research, 68*, 2125–2131.

Hobbs, D., O'Brien, K., & Westmarland, L. (2007). Connecting the Gendered Door: Women, Violence and Doorwork. *The British Journal of Sociology, 58*(1), 21–38.

Lee, M., Tomsen, S., & Wadds, P. (2020). Locking-Out Uncertainty: Conflict and Risk in Sydney's Night-Time Economy. In J. Pratt (Ed.), *Criminal Justice, Risk and the Revolt Against Uncertainty*. Melbourne: Palgrave Macmillan.

Lubman, D., Peacock, A., Droste, N., Pennay, A., Miller, P., Bruno, R., Lloyd, B., Hyder, S., Roxburgh, A., Wadds, P., Tomsen, S., & Brown, J. (2013). *Alcohol and Energy Drinks in NSW: Final Report*. Sydney: New South Wales Health.

Miller, P. G., Pennay, A., Droste, N., Jenkinson, R., Quinn, B., Chikritzhs, T., Tomsen, S., Wadds, P., Jones, S., Palmer, D., & Barrie, L. (2013). *Patron Offending and Intoxication in Night-Time Entertainment Districts (POINTED): Final Report* (National Drug Law Enforcement Research Fund Research

Monograph no. 93). Canberra: National Drug Law Enforcement Research Fund.
Presdee, M. (2000). *Cultural Criminology and the Carnival of Crime*. Oxon: Routledge.
Wadds, P. (2015). Crime, Policing and (In) security: Press Depictions of Sydney's Night-Time Economy. *Current Issues in Criminal Justice, 27*(1), 95–112.
Wadds, P. (2020). *Policing Nightlife: Security, Transgression and Urban Order*. Oxon: Routledge.
Winlow, S., Hobbs, D., Lister, S., & Hadfield, P. (2001). Get Ready to Duck. Bouncers and the Realities of Ethnographic Research on Violent Groups. *The British Journal of Criminology, 41*(3), 536–548.
Wood, J. (1997). *Royal Commission into the NSW Police Service, Final Report, Volume I: Corruption*. Sydney: Government Printer.

5

Doing Critical Drugs Research: From Deconstructing to Encountering Risk in the Field

George Dertadian

What Types of Research Have You Done in the Field?

The first time I did fieldwork was in 2012 when I was doing my PhD research. That project was on the non-medical use of pain medications. So sometimes that involves things that aren't typically associated with illicit drugs, like using medications at work to bulldoze through a stressful period, or mixing painkillers with alcohol to 'get more drunk'. Other times it involves things that are explicitly illegal like people using painkillers to come down from amphetamines after a big night of partying, as well as people who go from using pharmaceutical drugs to injecting and heroin use. I started doing this work by spending lots of time in the inner city of Sydney talking to people in street-based drug markets about pharmaceuticals. That is where I started, but I have broadened out what I do

G. Dertadian (✉)
School of Social Sciences, University of New South Wales,
Sydney, NSW, Australia
e-mail: k.dertadian@unsw.edu.au

from there to include an interest in how people who use and inject drugs become marginalised and the drug use of non-marginalised groups.

I've done qualitative studies with people who use drugs (PWUD) from really different perspectives, including; sociological research on the non-medical use of pain medications (Dertadian 2018); qualitative epidemiology on oral and injecting opiate use (Dertadian et al. 2017); and criminological research with young men who inject drugs and their experiences of violence (Dertadian and Tomsen 2019). It is a bit of a patchwork of areas, but that is relatively common for people interested in Cultural Studies, which is my training background.

In terms of where I have done this work, the main location has been the infamous inner-city suburb of Kings Cross. This suburb has been known for many years as the heart of the city's underbelly and a beacon for drug market activity. Although I have to say that having done research in the area over many years, there have been seismic shifts in the urban landscape in Kings Cross recently, because it's become really gentrified. When I first started doing research, it had a much grungier and urban vibe about it. The storefronts were aged, their signs a dull shade of the original colour. There was a constant and visible presence of people sleeping rough, using drugs and those involved in sex work. Compare that to the last time I did fieldwork in Kings Cross, which was last year—there were a bunch of fancy restaurants, with minimalist and slick middle-class aesthetics. Not to mention the fact that there were far fewer drug users and sex workers simply hanging around. They were still there, but you had to look a lot harder. This is one of the reasons I started to try different methods for recruitment.

Tell Us About Those Methods and the Impact They Had on Your Research?

I have used three main methods to recruit people to studies: cold calling people in the field; partnering with a relevant service that is embedded in the field; and online advertisements that attract hidden populations that are hard to find in a traditional field context. Each of them have their benefits, but also come with their own risks.

When you're doing cold calls, there are more immediate physical risks involved, because you are approaching people you do not know, in an environment you may not be familiar with. That's a pretty daunting thing to do as a student or early on as a researcher. And that's what I did. My first project, my PhD, started with cold-calling in Kings Cross. It feels really different when you are in the more comfortable space of a drug service and there are staff there helping you out. But for me, there are real risks involved in only doing research in environments where you feel comfortable. When you do that you are narrowing your understanding of the field to people who are in contact with a service and that is hardly the whole picture of drug use in a city.

As for the third recruitment strategy, when you're recruiting online you get this totally different group of people and all of a sudden there is this vast chasm between the experiences of people from street-based drug markets and people responding to online advertisements who, in my experience, often come from affluent suburbs. When you're using multiple of these methods in a study you start asking questions like, can I really compare this data? So there are different types of risks involved with different methods.

Can You Tell Us a Little More About the Risks in Your Field?

Actually, it's a little weird talking about risk for me. It's my Cultural Studies background—Cultural Studies is quite sceptical of the term risk. When it comes to research training, what you get in Cultural Studies is poststructuralist-oriented discourse analysis (Good 1995). So, my training was all about reading documents and analysing what they were saying, as well as paying attention to the silences. The emphasis is on the fluidity of knowledge and social practice, rather than any fixed categories involved in paradigms like risk assessment. Because of this, I have a strong conceptual commitment to the idea that the 'dangers' of drug use are contextually contingent and discursively constructed (Keane et al. 2011; Manderson 2011). This approach rejects the idea that drug use makes people commit crime, or that it necessarily results in homelessness, disease transmission, dependence or overdose. Instead, I'm interested in the way social contexts, like drug discourses, drug policies, drug cultures, and so on, work together to marginalise, stigmatise and criminalise PWUD. It's not an inherent risk; it's a constructed or co-produced risk.

I think another of my aversions to the word 'risk' comes from the fact that I see risk as a tool of governance that is used to mark PWUD as a 'risk to society'—because they transmit blood-borne viruses or are involved in crime—and in dispassionate claims about how they engage in 'risky behaviour' (Moore 2004). I am not saying these things don't happen, or that they aren't genuine concerns, just that they are usually presented without context, without any discussion of how these risks emerge, and this can leave the impression that they are somehow 'naturally occurring'. So I'm sceptical of talking about risk in the field, not because I think there is *no risk* in drug use, but because I think it's important to be aware of the way discourses of risk—how we think and talk about risk—actually contribute to the on-going marginalisation of PWUD.

Now, having said that, when I entered the field with this critical stance, it was quite a shock to have my conceptual commitments challenged so immediately by personal encounters of fear and danger. When I first started doing my PhD, I was riddled with anxiety over the possible risks: the risk of rejection; the risk of perpetuating unhelpful stereotypes; the risk of accidentally causing distress; the risk of being stigmatised by colleagues for doing this type of work; the risk of exposing myself to illicit activity; the risk of overthinking it. More than anything I was concerned about doing fieldwork wrong, about breaking one of the unspoken and difficult-to-decipher rules. At the start that made me a little too careful I think.

The reason for that caution was just simple things like witnessing very public disputes, often involving violence, about drugs. I heard people aggressively yelling across the road near me: "*You owe me money you fucking prick*" and "*I'm going to fuck you up you dog*". These are formative experiences when you first enter the field. Not just this, but the fact that these types of disputes are actually one of the only ways you can reliably identify PWUD. The idea that you need to approach and speak to people who are making violent threats or throwing fists at someone they were being quite friendly with only a minute ago is a little frightening. I mean I wouldn't approach them right after they were in a fight, but it just plays on your mind that violence is part of this world and I am inserting myself into it to do research.

So even though I was trained to deconstruct risk and question stereotypes about the dangerousness of drug use, that does not mean that I was numb from feeling a palpable sense of being 'at risk'. While I had significant training in critically assessing problematic narratives about drug use and risk, these ideas are so powerful that they constantly reassert themselves. It might come from the films you watch or the news you consume, but it's also there in everyday encounters with family, friends and colleagues who tell you to 'be careful out there'. It's hard to shake off that social conditioning when you are explicitly seeking out a social phenomenon that is symbolically charged with fear and danger. It feels like it's impossible to escape that and I had a lot of internal conflict about it. Was the critical perspective I was so focussed on being proven wrong before my eyes, in real-time? Was it my responsibility to find out what that fight was about? Was this work worth my own physical safety? But that self-questioning fades as you spend long stretches of time in the field. I became more settled in the idea that it was ok to avoid situations that made me uncomfortable. Eventually the pockets of violence become background noise. The big picture, which is hard to see when you first start out, is that I have never had any of that physical violence directed at me. In the end I actually think that the feeling of being frightened to even be around PUWD proves the point that critical perspectives are trying to make: the 'dangerousness' of drug use is, to some extent, a self-fulfilling prophecy. Of course, the embodied presence of risk as I walked the streets of Kings Cross was both concerning and exciting.

Can You Tell Us About Cold Calling and the Challenges It Presents?

Cold calling is probably the most field-intensive approach I have taken and the one that involves the most risk—well physical risk anyway. This is where you hang out in an area with a lot of drug market activity and approach people 'cold'. You are approaching strangers. No one is introducing you to them.

When I first started doing fieldwork fear of rejection stopped me from actually talking to anyone using drugs. But after a while, maybe a few weeks, I was getting a bit desperate to kick off the interview component of the study and so I mustered up the courage to approach people—the problem is the only way I had to identify people was to fall back on assumptions about the visual presentation of PWUD. So, I approached people whose clothes were 'untidy' and who were 'loitering' in the area. These are classic symbols of 'deviance' or 'criminality' that the deconstructionist perspective I was trained in constantly debunks. This was a source of self-doubt as I was doing fieldwork. I felt like I was just stereotyping people and that I was betraying all of those really important theoretical commitments. But it was out of necessity to move the study along. As you can imagine though, this approach had its downfalls.

For example, there were a lot of backpackers in Kings Cross at the time I was doing this research. They packed light and shared small accommodation spaces, which meant they also wore a lot of comfortable and loose-fitted clothes, and often hung around outside, in the street. Unfortunately, they fit the stereotype. In my desperation to make contacts, I approached a lot of them, and some of them were insulted at my mistake, my assumption that they injected drugs. While embarrassing, those encounters did help me refine the way I approached people, both the types of people I approached, and the words used in the approach. With the benefit of hindsight, I tend to only approach people if I have some significant indicator that they are involved in an illicit drug-related activity, like if I have seen them buy drugs, argue about a drug deal publicly or visited a drug service.

One of the major things I changed was that I started by hanging around a unique service called the Medically Supervised Injecting Centre (MSIC). The injecting centre is a clinical space where people can go to inject drugs, and then get health advice from nursing staff on how to minimise harm. I wouldn't approach people as they entered the centre because that would run the risk of having someone with drugs on them being publicly exposed out front of the centre just to speak to me. What if a police officer saw us talking and walked over to investigate? I had to be discreet. Discretion is an incredibly important part of this type of fieldwork. Also, people often head straight to MSIC after they have made a drug purchase and are anxious to use—so there's no sense putting people offside by interrupting this. However, knowing who went into the facility did make it easier to approach them later that day or week.

From those early experiences, I also learnt that the wording of the approach should avoid assumption as much as possible, because depending on the way you say it, even people who inject can be insulted at the assumption that they inject. And just because they inject does not mean that they want to talk to you about it. Of course, they will make this loud and clear to you. On approach in public settings, I've often had people loudly yell *"get the fuck out of my face"*. It is pretty embarrassing, but it is important to respect that request for a few reasons. The first is obviously your own personal safety. The second is to avoid any reputational damage, because other people see that and they might 'clock' you as the guy doing shady things, as the one *not* to talk to. But the most important reason I think is that you never know what that person has been through that day, and what kind of stress or trauma you are adding to. Has she just been robbed by someone she thought was her friend? Did he just get strip searched in public for no good reason? Did their partner just overdose? These are all stories that I've heard, and they are all part of the landscape of things that people who inject have to deal with on a daily basis. I know that if any of those things happened to me, I wouldn't want some random person from a University asking me to take part in a study.

Another thing about cold-calling is that you spend a lot of time walking the streets. I would say most of my time in the field was spent walking the streets of the drug market and its surrounding suburbs. I'll just be talking to people about issues related to the study, not doing formal interviews. When I say that, I mean I will talk to a lot of people who will not be included as part of the actual 'data' of the study, but who provide essential information about the social and physical setting of drug use. I want to find out where PWUD hang out, where they eat and sleep, as well as where they use and buy drugs. I do this so that I can actually find PWUD but also to get a sense of the world they are occupying. The value of doing this is well documented in the literature, but I have to say that as you are pacing around random streets and talking to an assortment of locals, it hardly feels productive in the moment. When I first started doing field-based research, I felt very self-conscious about what outcomes I was achieving by 'hanging out' in the field. I constantly wondered if I was wasting my time. The reality is it's really hard to understand the value of hanging out until you have been in the field for a while and you have enough local knowledge that it is informing the routes you walk and the people you speak to. The longer you spend in the field the more comfortable you get. Also, feeling like you are familiar with the field is essential to building the confidence to approach people who are used to seeing you around. They might even start to become curious about why you have been hanging around lately.

One good example of the value of hanging out in the field is when I was in King Cross during 2015 doing a project on young people's patterns of and experiences with the non-medical use of pharmaceutical opioids. I hadn't been in the field for a project involving injecting drug use since my Ph.D. fieldwork, so many of my contacts were no longer around. This is a particular issue in the drugs field because, especially when dealing with injecting drug use, you are talking about people that, by virtue of their circumstances, can be quite transient. They are being pursued by law enforcement constantly, they sleep rough or rarely have a single residence for long, and they often change phone numbers because of theft and the difficulty of keeping personal belongings safe while living and working 'on the street'. So, you constantly need to update your knowledge and local engagement. After spending a good deal of time walking my old routes, I realised the alleyways and street corners I used to frequent were now the domain of a trendy café culture. Following several conversations with those in and around these cafés I began to hear a consistent story that people who use pharmaceuticals and injected drugs hung out in a park opposite the local hospital because hospital staff and patients provided a good source for the supply of pain medications.

After visiting the park, I met a man, who I came to know as 'Tim', in this park. He was on my radar because of the large backpack he carried, which was a sign that he was keeping all of his belongings on his person: meaning he probably slept rough. Tim always came to the park with his dog to play fetch and I love dogs so I thought that would be my best way in. I sat close to where the dog's ball was being thrown and waited for it to land close enough to me so that I could pat the dog, then used this as a way to spark a conversation with Tim. As it turned out, Tim was over the age bracket for the study, but I spoke to him about the topic and took his number to keep in touch as a sounding board for any issues I was having with recruitment.

A few days later Tim told me about a spot where many people who inject drugs sleep under a bridge in Woolloomooloo (a nearby suburb). He also explained to me that the 'injectors' and the 'drunks' slept on different sides of the road; a strict separation between these groups that was a result of their intense dislike of one another. So, I added it to my list of regular spots to walk by. After regular visits there I learned that the spot was popular because it partially protected against the rain, which is important when you are sleeping rough, and was also nearby to a public toilet. I hung around for a bit but was totally intimidated to approach a big group of people who injected in what was essentially their street home. I did notice that a few of them smoked though, and so one day on the way to do fieldwork I bought a lighter. I felt like that would be a little less daunting way to approach someone, for them and for me. I recruited a participant named 'Destiny' under the bridge by offering to light her cigarette.

Can You Tell Us About Partnering with a Service? How Is It Different to the More Street-Based Work?

It feels very different, I will often partner with a service when I am looking for a really specific group of people. The main partner I have worked with is the MSIC in Kings Cross, which has highly marginalised clients, lot of them are from low socio-economic backgrounds and have significant histories of trauma. It can also take a lot less time because the design of the study will often mean that MSIC helps recruit participants. Most of the time this means that I provide the service with the selection criteria and the staff then identify clients that fit the criteria and ask them if they want to participate. So, the staff at the service do the recruitment and you conduct the interview on-site. There is definitively less physical risk involved. Firstly, the atmosphere is much less tense in a service—everyone is there for the same or similar reasons and there is a much-reduced threat of publicly exposing someone's drug using status. There are also other staff around and usually a security guard as well. Of course, there is a trade-off, because you have less control over who you interview. Rather than approaching people you feel comfortable to approach, you are simply brought people to interview, whether you feel comfortable with them or not.

For example, in January 2016, staff at the MSIC introduced me to a guy called 'Geoff' in a clinical service room where I was doing interviews with clients about their experiences of violence. As I shook Geoff's hand, I notice that his right hand had the letters W-H-I-T-E tattooed just below the knuckles on his fingers—during the interview, I noticed the letters P-O-W-E-R tattooed on each finger of his left hand. As I spoke to Geoff, it became clear that he was a white supremacist. As someone from a migrant family, it made me a little uncomfortable to be in a small room with a white supremacist talking about violence. But I wanted to be professional and so I pressed on.

Towards the end of the interview Geoff was explaining why he thought violence was necessary, saying "*Them Middle Eastern cunts they have violence, they'll cut your fucking head off and take your gun*", "*We need to fight back with the same… Violence needs to be used"*. At this point it is worth noting that my background is Armenian and I have a moderately dark skin tone as well as dark hair and a beard—in other words, I match the description of a person of 'middle-eastern appearance' that Geoff was advocating violence against.

How Did That Make You Feel?

Uncomfortable. I was holding back squirming in my seat. And I think Geoff was happy about that. He seemed to indulge in a range of physical gestures geared at intensifying my discomfort: his tone of voice became progressively more combative, he spoke in shortened breaths, he leaned in closer to me and he constantly touched the tattoos on his fingers.

While I didn't feel like I was ever in any real danger (there were security staff just outside), in the moment there was still a palpable sense that he didn't like me and that he was intentionally trying to agitate me. I tried hard to control my face from expressing disapproval, because this is generally discouraged. The usual advice in the literature and from colleagues is to have a human response to what people are telling but to avoid being judgemental. But that advice is usually given to make sure middle-class interviewers avoid compounding the moralisation and stigmatisation that comes with practices like the sharing of injecting equipment or injecting while pregnant. That advice doesn't really relate to a personal attack on the interviewer though and I was confused about how to respond. Instead of addressing it in the session, I tried to defuse the tension by bringing up issues like his financial disenfranchisement or how he felt ostracised by his class status—the topics I felt most 'at home' talking about, and to be fair it sounded like he had genuinely experienced it in his life. I gave Geoff the opportunity to expand on these issues I could sympathise with. The interview ended shortly after this.

Afterwards I wondered how my discomfort impacted the interview. Should I be able to do an interview with someone who is trying to make me uncomfortable? Was it as bad as I was making it out? With hindsight, I am still glad I did that interview. I mean, at the end of the day having a staff member bring Geoff to me bypassed my own personal bias in the sampling. And while generalisable sampling is not the goal of qualitative research, hearing views that are personally uncomfortable for me can be a powerful thing and it is worth pursuing. I don't have any specific thing I would do to avoid discomfort next time, but I would certainly feel more prepared if it happened again.

What About the Research You Have Done Using Online Advertisement? Is That Different Again?

Using online advertisements is probably the least field intensive approach that I have used. It generally involves setting up advertisements on social media sites like Facebook or in classified ad sites like Gumtree. I have also used Airtasker which is an errand outsourcing website where you can ask people to do different jobs for you.

Once people respond to the advertisements, you can then do an assessment to see if they fit the criteria. You have to be careful about how you do this assessment though, because sometimes the wording can throw people off, especially if you are communicating over text. A lot of these websites only allow you to contact the person who answered the ad with an internal private messaging service. So, for example, one time I was trying to determine if a potential participant named 'Jennifer' had used a pharmaceutical pain medication non-medically at least twice in the previous six months to see if she qualified for the study. Jennifer answered 'yes', and we organised an interview, but as the interview got started, she was talking about the use of Xanax, which is not technically a pharmaceutical analgesic as outlined in the study's inclusion criteria. Xanax has similar effects on the body to many painkillers, but the participant simply did not fit the criteria now. So, I conducted the interview, but it was disappointing that her story could not be included in the project. After that I adjusted the questions and asked what medications a potential participant had used non-medically. That way I am asking for a specific drug and I can assess their eligibility with more information.

The other thing about online recruitment is that you get a really different batch of people. Advertising online is especially useful if you are trying to locate people that are part of a hidden population that do not rely on street-based drug markets. These are often people who live in affluent suburbs, who have access to private spaces when using drugs and who mostly get drugs through valid prescription, or in the case of younger people by taking medications from their parent's cabinets and sharing them around. A good deal of participants who are recruited online also buy drugs online. So, if you ever want to speak to PWUD that are not part of marginalised communities, the internet is a good place to start.

A lot of the rules of engagement are also different when you are dealing with a wealthy middle-class person, at least when compared to the marginalised groups you most commonly encounter at street level drug markets or at a service. Something as basic as where you do the interview has different implications. For example, in 2015 I made contact with a participant named 'Ben' online and organised to meet him at a local shopping centre in a well-to-do suburb in Sydney's North, where he lived. I had always done interviews with people who inject in public locations, like cafés or parks and so I arrived early to look for a spot. I found a local park that was far enough away from the local shops that not many people were walking by and let Ben know where I was. But when Ben arrived, he was acting very cagy and was clearly uncomfortable. He was jittery and constantly looking around. His answers were short and rushed too. Eventually he asked *"Can we go somewhere else? Do you have a car?"* I was happy to oblige. Once we got into the car and closed the doors, Ben let me know that I was the first person he had ever told that he was dependent on OxyContin. He was scared that someone in the local area would notice him talking to me or overhear the conversation, and that his status as a 'drug user' would be exposed. This could not be more different from my experience interviewing people in Kings Cross, because their drug using status is usually so public that it is assumed. When I'm interviewing in Kings Cross, a participant might speak quietly when discussing traumatic or sensitive material, or we might break while a large group walks by, but there is very little assumption that a private space is even possible. Of course, it makes perfect sense that people who do not use drugs in public would not want to talk about using drugs in public.

With that experience in mind I now try to pursue a private space, like my car or a room in a library, for all participants. It's not always possible, but it is worth trying to give them as much privacy as possible. I also wonder how access to a private space changes the kind of information a participant is willing to share. I mean at a human level I would be more willing to talk about trauma or crime if there was a closed door.

What Are the Ethics of Doing This Type of Research? Have You Had Any Challenges with Ethics?

You never know what is going to happen when you are hanging out in a street-based drug market, walking around a service or trawling the internet looking to find PWUD. There is no neat and tidy way of doing this work. Because of this, there is a tension between preparing for what are genuine practical and ethical dilemmas by setting some boundaries, but also the need to be flexible enough to seize moments that are presented to you serendipitously (Bryan Page and Singer 2010; Maher 1997). This is why the ethics application is so interesting. I am always torn about the ethics application. If taken seriously it does provide the opportunity to be forward thinking about the risks that the researcher and participant can come up against. For instance, as we will get to later, you need to know how to deal with the trauma you will encounter in the drugs field. Not how to literally *treat* it, but how to help people find help should they want it. However, the modern University is so risk averse that ethics committees often suggest rigid protocols to respond to dynamic situations. As an example, the protocol for recruiting a participant or conducting an interview, which is cleanly laid out in your ethics documents, often looks very different in the field. These documents assume that interviews are going to be done in static conditions and in one block of time. Of course, participants are on their own schedule and they don't always care about your protocols. They might, for instance, need you to come along for the ride on one of the many adventures, tasks and errands they have planned, or when they get a free moment. While you do not need to follow participants around all day, and should avoid it if you feel unsafe, it can be very informative to go along for the ride. You need to be flexible.

A good example of this was with a participant I met when I was pacing the streets between the main strip in Kings Cross and Woolloomooloo: her name was 'Megan'. Megan was very generous with her time, spending hours walking around with me and introducing me to other people. She would say, *"I really want to talk to you, but I just need to meet this guy first"* or *"I've just got to go sell this first"*, followed by an invitation to *"Just come with me quickly and then we can talk after"*. These offers to accompany Megan on her daily activities provided some good opportunities to observe aspects of the field I might not otherwise have had, but it also meant that I was witnessing criminal activity that was not directly of interest to the study. Boundaries are important here and asking people to avoid telling you about or showing you criminal activity that is not central to the study is an important starting point, but this is not always easy to enforce. You have to make an assessment in the moment. Is this person, or what they are showing you worth the risk of dealing with the can of worms it might open? If it is, then tactically ignoring it is sometimes the only option. It's not like you have a lot of time to decide either. She's in a rush and has asked you to come along—what are you going to do? I said yes to Megan, though I haven't with everyone who asked.

On one occasion I went with Megan to a bench across from a local pub in Kings Cross while she sold a small amount of methamphetamine to a customer. The man buying was named 'Elijah' and he did not like the fact that I was there. He became very nervous, asking Megan *"Who is this guy?"* and *"What's he doing here?"* My presence felt like a risk to his safety and to Megan's sale. Megan tried to calm him down by saying *"I know him, he's fine. You can talk to him, he's from the Uni"*. I offered to leave to avoid any escalation—his nervousness was making me nervous too. But Elijah did become more comfortable and we spoke more freely. I did eventually ask him why he got so nervous around me, and he told me *"your shoes were too nice, so I thought you were dodgy"*. That day I was wearing loafers because I had come straight from a meeting on campus. For the record, it was a cheap pair of loafers from a low-end retail store, but loafers are loafers I suppose and the symbolism of having 'nice shoes' goes a long way when you're in the middle of buying methamphetamine in Kings Cross.

How Do You Deal with Trauma in the Field?

One of the things that I have found hard to deal with is the amount of trauma you encounter in the field. I am not a trained psychologist and I have no qualifications in counselling. Of course, research is not a therapeutic encounter. That's why you have protocols in place when doing this type of research, so that you can refer any incidents to someone qualified to deal with them. Now that sounds nice and simple, but in reality, when you actually have a person in front of you that is suffering, it's so much more complicated than following a protocol.

In 2014 I was interviewing a man named 'Mark' in a semi-private space at MSIC, when he described thoughts of self-harm, telling me that he felt demoralised by his drug dependence and the fact that he slept rough. He said that it was so difficult that he considered sleep "*A bit of a relief or release from the consciousness of the hell that I'm in*" and went on to say "*That's why I thought it would be better off if I just fell asleep and didn't wake up*". This was the first interview I had ever done at MSIC and it was the first time I had heard a disclosure of thoughts of self-harm in the field. What played on my mind more than anything was that it happened in a semi-private space—leaving me concerned about my ability to contain the information shared, process it myself and then deliver an appropriate response. I wondered had anyone on the other side of the partition heard what Mark said? Had I put him in a compromising position by doing the interview in a space that was not private enough? What, if anything, did Mark want me to do with the information he had just shared?

As per the protocol set up as part of the ethics application, at the end of the interview I provided Mark with the contact details of a counselling service. Mark took the referral but told me "*Nah I don't need this*". I had fulfilled the official ethically approved requirement related to incidents such as this, but I still felt a deep sense of responsibility to Mark's wellbeing after asking him to discuss his drug use for the purpose of research. I texted Mark a few times over the next couple of days and weeks, not directly about the disclosure, but to just generally check in: "*Hi Mark, how are you feeling since we spoke yesterday?*" and "*How was your week?*" things like that. He always responded, though mostly with vague language like "*Doing fine*" and "*Yeah good*". Not being able to do much more than that makes me feel a bit useless. I mean the whole reason I do this work is to help people like Mark, and yet when he is saying something so vulnerable all I can do is give him a card he won't use or text him a few times. That is one of the hardest parts of fieldwork for me. I still have not figured out how to reconcile how useless I feel in moments like this, because it's not the only time this type of thing has happened.

In 2016 I was doing field interviews at MSIC and staff brought a young man named 'Jason' into the room. Jason was the one-time partner of Megan (mentioned above), and I had met, interviewed and spent some time with him as part of a previous project. While I had a good sense of Jason's history of drug use from hanging out as part of the previous study, I had never asked him about his experiences of violence, which was the subject of this study. As he detailed past experiences of violence, Jason started to tell me about a traumatising story of abuse at the hands of his father. During his early teenage years, Jason was in a car accident where he unknowingly broke his collar bone and a bone in his shoulder. The pain was so severe that he was vomiting from pain. After telling his father what happened, his father started to make fun of him for not being able to cope with the pain. He then forced Jason to hold a beer can above his head using the injured arm. Jason explained that every time his arm dropped "*he punched me in the face*" saying "*fuck I can still feel it today just imaging the crunch*". This was repeated several times, and each time Jason described the punch to his face he punctuated it by punching his closed right fist into the open palm of his left hand. Each time he punched his hand it increased in force, and so did the visible distress on Jason's face.

After the fourth punch to his open palm, I interrupted and nervously asked: "*We can break? Do you want me to get you some water?*" Jason agreed and we left the small clinical room where the interview was being conducted, walking past the reception area of the service to until we got outside in the hustle and bustle of the street. As soon as we got outside, Jason began to pull out a packet of cigarettes, offering to share one with me. While I don't normally smoke cigarettes, I felt an overwhelming human need not to reject Jason after the horrific story I had just heard. I accepted and Jason smiled with delight.

I guess the point I am making here is that with both Mark and Jason, the protocols and set boundaries missed the point. Even though the conditions of the study did not require me to follow up with Mark, he had given me his number and invited me to stay in touch. I am glad that I texted him in the days following the interview to check in. However, it may not always be a good idea to text participants after their participation in a study that does not involve on-going contact—they might not want to hear from you. With Jason, after exiting the building with him I had to make an unexpected decision as to whether I would break a personal boundary—to not smoke—and share a cigarette with Jason in that moment. Participants often feel more comfortable speaking about traumatising or stigmatising topics if they can do something familiar and intimate and can share this with their interviewer. Of course, you should also think about the appearance and implications of 'using drugs' with your participants. It felt right this time; it might feel different in other circumstances. Each of these felt like the right choice for that moment: a human response to someone in pain. How 'right' it feels will change with circumstance, participant and environment. I suppose I learned that you have to have some boundaries in mind when you enter the field but must remain open to embracing the way those boundaries need to be altered by human contact.

What Role Does Being 'Critical' Play in Your Fieldwork?

The 'critical' part of doing critical drugs research is really important to me. Mostly it's about avoiding assumption as much as possible in the field. So, for example, there are two areas where I try to be conscious of the assumptions I'm making: the language I use in the field and the type of participants I recruit.

Talking 'like an academic' risks obscuring your goals. I try to avoid using patronising or inaccessible language in the interview itself—not because PWUD would not understand these terms, but because hardly anyone outside professional researchers or those in your specific field of research would understand them. Not to mention the fact that it would be an inappropriate way of pushing your status as a supposedly 'important person' from an 'important University'. The approved set of questions for a study is often a sanitised, clinical document, which has been through several rounds of review by an explicitly risk-averse Ethics Committee. This means that approved questions can come off as either oddly phrased or even unclear to participants. Most of the time, they are not appropriate to ask as written. So, what you have to do is practice rephrasing the questions in ways that incorporate them into conversation. For example: *"Can you tell me about your experiences with health care services?"* becomes *"You mentioned that you had gone to emergency at St Vincent's Hospital. How did the staff treat you there?"* Now sometimes the question is too big to simply rephrase and what you actually need to do is build up to it slowly over the course of a conversation.

For instance, let's take the question: *"How did any victimisation from violence impact on your own sense of being masculine?"* That's a big question about people's experiences of violence, and the way that violence is connected to drug use and masculinity. It needs to be drawn out slowly and in stages. In an interview with a young man who injects drugs named 'Jinan' in 2016, I was struck by the passing mention of him being beaten by his cousins when they found out he had been injecting. Later on in the interview, I brought up the incident to ask for more detail and got a fuller description of how it started with punches to the face up against a wall, then moved to the floor where he was kicked. He ended the description of the beating by saying: *"But until now I actually thank them for that. It taught me a lesson, kind of"*. Jinan went on to explain that his family were 'trying to help', that doing nothing after they found out he was using drugs would have meant that they didn't care if he was 'killing himself'. As I saw some vulnerability emerge in the conversation, I asked: *"How did that make you feel as a man?"* He gave an answer that threw me off big time, saying that he approved of the beating, taking it on as a masculine duty to protect people from themselves. While Jinan's answer was confronting to me, it was a very rich explanation of his understanding of the apparent immorality of drug use, and how violence and masculinity are linked. I doubt I would have got this answer by simply asking the question as approved.

Now that is a story about a young man recruited from MSIC, and I find that people at the injecting centre and people who hang out around drug markets more generally are usually the most marginalised. For the most part this is appropriate for research, because marginalised people are disproportionately impacted by the harms of drug use. Disadvantage compounds harm. But you also have to think critically about why groups of marginalised people are almost always the subject of drugs research. There are a lot of people who use drugs and never come into contact with police or hospitals or treatment services. If we never talk to people from more affluent communities, then we risk presenting the harms of drug use as inherent rather than coproduced by discourse, policy, social status, and so on. So, part of being critical is actively doing work that expands the field's understanding of PWUD beyond categories of risk. Sometimes the diversity of participant backgrounds can be built into the design of a study, other times it will happen through critical reflection on a project in-progress, and other times, it is just part of a broader program of study in your career. Either way, being conscious of this helps to diversify the stories you hear about drug use and by extension the things you write about.

Of course, seeking out people with different social backgrounds can invite some pretty confounding ethical dilemmas. For instance, in a study comparing oral and injecting pharmaceutical opioid use, I found myself recruiting a lot of the oral users from the Northern and Eastern suburbs of Sydney (affluent suburbs) who were describing a more affluent upbringing than most injecting drug users in the study. I came up against an issue I found quite difficult to deal with around the role of stigma. I found that everyone who injected drugs told me that stigma had a devastating impact on their lives, while the oral users told me that stigma was one of the reasons that stopped them from transitioning to injecting or heroin use. The oral users would say "*I don't want to inject because I don't want to be a junkie*" or "*I won't use heroin because I worry about what people will think of me*". As someone who strongly advocates for breaking down the stigma attached to drug use, and especially for people who inject, it was really hard for me to work through how to present this material. Personally, I can intellectualise the fact that there is a disproportionate amount of harm caused by stigma in marginalised communities and that this is more significant than any imagined potential harm that might be caused to affluent middle-class young people from the theoretical removal of stigma. But I am not in control of every single way that my work is used. Will someone take this work and use it as a reason to say that we should keep stigmatising people who inject drugs? Those are the types of questions that keep me up at night.

So by doing critical research in this way you do run the real risk that your work will be used in ways that are counter to your own personal commitments. But dealing with these complications is worth it because it means you are also able to present a picture of drug use that is more realistic. Talking to people from wealthy backgrounds provides an important counterbalance to those that are from disadvantaged ones. It gives me the chance to show how the harms of drug use are not inherent or inevitable, but structural and co-produced.

Any Final Thoughts? What Would You Tell Others Looking to Do Fieldwork?

I think for me fieldwork is an opportunity to challenge the idea that drug users are damaged and depraved risk-takers. It can be used to help foster counter-narratives to stereotypes that assume that crime and deviance are inherent to drug use or the result of the moral failings of the drug user. The purpose of critical drugs research is to identify the constitutive elements of risk, to explain to academic and other audiences the actual interactions, events and contexts that make risk in drug use. Just being around a drug market meant that even I was exposed to those risks: witnessing public fights over drug use; being caught up in drug deals; hearing stories about traumatising violence. There is always the worry that being in an environment where this happens means it is more likely to happen to you. But the reality is that the risks I take by doing fieldwork pale in comparison to the risks that PWUD are forced to be exposed to. Imagine for a second what it feels like to be pitted against your friends and family by punitive attitudes to drug use, to be on the other end of a loved one's fist when they find out you use drugs or to overdose and have your friend not call an ambulance because they are scared they will get in trouble. Not all risks are made equal.

References

Bryan Page, J., & Singer, M. (2010). *Comprehending Drug Use: Ethnographic Research at the Social Margins*. New Brunswick: Rutgers University Press.
Dertadian, G. C. (2018). *A Fine Line: Painkillers and Pleasure in the Age of Anxiety*. Singapore: Palgrave Macmillan.
Dertadian, G., & Tomsen, S. (2019). The Case for a Second Safe Injecting Facility (SIF) in Sydney. *Current Issues in Criminal Justice*. https://doi.org/10.1080/10345329.2019.1689787.
Dertadian, G., Dixon, T. C., Iversen, J., & Maher, L. (2017). Pharmaceutical Opioid Use Among Oral and Intravenous Users in Australia: A Comparative Study. *International Journal of Drug Policy, 41*, 51–58.
Good, M.-J. D. (1995). Cultural Studies of Biomedicine: An Agenda for Research. *Social Science & Medicine, 41*(4), 461–473.
Keane, H., Moore, D., & Fraser, S. (2011). Addiction and Dependence: Making Realities in the DSM. *Addiction, 106*(5), 875–877.
Maher, L. (1997). *Sexed Work: Gender, Race and Resistance in a Brooklyn Drug Market*. New York: Oxford University Press.
Manderson, D. (2011). Possessed: The Unconscious Law of Drugs. In S. Fraser & D. Moore (Eds.), *The Drug Effect: Health, Crime, Society* (pp. 225–239). Melbourne: Cambridge University Press.
Moore, D. (2004). Governing Street-Based Injecting Drug Users: A Critique of Heroin Overdose Prevention in Australia. *Social Science and Medicine, 59*(7), 1547–1557.

6

'I Hope Little Worms Die in Your Arse': Fieldwork, Anarchists, Fascists and Academic Snitches

Nicholas Apoifis

Can You Just Start Off by Giving Us a Bit of Background About the Field Research That You've Undertaken?

My first real taste of academic fieldwork began when I was writing about environmental activists at a sit-in in Eden, New South Wales, Australia. Activists were protesting a pulp mill where native old-growth forests were being logged for woodchips. I had a few interviews with different activists including a few who were part of a sit-in up in the trees. I had been in loads of protests before. But while there, I began to understand the relationship between committed fieldwork and good research; the importance of being amongst activists, experiencing to varying degrees what

---

N. Apoifis (✉)
School of Social Sciences, University of New South Wales,
Sydney, NSW, Australia
e-mail: n.apoifis@unsw.edu.au

they were experiencing, the emotions, the impacts on the body and mind, the smells, the sounds, the highs and the lows. And that's kind of driven a lot of what I've done. At its core though, it married my want to research and understand and share activist insights, with my political solidarity with these causes and actions.

So for my next big body of research, as part of my PhD dissertation and subsequent book *Anarchy in Athens* (Apoifis 2017), I went and lived with militant Athenian anarchists and anti-authoritarians in Greece, in 2011, and I went back for a little bit more in 2013. A little over three months all in all. The Athenian anarchists and anti-authoritarians, radical anti-state leftists, were and maybe still are the most militant activist, anarchist community in the world. In their χώροι [spaces], they are living their politics through targeted interventions and actions that reimagine and reconfigure political, social and cultural relationships in this ancient city.

By the end of my time there I had squatted with activists, had hundreds of lazy meandering conversations over coffee and cigarettes, and participated in assemblies and countless meetings. I had seen and marched in intense and mostly violent street-protests polluted by tear gas, and heard about or witnessed numerous targeted property attacks against capitalist institutions. Plus, a ton of other things that go on in the space, like serious community building projects, in Athens, near Exarcheia, the heart of the anarchist and anti-authoritarian milieu.

How Did You Get Access? Was It Difficult?

Yeah access was tough. But my approach to the space helped. Framing my research was a field work methodology called 'militant ethnography' (Juris 2007; Juris and Khasnabish 2013; Russell 2015; Apoifis 2016). I love ethnographies, I want to do them all the time! Ethnography is the study of cultures and peoples which, importantly, encourages this intense engagement with the writing-up process of those stories. And the *militant* bit is the vigorous pursuit of, and dissemination of, partisan insights. That was really important—I can't escape the political nature of my work—and nor would I want to. I was very open about that and it

6 'I Hope Little Worms Die in Your Arse': Fieldwork, Anarchists... 109

certainly got me the access and the relationships that made much of that research so productive, I guess. Because militant ethnography mirrors the way activists, and anarchists and anti-authoritarians are producing their own analyses and commentary on their space—as insiders producing politically relevant work to their movement. I had to be part of that space. I had to live what they were living, feel what they were feeling, because not only does it produce richer insights, but politically, it is critical: how dare I just come in, extract knowledge and then leave without participating.

And as you can imagine, this involved me getting my hands dirty so to speak. I was participating in these actions in some parts to gain their trust, in some parts to experience what they were experiencing, and of course, to act on my own politics, which can't be excluded from this. And when I say gain trust, well, some people there trusted me. And others there are still pretty pissed off at my work—hostility towards academic research is *robust* in some sections of this milieu. Plus there was loads I wasn't invited to see. But I saw enough.

So yeah, I had to gain trust. I had to make connections. And it was tough. Let me set the scene then:

I am super nervous, I'm in Exarcheia, in Athens, going up to people cold, trying to initiate conversations. And it's not working. Academics tend to be seen as part of the State's apparatus. "Hi, I'm from x University, and I'm here to learn about ...". Immediate cut off. No chance to do my spiel, to talk about consent, to have them sign the consent forms. No time to turn on the recording. At best, I get a classic Greek raised eyebrows flick of the head response, with a *tntt* sound. This means no, imbued with a healthy dose of *go away*. Or clearer yet, and I heard this just as regularly, "Fuck off *re malaka*".

I had to devise another approach.

I noticed many people smoked cigarettes in Greece. Hardly a groundbreaking insight. So I bought some tobacco, filters and papers, and reconnected with a long, dormant habit. There's a wonderful, beautiful albeit horrifically cancerous thing about the time it takes to roll and smoke a cigarette. You stand next to someone who you want to talk to. You roll your cigarette. Maybe you ask to borrow their lighter even though you have one in your pocket. You strike up a conversation, you share a quick chat, and once the cigarette is out, you can go your separate ways. But if you do enough in that time to capture a little bit of a connection, you have your in. You explain why you are there. No signatures on forms. No recordings. Just honest conversations about your personal motivations for being there. Who you are! "I'm here to learn more. I want to learn more. I know this is a burden. But could I buy you a coffee and chat?". And then you talk about consent and recordings.

And at this point I smashed headfirst into a wall, a potential barrier to the access that I needed for my research; the institutional obligations set out by my University's Human Research Ethics Committee (HREC). The ethics guidelines set out in my approval letter sort of insisted that I have (1) a voice recording device and (2) written consent forms. But here is the major problem: I was stupid to think people would sign a piece of paper and be forever identified as fighters against the State. I was stupid to think that anyone wanted to be recorded. The formal ethics expectations were so out of place in my research context.

Seriously, during my first proper field interaction of depth (field—that's an ugly word but anyway), I was speaking to this really nice activist, when out of nowhere we saw a bunch of anarchists attack a police van, start pelting rocks, one of which hit a cop, and straight away blood starts spewing from the policeman's head. At what point was I meant to say to the person I was chatting with, "Hey before you tell me what's going on here, before we find a place to hide lest we get arrested if they think we are involved, can you just sign this consent form and let me just turn on my audio recorder so there is a record of our conversation?"

It doesn't work like that.

When you're trying to build personal relationships, they can be undermined by the formalities of the ethics process. This is a serious risk. Imagine if a cop, totally understandably, had come up to me during that melee and asked what I was doing. And then I also tell you that one in every two Greek police officers at the time I was there had voted for Golden Dawn, Greece's neo-Nazi party. And then they found the signatures, the signed consent forms, or worse, my audio recordings. I'd be putting myself and my collaborators at serious risk of arrest and possible beatings.

I remember on the second or third day being told—"put that fucking recorder away!"

Of course! What a naïve fool I was. The formal ethics process had encouraged this borderline dangerous behaviour. Actually, not borderline; it is dangerous behaviour. It could have easily put me in harm's way. And don't get me wrong, informed consent and accurate notes of conversations are crucial, critical, no question! But pretty quickly I learnt to get oral consent, and on the advice of Athenian anarchists and anti-authoritarians, I was encouraged to hand write notes from conversations (Apoifis 2016, pp. 11–12). Basically, what I would do was chat to the person and take some notes as we were going and add to these notes after the conversation. Then, I would meet up with them, usually a few days later, and share my notes—encouraging them to edit and clarify points as they saw fit. I liked that approach as it allowed people to fine-tune what they wanted to say. Clarify their thinking. It gave people time to think of other examples to add to their stories, but also gave them the space to reflect on their own positions. You know, a bit more insight, pondering why they thought the way they did. Anyway, it helped me get access to some amazing stories and perspectives.

A few times though, I didn't get the chance to meet with the person again, after that initial conversation because of the tear gas. I would be having a chat to someone in a protest or demonstration, loving the talk, amazing banter and then a tear gas canister would explode and we'd have to disperse. It's a bit hard to reorganise an interview with someone when you have no idea what they looked like because they were wearing a bandana around their face, or a hoody or a gas mask. Especially because I was a bit sloppy sometimes, failing to organise a meet-up before our eyes started tearing up from the gas! As time went on, I got better at organising follow up chats *before* the protests properly kicked off, but sometimes I would forget or sometimes the protest would explode unexpectedly. Like you can ever predict when a protest will ignite!

And of course, a few other times, I would get stood up at the second meeting. I would be waiting at a meet-up location, and waiting, and waiting. But that comes with the turf, it's not unexpected. People have their reasons and I respect that. So, for all these people, the ones I couldn't confirm a quote with, I didn't direct quote them. Not at all. But they helped shape my understanding of the space.

That's the first aspect of getting access. Finding ways to chat to people without unnecessarily putting their lives and yours at risk. The second thing that was key for me was that I knew the language of their politics, I knew loads about anarchism. I knew about anarchism and insurrectionist literature, the actions and its history, plus I had a fair idea of the history of the space. I had consumed every piece of literature, every website, every scrap of audio and video I could get my hands on before I went there. About Athenian anarchism. About Greek anarchism. About anarchism in general! And I knew enough Greek to get by. I got access as a result of all this.

But no matter how much I talk about being part of the space, I was always an outsider. I could always leave. As much as it was insider research, I was still a *xeno*, an outsider, foreign to the space. Some might even say an *anarcho-tourist*. I know that. But no researcher had gotten decent access to the space before then. So, I needed to commit to the space as much as I could in order to gain some sort of trust, so I could hear their stories and see some of the things they see. And that was so hard.

And with all of that, plus a dose of luck that no activist genuinely thought I was a cop—I was able to participate in the space and learn from the experience.

Is There a Line for You? How Far Are You Willing to Go to Get Your Story? How Much Risk Are You Willing to Take?

I've been thinking a little bit about this recently, because you know, how much do you need to do to get good stories? I wanted to capture some really important stories that I thought were critical to share, about this vibrant, conflicted, productive movement, and I saw myself as a curator of some of these stories. In order to access these stories, these insights, these activist wisdoms, I was engaged in risk. But how much risk do you need to take?

I think participating in a protest is one thing. That was doable and I did do a fair bit of that. Watching someone get beaten is sickening, like a proper beating, where you are not sure if they'll walk again, that was hard to deal with but also telling and important to the story. I don't think that was my line. A big part of what I subsequently wrote about is why people use violence (Apoifis 2017, pp. 108–127).

But the whole time, with everything I did and I got involved in, I had in my mind: avoid arrest. That was a line. Easier said than done though. I don't need to be arrested to tell the story. I don't need to be arrested for authenticity's sake. And I don't need to be beaten or tortured. No way! And what a burden that would be for my collaborators! Here was this researcher putting them in harm's way. They'd have to bail me out. Tend to my physical and mental wounds. That's so unfair on them, they have enough shit to deal with. Fascists use to go into local neighbourhoods and bash up migrants, and anarchists would get on mopeds to help defend these neighbourhoods. And then I was going to take away resources from that by needing their help? No way. I had to avoid that.

I don't *need* to put my life on the line. That's what I also learnt in Greece. Notice, I said *need*. I can if I want to, if I think it is worth it. But I don't *need* to. That distinction helped me a lot. I wanted a 'holistic' experience, to inform my writing, my research, my understanding of the space. But to capture a 'better', richer story, the danger then becomes that you get hungry for it—and you think that you *need* that heightened experience of participation, and so you take more risks. That line is always moving but yeah mine at the time was to see, hear and do everything I could while trying to preserve my life and liberty. Again, easier said than done.

So I developed strategies to help me do the things I wanted to do in the field.

What Kind of Strategies?

The most significant event happened at an interdepartmental talk at uni before I left for Athens, when I presented my initial idea to go and do this research. I was presenting my thoughts and plans and someone from the

Department of Security Studies and Criminology in the Policing, Intelligence and Counterterrorism program at my (then) University was in the audience. And this hulk of a man, a former cop, came up to me afterwards and he said something like "great idea, great talk, I can't wait until you get home because I'm coming for your notes". Just like that! So I am about to go to Greece, where you've got a largely right-wing police force, successive Greek governments—conservative and socialist alike—who despise the people I am planning on staying with, and I had this Australian former cop saying "I want your notes"!

I panicked.

And to be perfectly honest, that was the best thing that could have happened. Because it prepared me for the reality of the field. I cannot stress enough that the most important thing when dealing with risk and engaging with the field is to actually over-prepare your security concerns—you just can't prepare enough for that, because if it goes wrong, which it inevitably does, you need to have strategies in place. Multiple strategies! You need to be ready. You need to have an awareness of what other people have done in certain circumstances to get out of trouble, and what *your* strengths and weakness are in getting out of those situations—to underprepare could be catastrophic. And even then, things still go wrong.

So, knowing that this person was interested in my notes, I went oh my gosh, I have to prepare—I have to be ready for lots and lots of different things that are going to occur over there. For example, what do I do with my notes? Right, if this guy is serious—which he definitely appeared to be—and I get back and he comes after my notes, what am I going to do? How do I protect my collaborators? I don't want my words causing harm to them!

As I mentioned, I hand wrote interview quotes, all of them. So rather than massive pages of transcript, I selected quotes from individuals. Usually a couple pages for each person. Maybe a bit more. And when I was finished chatting with the person for the second or third time, either on the day or soon after, I would physically send the transcripts to different mail addresses of my friends throughout Europe. I bought loads of stamps. And then just daily would carefully go off and post letters, maybe with three to four pages of notes in each letter. Never enough in one letter to tell too much of a story, but certainly there were some gentle descriptions of places, people and events. And at the end of my time in Athens, I got everything sent back to me to different mailboxes of friends in Australia.

I asked all my friends not to open the envelopes and I didn't tell them what was going on, beyond that it was for research. Was I putting them in harm's way? I don't think so. They just had a few envelopes from interviews and field notes. They would have handed over the envelopes if they had to and be done with it. I wasn't worried about them.

It also helps that I have borderline illegible handwriting which was certainly helpful. Sometimes I can't read my own handwriting! There was no way that people were going to be legibly reading those notes. And I took field notes, not shorthand notes, but pages of field notes that only I could understand, a mixture of Greek, French and English filled with slang-words from home. These were also sent off to friends. Plus, I deidentified people by using real people in my life; so, like, their names in place of real names, to help me understand who everyone was. I'd match my collaborators' social cues, idiosyncrasies, things like that with people I knew back home, and name them accordingly. So, my notes might say '*Phil*', who is an activist I know from home, who shared an idiosyncrasy with let's make up a name… *Vangeli*, who might be an activist from Athens. This kept *Vangeli*'s name out of it but allowed me to remember who was who in the notes.

I told no one about this whole—sending notes to different locations thing—by the way, not even my academic mentor (who I adore and respect so very much), no one knew that I was doing this. I actually didn't tell my mentor because I was a bit embarrassed about this process, aware I may have appeared overly paranoid. Maybe it was over the top, but I was worried. I had to protect my collaborators—I was dealing with a militant group whose participants are regularly beaten up and arrested. Yeah! I made an ethical decision to adjust my data collection plan because someone from my own institution had let me down.

What Happened When You Got Home?

I bunkered down and I got all my field notes and interview quotes out that had been sent back, put them all together and did two months of hardcore engagement with them. This idea of coding in the formal sense, like with *Nvivo* or something, it's not really my thing. With an ethnography like this one, I was coding in an informal sense as I was going, could you even call it coding—I was definitely co-creating themes as I went. It was more a matter of putting all the quotes, all the field notes, and all the stories into a narrative.

I avoided campus during this time, and I got stuck into transferring the notes from their original form into the cleanest form I could: the rabid deidentification process! I had deidentified people's names while over in Athens, of course, but as I said my field notes had some descriptions of characteristics, idiosyncrasies, events and places. You know, things I'd seen and heard. And yeah, I set to work removing any, even slight descriptions of people. I removed all fragments of identifications of places. All descriptors removed that could identify the location of anything really. The last thing I cleaned up was a field note that had some crappy, pathetic amateur-poetic thing about the 'rejuvenating warmth' I felt leaving a cold squat, as the sun hit *something*. And that *something* would have given the location of the place away. That was a good mistake to catch before publication!

Having deidentified fully, I then kept a copy of the quotes and descriptions I thought I needed, I made a backup file with some reserve quotes I thought I might use at different times later on, stored both those copies at a special location, and then I literally burnt my old notes.

I literally burnt them. It was kind of cathartic in a way.

Now again, did I go too far? Did I need to do that? Certainly, there was an institutional Ethics issue associated with that, right? As you're meant to keep your notes, locked in some cabinet. But I felt like I could honestly defend my practices, because I had an ethical obligation to protect the communities I had spent time with. I didn't think a locked drawer in a so-called secure cabinet on campus was enough protection for those communities. The notes could be subpoenaed, they could be raided. Do you think the security services, the Federal Police and co. care about the University's ethics requirements? The most important thing you can do with your research, when you are dealing with the State, with a hostile police force, is protect it anyway you can. To me, that is critical.

What Other Issues Did You Have to Deal With?

On the ground, in Athens, I had other more physical issues to deal with, too. I had to be constantly cognisant of what was going on around me.

Straight away you have this awareness, you feel it, that as soon as you enter the neighbourhood of Exarcheia, where most of this sort of semi-autonomous community exist, you're being watched. There are police sitting around the area watching. You're aware that if you're going into the space you're being watched, and if you're coming out also you're being watched. Not followed so to speak, but watched, gazed at. But for whatever reason that didn't bug me, like I didn't have any genuine fear about it, and I wasn't freaking out when I went there. Not in the slightest. In some ways it is just a neighbourhood, right? With cafes, and folks walking the streets, small shop fronts and some little πλατεiές (town squares). But it's also a neighbourhood with an enormous history, the heart of the anarchist and antiauthoritarian milieu, with quite a lot of cops on its periphery.

So, I became hyper-aware of my surroundings, particularly when I was interviewing people in cafes. Squats were different, far more relaxed, but outside, you should be on your game. And so if you see the person you are chatting to looking elsewhere, fidgeting, stirring, you see their eyes move, well, be ready to run. A couple of times we were mid interview, during or just after a heavy protest, and we'd have to do a 'runner', move quickly out of the area, as there were too many police around. And it's not like that goes down slowly. You have to be ready to grab your pen and paper, and actually know where to run. I was constantly aware of my surroundings. My exits. Oh, and I had a buddy system of sorts.

Can You Explain the Buddy System?

For my personal safety, I identified someone that looked like I could kind of trust them to do something if I got into trouble. And, that they could protect me from other people within the community that didn't know me yet—they could vouch for me. Someone that liked me, that I got along with, someone I had got a sense would be good in a tough situation.

And yeah for about a three-hour period I would not leave my buddy's side. Just someone that I had a connection to, a relationship of sorts, and I'd stick to them for a period of time.

The only thing was they didn't really know that they were my buddy. I just said to them I was going to hang out with them for a bit, I didn't say hey, you are my informal security system. I just asked if I could hang out with them for a bit and stay close by. And most people were cool with this. And probably understood what was going on. In assemblies and meetings, it was good to be next to someone who was known, and that way people weren't hostile to me if they didn't know me. It allowed me to relax a bit and be more myself when talking to people, less uptight and concerned about the surroundings. It was helpful just knowing that I had this person nearby should stuff go wrong.

And it was a particularly good system in protests, it's a system that activists use in protest spaces worldwide. It's weird you know, there's often a pause at a key moment in a protest, just as you hear the tear gas being shot, and the canister rattle on the ground, before it smokes up and the craziness starts. I made sure that my buddies were experienced in this space, the ones that didn't panic, didn't run when the tear gas started. Because the panic is what often causes the problems, right? So, I buddied with people who were more relaxed and more experienced: the ones that were lighting the fires to prevent the noxious fumes from the tear gas coming in; and the ones that knew what to do or had gasmasks, for example. I started to identify and recognise people who would be good in protest situations—you build up experience, identifying people who were appropriate to help you out in that space. I was knocked over a few times in a stampede in a handful of protests, and your buddy is there to pick you up, and you would do the same back. It was very helpful. Until I stuffed up, pretty badly actually.

I was in the middle of a protest; it was a particularly heavy protest and I just needed to get my field notes written down. I'd seen a fascinating interaction between some fascists and a policeman, and I had to get it down on paper then and there. So I slipped away from the protest, off to the side of it, without my buddy. I prioritised getting my thoughts down on paper. I prioritised the story. I got to the side of the protest, sat down and started to write. And then I felt this forceful hand on my shoulder gripping my shirt, and it was a police officer from the riot squad. He was really aggressive, as he started speaking to me sharply in Greek:

"Σε έπιασα, σε έπιασα, τώρα έχεις πρόβλημα" [I got you, I got you, you're in trouble now]!

"Sorry, I don't speak Greek", I said in English, "I'm just a tourist". A lie. I knew exactly what he had said, and you bet I was shitting myself in that first instance, but my response settled me, which gave me a quick second to think.

"I saw you in the protest" he barked in good English. He had, of course. He had reason to bark! "Why are you taking notes?"

I pieced together a response super quickly: "Yeah, I just wanted to go and see what was happening. I'm just learning about Athens".

He still had me in his grip. He looked at my scribbled illegible notes, I could see he had slightly changed his tune, but still wasn't sure. Then he asked me to open my backpack. Now in my backpack I had a Lonely Planet book on Greece, and I had a hand drawn map, drawings of places in Athens that were totally tourist-places. The Acropolis, Lykavittos hill, and I think a few museums from memory. The cop relaxed, loosened his grip. He had enough doubt now. "Go!" he said, while aggressively lifting me up by my shirt, sort of clipping me across the ear as he did it and shoved me away from the protest.

Was That Planned? The Map, the Book?

Totally planned, absolutely planned. And it worked, the policeman was convinced by the argument. If I didn't have that backup plan, I would have been arrested. But I stuffed up by even being there in the first place. Alone, easy to be picked off. That was dumb. And I got lucky. But as I said earlier, over-prepare. It saved me, that time.

All of This Must Have Been Quite Emotional, How Did You Deal with That?

Look, with that moment, with the cop in the protest, I was more annoyed at myself for getting into that situation. If I am being honest, I also remember being quite proud of myself for staying cool and having that backup plan with the maps. But no, I wasn't emotionally affected by that incident. The violence though, that's a different story. I saw some pretty intense violence while I was in Greece; I saw activists beating cops and vice-versa.

I wish before I had left, I had read more about researchers who had participated in or witnessed violent events, because I was so fresh and so green. I had seen protest violence before, but I hadn't seen anything to this extent, the intensity on both sides and the violence. I definitely didn't enjoy it. It was the worst part of the research. But there was a good support network there amongst the community, debriefs after events so that was helpful and important.

That said, it was all such a rush, it was all going on so intensely at that time that it didn't affect me then. What I think is key, though, is putting strategies in place to deal with the intensity of that risk, and dealing with those things that you see, when you get back. Because while in the space, no matter how normalised it became for me, I was still 'away'. I knew that I wasn't home, right? So in my head being away meant, subconsciously I suppose, that I didn't have to deal with what I saw there. I had to capture it, I had to note it, I had to write about it, but I remember not being affected too much while there. Ok maybe once, where I saw a brutal beating and then got blind drunk that night, probably to get that image out of my head. And sidenote, it works for a few hours and then the next day you wake up super-hungover, and that image is still in your head. Not recommended.

In Athens, I just got on with the research. I just kept working. And probably just pushed things down, down, down into my belly. "Move on, that's real, that's the reality of it, you need to capture it, to tell the story and you need do it well." I did write in my own notes about how I felt, "this is sickening", "'disgusting", things like that. But I don't think I thought, "just get home and deal with it". I just pushed it down.

I was so fiendishly pursuing those narratives while I was there, that I was able to just get on with the job. It wasn't until I got back, it was probably about a good year later, that I was in the middle of a talk to a class about protest-violence, literally in the middle, and I lost it, I kind of froze. All the blood left me. I felt weak, drained and exhausted. And I just had to stop, and I was like I can't do this. I had to stop, and I left the room. It kind of all hit me—bang!

That was a really intense moment and it definitely snuck up on me. I wasn't expecting to be hit by this emotional response so long after my time in Athens. Yet in hindsight, it is probably not surprising that it happened. It makes sense, because when I returned to Australia, I didn't have a proper debrief about the things I had seen. When I got home from Greece, my partner gave birth to our first kid, I had to finish the PhD, and I was in the book writing phase really quickly after that (because I wanted to get the story out as soon as I could). I was also speaking at a lot of anti-fascist events, it was all happening. And there was no debrief at all, really.

While there, and even back in Australia, I had concentrated on the reward—the story, the research, the dissemination. And I hadn't properly dealt with what I had seen. We have counselling services ready to go for the participants, but certainly I didn't put things in place for myself. I will never make that mistake again.

Was This the Most Difficult Thing to Deal With?

No, a bigger fear, the thing that kept me up at night and still troubles me, the thing that worries me so much is how my work will be used. Risk to myself is one thing. I can deal with that. The real risk is what happens to the knowledge; produced and disseminated, it takes on a life of its own. And that's so scary.

A big part of my ethnography didn't finish when I left Athens. One of the things I discussed with and was encouraged by my collaborators to do was disseminate these field-insights. So, I did loads of talks, hit heaps of anti-fascist, anti-racist and anti-authoritarian and anarchist spaces up in Australia and elsewhere, to share the insights that had been generously shared with me in Athens. This was a key component of the militant part of the ethnography. This was a part of my commitment to the space.

And from this comes one of my biggest fears, one of the biggest risks, if you will, and speaks to the dangers of the field work and what happens after: I have genuine concern for the way these insights are acted on in different geographical contexts.

Let me explain:

So again, you've got this pretty hostile space in Athens. The anarchists and anti-authoritarians have to deal with neo-Nazi sympathising cops. They are also protecting migrants from fascist beatings, housing refugees and asylum seekers, and they're hated by many. So a lot of anarchists and anti-authoritarians deploy violence; because they're violently attacked in the first instance. That's their reality, whether you agree with their responses or not. And my experiences have been that this resistance in Athens is romanticised elsewhere in anarchist and anti-fascist milieus, perhaps even exoticised, where fragments of heroics are reproduced in stories and become the pervasive *truth*. But these stories are incomplete and problematic. They lack insights into personal motivations and experiences. They lack historical and contemporary contexts and nuances.

Which brings me to my issue. How do I go into an activist community, in Australia, in Canada, with activists who want to do *stuff*, they're praxis driven, they want direct action, they know about this romantic other, the Greek anarchist, how do I talk about violence while ensuring that the people listening understand that this is super contextual knowledge? The Athenian activists knew this. They specifically told me, *don't go telling people we just fuck shit up. We don't. We build. And we use violence when we have to, because we have to.* The local matters.

So, the danger then becomes that I, without context, repeat stories from Athens of a particular form of radical and resistance politics. I am an academic. There is power attached to this. I have a form of authority (even in anarchist spaces), people listen, they invite me to talks, to do radio interviews and presentations. And there is an enormous responsibility to that, a responsibility I was never taught about. This is painstaking work. In each talk I have to stress context. I have to speak of the history of the region. The military junta. The arrests and tortures. The personal experiences that I heard about. The interventions and role of the Greek state. I spend ages setting up the background, because my fear, to this day, is that activists might uncritically replicate the tactical repertoires enacted in Athens, basing their decisions on fragments of romanticised narratives.

And in the written work, there are the same responsibilities. The way you tell your stories, the way you represent a space, there is an immense weight attached to this—because you have to ensure that you are sure of your observations. As sure as you can be. That's what good research is, and ethnographies help produce such knowledge, for sure. Because once the research, the stories, and the narratives are disseminated, they take on a life of their own.

This Troubles You a Lot?

Totally. Yeah this is another core part of risk. It's dangerous. I'll give you another example. I was presenting this work at Jura Books in Sydney, it was a book launch, and a question came from a group of three activists asking me to talk about gender politics in the space. In *Anarchy in Athens*, I wrote about sexism, homophobia and transphobia. In the talk, I told an anecdote about gender politics, it was about how I'd seen gendered divisions of labour within a squat, and how this guy who lived in the squat asked me not to include that story in my work. I said I would put in, we had an argument, and I never spoke to that Athenian anarchist again.

Then, in the talk, I spoke about sexist and homophobic behaviour, and violence and masculinity. And I didn't notice but those three people that asked that question left shortly after. It was well over a year later when in a random conversation, the moderator of the talk, a good friend, asked if I knew why those people had left the talk. I said to be honest I didn't even notice that they had left and had no idea why they would.

Turns out they were furious about my representations of the space. Their question about gender politics, while not articulated as such, was underpinned by my lack of engagement in the talk with what they felt were persistent rumours of sexual assault in the Athenian anarchist and anti-authoritarian community. I hadn't mentioned it in the talk, and they believed I had not included anything of substance in my book. When I heard this, I was devastated by the fact that I might have misrepresented a space, particularly on such a critical issue. Had I created a narrative that masked this issue? Was that the takeaway for listeners of my talks, and readers of my book? If so, that's horrendous scholarship and politics.

I had to think long and hard about all of this, specifically my research practices. In Athens, I'd asked many questions about sexual assault in that community. I did so because it is prevalent in many communities, activist and non-activist alike. But no one confirmed this to me in Athens. I found only one reference to this issue, in a conference paper about sexual harassment in an activist camp in Greece (Sullivan 2004), and included it in my book (Apoifis 2017, pp. 109–110). Since the conversation with my friend and moderator of my talk, I have spent ages going over online evidence and journal articles, but have still found no documented evidence of sexual assault. Of course, this doesn't mean anything regarding the validity of claims, merely that they have not been published.

And I reflected on why I may not have been told of these stories. I talk about gender politics in my work, sexism, my positionality as a cisgendered male, and how this gave me access to certain spaces and conversations and insights, while closing off other spaces. But I didn't have any evidence to talk about sexual assault, so I couldn't say so. No one would speak to me about it, and I never felt anyone was hiding things from me. I heard no supporting stories.

Which means, all in all, I probably should have asked a lot more questions about this while in Athens.

That's risk isn't it? It's heartbreaking. The production of potentially flawed insights. That's why you have to exhaust yourself, bleeding fingers so to speak, trying to get as much information as you can when telling a story. And it's always dirty and messy. And all I can do now is learn from this experience.

You've Done This Political Research, or It Has a Political Edge to It. Are You Worried About Threats to Your Personal Safety?

Not as much these days, but I try to stay on my toes. If I give a talk in a community context, I'll try not to arrive or leave alone. When I go to Greece, I play it safe. I have a lawyer who knows I'm coming. I let my University know I'm going. Things like that. And most critically, I severed all contacts with anyone I knew in Greece who was connected to the project. That was key. I can, without a word of a lie, say I have had no communication with anyone from that fieldwork time in Athens since 2013. I had to do this. For their safety. For mine.

That said, I did write an article in 2015 in the Sydney Morning Herald discussing Golden Dawn (GD), the neo-Nazi party in Greece, and their presence in Australia. That article inspired quite a lot of animosity towards me.

GD had been doing some dodgy stuff in Melbourne, where they had been packaging clothes that they had collected from the Greek-Australian community and sending it over to Greece, labelling it as if it was solely from Golden Dawn members. When people were donating, many in the community didn't realise that it was for Golden Dawn. GD hid that. Plus, they hid that when the goods arrived in Greece, they were labelled, for 'Greeks Only'. None went to the massive refugee community there, for example, some who had escaped the horrors of the Syrian war. The Melbourne Greek-Australian community were up in arms about this and so partly I wrote about that, but more so, the article was highlighting the re-rise of the far right in Greece, this pernicious beast.

Well fascist elements within the Greek diaspora lost their shit at me. I got some colourful responses, some emails, some aggressive Twitter abuse, some violent descriptions as to what would be done to me, and some death threats. My favourite one was (translated): "I hope little worms die in your arse, and you die too". And I thought well, at least that's poetic.

I joke about it, but this is a serious thing. I had to be super careful during that time, I had to be aware—and most of them are keyboard warriors, but, as we know of the far-right in Australia, just one needs to turn. So, I had a sort of abeyance in my concerns about my own safety, but once that material hit, particularly through that major newspaper story, I did realise that I had to be aware again. And certainly, with the publication of the book I had to be again aware that there were people that were very unhappy with what I had written.

What Advice Would You Give Your Younger Research Self, to Deal with Risk or to Make the Research Experience Less Potentially Hazardous for Yourself?

I think it's critically important that you speak to people before you go, while you are there, and after. I take phone calls from journalists and PhD students quite regularly, who are in high-risk settings and want to chat about what they are doing and what strategies they have in place. It can be a little emotionally taxing for me to constantly have these conversations, but I have insights gained from over a decade of fieldwork, that people want to hear about. So you got to share if asked, right? A lot of the time it's just listening to people's plans, picking it apart, finding potential issues. I think it is an excellent strategy. And unequivocally, the thing I do with my students and encourage any field worker to do is speak to people when you get back. Debrief. It is super important to the work and to your mental health.

And over-prepare! I do get very worried for my PhD students. I don't want them thinking that high-risk fieldwork is necessarily amazing. Fieldwork is tough, it's brutal, so I probably go over the top conveying that it is very hard work, and that it is intense and wild. It is so fluid, so on the go, that you need to have things in place before you commence. You have to have strategies in place so you are ready to chase down a lead, or to witness something on a whim, but also when things go wrong, as they do, you have this arsenal ready to help you out. A way to do that is to know how people have done things before you. Mitigation strategies that you can adapt at the drop of a hat; "I know what five people before have done in x situation and I can adapt these to come up with a quick solution in another". Dissemination of activist knowledge is so important to me and many others. It is just a matter of doing everything you can to prepare, learning from others, capturing as much info as you can before you are there, and having a dose of luck.

And since it was asked, what I'd actually say to my younger self is mate, I love that you want to pursue narratives that speak to the richness of human experiences. But that journey is going to put you in harm's way, put your collaborators in harm's way, and you will co-produce knowledge that can be interpreted and acted upon in ways you can't even imagine. The rewards are these beautiful research stories that enrich our lives and our understanding of the world, but just know that you will be opening up a can of worms: and like that Greek neo-Nazi said, those worms might end up dying in your arse.

References

Apoifis, N. (2016). Fieldwork in a Furnace: Anarchists, Anti-authoritarians and Militant Ethnography. *Qualitative Research.* https://doi.org/10.1177/1468794116652450.

Apoifis, N. (2017). *Anarchy in Athens: An Ethnography of Militancy, Emotions and Violence* (Contemporary Anarchist Studies). Manchester: Manchester University Press.

Juris, J. S. (2007). Practicing Militant Ethnography with the Movement for Global Resistance in Barcelona. In S. Shukaitis, D. Graeber, & E. Biddle

(Eds.), *Constituent Imagination: Militant Investigations. Collective Theorization* (pp. 164–178). Oakland: AK Press.

Juris, J. S., & Khasnabish, A. (Eds.). (2013). *Insurgency Encounters: Transnational Activism, Ethnography, and the Political.* Durham: Duke University Press.

Russell, B. (2015). Beyond Activism/Academia: Militant Research and the Radical Climate and Climate Justice Movement (s). *Area, 42*(3), 222–229.

Sullivan, S. (2004). *'We Are Heartbroken and Furious' (:2): Violence and the (Anti-)globalisation Movement(s).* CSGR Working Paper No 133/04.

7

Doing Elite Interviews in Feminist Research: Confessions of a Born-Again Observationist

Louise Chappell

Can You Tell Us a Little Bit About the Type of Research You've Done and About Some of the Field Experiences You've Had?

I am a qualitative researcher. In my PhD and early research phase, my main method of data collection outside the literature and primary text-based sources was largely interview based, but increasingly I became interested in participant observation work and now I'm a big fan of that sort of approach. My research is really focussed on the formal and informal gender rules that operate across a range of institutional arenas—political, bureaucratic, legal and corporate. I find an observation and shadowing approach very useful for identifying which rules are at work when, and how they coincide and collide to produce gendered outcomes.

L. Chappell (✉)
University of New South Wales, Sydney, NSW, Australia
e-mail: l.chappell@unsw.edu.au

My work shifts across a lot of different field sites. I started off working on public policy issues, talking to bureaucrats, politicians and civil society activists seeking to influence policy. Then I moved on to focus on courts, specifically the International Criminal Court (ICC). In that project, it was one of those 'yo-yo' processes (see Mackay and Rhodes 2013) of going back and forward to the court, observing ongoing developments, doing lots of interviews with personnel in and around the court. This wasn't what I'd call an ethnography per se, but the longer-term engagement meant it was inching closer to that approach.

More recently, I've taken this approach a step further with probably the most interesting and methodologically exciting work I've done—undertaking on-site observations in the construction industry. In this project we were looking at how gender works in the construction sector to block women's recruitment, retention and promotion. That required me to, for the very first time in my life, go on-site to big construction projects and monitor what was going on and try to detect the existing gender power relations. It was really fascinating work and now I'm trying to bring that approach into other field sites because it produces such revealing findings.

What Challenges Have You Encountered with Formal Ethics Processes?

Increasingly over the years I feel university ethics processes have become more formalised which, in some senses, makes it much more difficult to do social science research. I believe that the core function of these processes, which is to protect our subjects from harm, has been overtaken by a risk assessment by the university to protect itself. This is not just a problem at this university—I hear from colleagues across the sector, inside and outside Australia that it's a growing problem everywhere. I'm feeling this shift quite acutely right now because I am trying to get a project off the ground to do work on sexual violence on university campuses, and some of my students are also doing university-based research, and we're all experiencing push back, delays and petty interference making it almost impossible to pursue the questions we're seeking to ask. I think it says something too, about how universities, the producers of knowledge, do not want to be interrogated themselves, particularly around these sorts of controversial issues, where it's clear their processes are just not up to scratch. They don't want their own researchers looking at them.

But it's not just with university-based gender research where I find this ethics problem. I've never really come up against these frustrations doing elite level interviews—whether with a senior judge or a senior policy maker or whatever, it seems entirely uncontroversial. But the more you want to go down levels, the more you want to see what's really going on the ground in terms of gender power relations, with mid to lower level personnel, it's very hard to get ethics support to do this sort of research. I understand there is a need to protect more vulnerable individuals who experience discrimination based on their sex and/or gender, but it's where the knowledge of institutional gender rules rests, so it's critical to be able to engage with these people.

In my darker moments I think the challenges with the ethics process are deliberate: they are there to frustrate you to the point that you give up and walk away. Or that you change your research design completely, and end up chasing different, more palatable questions. As an example, in the construction project we wanted to *observe* gender relations, so we didn't want to flag with people that's what we were looking at—we wanted to see the messiness of it, the embeddedness of 'taken-for-granted' gender relations. But the ethics committee made our research conditional on telling everyone on-site that we were there as gender researchers, which completely undermined the research as it made all the subjects hyperalert to our presence and not surprisingly, they acted accordingly—at least at first. I suppose showing the value of this method, we were there long enough that we gradually blended into the background, and then the site workers just sort of fell back into their usual sort of practices. But we were hugely frustrated with that ethics decision; we went back and forward with the ethics committee to try and change their mind but they just wouldn't budge. This wrangle added months to our preparation time.

One last thing in relation to ethics processes, I've always had a concern about having to provide interviewees with the questions up front. I have no problem with consent forms, and all the processes to allow participants to withdraw and so forth, but requiring us to share our questions undermines the value of the material because the subjects usually prepare in advance and give pat answers, especially when you're asking them about power relationships. This is the subject I'm always asking them about, and they'll just go and find out what the party/company/government line is, which is of little value in terms of data gathering. By not wanting to reveal questions, I'm not seeking to be a journalist looking for a 'gottcha' moment, but I am aiming for more authentic, genuine responses which provide valuable data. So, in general I'm concerned because I see the whole ethics process narrowing, narrowing and narrowing.

What Sort of Things Do You Put in Place, What Strategies Do You Have to Attend to Ethical Concerns About Protecting Subjects?

Well, of course, I always try to anonymise to the extent I can. One of the problems in feminist research and no doubt in other research areas with marginalised communities is that it's a numbers game. Your subjects, such as women politicians, are much more identifiable because there's usually fewer of them. So, you've got to think about how you can protect them, and sometimes it means not using their material directly, but relying on it as background. At times I've had to make hard decisions where I've just not been able to add that 'golden' quote into my writing because I know it'll alert readers to exactly who that person is: it a matter of constantly walking a tightrope. At any rate, on contentious issues I show the subjects the material and see if they're happy with it being used. Which is another challenge of course, and I have had a few awkward situations where people have wanted me to change my analysis based on their quotes, but I've rarely done so.

What's One of the Most Important Issues in Terms of Getting Good Interview Material?

Without a doubt, it's all about trust. Trust is such an important part of doing this sort of work. Unless you're able to build those relationships of trust, you're never going to get good material. On reflection, I suppose it's one of the things that gets easier as you go on in your career, people see that you've done a lot of work and obviously you've gained the trust of other people so they're more likely to trust you too. And I think that might be something that just comes with years in the field rather than anything else. This is fair enough from the participants' point of view but doesn't make life easy for the early career researcher.

What Do They Trust You About Though? Your Integrity?

Yes, I think that's right. With my colleague Fiona Mackay at Edinburgh University, we have landed on a position that we call a *critical feminist friend approach* (Chappell and Mackay 2020). Even when I'm working at the elite level, because of the nature of my work, I'm dealing mostly with institutionally marginalised female/feminist actors, whether they be internal policy makers, judges, prosecutors or external people trying to challenge gender power relationships. I'm very open with them about the fact that I want to recognise their dilemmas and their struggles, that I'm not there to measure whether they are being 'good feminists' if you like, or even to see whether they are achieving their objectives. Rather I want to work out the dilemmas and challenges they face, including being marginalised and suffering backlash, as well as their successes, and why these occurred. I don't completely buy into a co-option thesis, I think that there's a line that people within institutions can walk to make a difference but the line is not always obvious, that it's important to take account of 'micro wins', to understand that these can still add up to something more transformative in terms of gender justice. That's the dynamic that I'm interested in rather than a story of 'success' or 'failure'. Just to be able to have that conversation and express empathy with them, I think that really contributes to developing trust. I still call out the limitations when I see them, and occasionally get pushback from interviewees about my analysis at times, but it seems to have worked for me.

What Are You Concerned About in Research in Regard to Risk to the Participant?

I think in terms of risks for the participants there are quite a few. One is that they can be quite critical of the people that they're working with and for and, so, their own careers can be on the line. I'm very conscious about that. In political environments too, they can be seen to be too aligned with one faction or another, and so I'm very cautious not to put words in their mouths or misrepresent what they say. More acutely, but not a situation I've dealt with directly, is the risk to someone's freedom or indeed life. I don't deal directly with victims, so I've not had to think through these critical risk factors, but working in the human rights field, I have colleagues who do, and they must think very carefully about how to 'do no harm' in their work.

Generally, I think it's important to be very sensitive about the context in which your participants are working. And then through the production and dissemination process, making sure that I keep them aware of where I'm at, feeding back to them, getting them to read that material so they know how they and the context are being portrayed. So, I hope that by the time that findings are in the public domain they've had a number of opportunities to say to me, that's inappropriate or risky from their perspective. This process can be challenging because you know how slow these publishing processes are, which means someone might have moved jobs or roles and they might want or need to have the material pulled. And it is my responsibility as a researcher to respect that. I've never taken the position that my research is more important than someone else's career, life, safety whatever, it's just not worth it.

What Is the Value of Elite Level Interviews?

It really depends on the person and the context. I've got the image in my mind of me sitting in the Hague in the office of the President of the ICC and he just rambled on and it didn't matter what questions I asked him he just wanted to chat about how important he was and on and on… and then he started giving me his insights about his women peers and how they all boss him around and how there's too many in the court. I remember stepping away from that and thinking there wasn't one thing worth quoting from the interview, but in terms of contextual material, it was so valuable. At that point the Court was in, well it's constantly in, crisis, but in that particular moment of crisis and it helped me understand one of the reasons why, which was that the leader was so lacking in a strategic vision and seemed to have no clue whatsoever about gender justice. So, that was in itself really revealing and helpful, even though I don't think I've ever quoted a word from that interview.

In elite interviews, more often than not what I expect is that I'll probably only get some version of the corporate line, the party line, the university line, whatever context it is. Those interviews can be tedious and boring and not help me understand what's really going on in terms of gender power relations. This is why I was so excited to find out how much more revealing observations and shadowing can be, especially for excavating informal rules. In the construction project we visited some mega construction sites where I was shadowing fairly senior people, big project managers and so on, with huge levels of responsibility. After spending a day or two with them observing their daily lives which gave us great insights, we'd also ask to interview them. These interviews were so rich in detail. They would just download everything. Details of their divorce, their relationships with their kids, what they thought about head office, what daily, weekly and project pressures were really like, everything. They'd often talk to you for two hours, at the end of an extremely stressful day. Mostly, you had the sense that they were relieved to be asked and to have the opportunity to off-load. These experiences reinforced for me how important building trust is and how hard it is to achieve this with 'fly in and fly out' interviews. I really came to understand the relationship has to be more substantial than that. It has to be more of a dialogue and a sharing process, rather than an extraction of material from the interviewee. On these construction sites, the interviewee would often turn the tables and want to know more about my work and life, which really did change the dynamic enormously.

Have There Ever Been Situations Where You Knew Your Work Was Perceived as a Threat? And Have You Had Any Adverse Responses to Your Research and How Have You Managed That?

Well, I've got two examples. The first was an interview with a fairly senior woman gender expert who had been told by her boss that she had to do an interview with me. From the moment I walked in, you could have cut the air with a knife. She was so hostile towards me wanting to ask questions about their program and especially probing her about the challenges. After asking my first relatively mild question she said, "you're the one doing this research so you should already know that answer". From that moment on, I just wanted to get out of that room. Whatever I tried, my usual critical friends' explanation, how I viewed my position as a researcher, and so on, just fell flat—she wasn't having any of it. Through her body language and curt responses all I could intuit from her was "I think what you're doing is just nonsense, you'll never understand the inside story of what is happening here, I know you're going to misrepresent us, go away". And so, I remember leaving there and feeling very shaken up. I think I used one or two quotes in the book I was writing, which she approved, but they were really anodyne. Interestingly, I saw her two years later at a workshop after my book had been published, she raced up and gave me a huge hug. I was so taken aback. It taught me a lesson I guess, that we can have different impressions of these experiences, and they may not be as bad as you think they are.

My second experience was a deeper ethical challenge. I had built up a very good relationship with someone who was involved in a feminist civil society organisation, over a ten-year period. I guess I would have seen her 12 or 15 times, and every time we'd either do something formal or we'd have some sort of interview or check in with each other or go for a coffee or meal just to stay in touch. Her work was critical to a book I was writing, but we agreed I would only use the formal interview material. I quoted her extensively throughout the book, and in one section advanced a mild criticism about the work of the organisation she headed in relation to one specific issue. I sent the manuscript proofs to her and because she was mentioned quite a bit, gave her two months to read it and return it to me. After sending it, I heard nothing, so kept sending her updates saying "I'm going to need this in five weeks" "in a month", "in three weeks", "in a week". With the publisher on my back, I eventually wrote to say if I don't hear from you by a particular date, I'm going to assume that you've read it and you agree with it. Eventually she responded well after the deadline, with a long screed suggesting I'd misrepresented her and so forth. That was very challenging, not because of the subject matter—I stood by my analysis—but her defensiveness. I felt as if she saw me as invading her turf and she wanted me off it. In this case I actually felt that I just needed to trust myself because I knew how much I had restrained from really going in harder. This was a case where I was guided by my critical friendship role. I could see the limitations of the context in which she was working, and how difficult it was for her to make traction in this area but I could also see that she had also made some missteps along the way, and I needed to document these as well.

So, that was a challenging relationship, much longer than just one interview. And sadly, I think that relationship is broken permanently. The trust has gone on both sides. I wouldn't have ever called her a friend, but you know, a good colleague and collaborator and I really admired her work, she's moved on out of that role now too.

Had She Responded in Time, Would You Have Responded in Full to Her Concerns Within Your Text?

On the key issue that she was upset about, I had already given her my opinion, so I was saying something that she had already heard directly from me. And it was something that I knew I absolutely had to include in the analysis because it had been a major issue with the organisations she was involved with. I was definitely not the only one who took a critical view of her decision, a lot of other academics and commentators had discussed it in their work, so it would have looked very weird if I had not at least raised that issue. So to come to your question, I would not have changed the text. She wasn't concerned about being misquoted, but she took issue with my analysis, which I stand by. But I do wish I had had a better opportunity to have a dialogue with her about it, but it was one of those things you know, I couldn't make her read it any faster.

How Do You Engage with Concerns About Your Personal Safety, Mental Health and Concerns About the Consequences of the Dissemination of Your Information?

As I mentioned earlier, one thing I haven't done, like some of my colleagues, is deal directly with victims. I interview their advocates, I read firsthand accounts of their experiences through court testimonies, submissions and whatever, but don't speak to direct victims. And that gives me one layer, a huge layer, of protection. But still, reading this stuff can be disturbing and there have been different times when it's been more disturbing than others. I remember I was reading a whole lot of testimonies from the Yugoslav Tribunal when I was heavily pregnant with my first child and I just couldn't handle it. Much of it was about violence against men and I knew I was having a son, and the brutality disturbed me so much I put that down for a while and went back to it many months later when I could manage it again. At other times it's a little bit like watching violence on TV in that you do become de-sensitised to some extent, but that can also be a dangerous thing. I had a PhD student start on her work on conflict-related sexual violence and she was reading through mountains and mountains of court testimonies, and it affected her deeply. She didn't tell me how she was feeling for quite a long time, I think she thought I'd be critical of her or something. And I think, because I'd become de-sensitised I was remiss in giving her the support she needed early on. I felt really bad about that. But when we did finally debrief about it, and I checked to make sure she had support structures in place, and gave her time out when she needed it. She's chosen to continue in the field, she did an excellent PhD, she's written a book out of it now and she's still doing a lot more work in the area. But it did make me realise that you know there are times when you can shut yourself down and it can have major consequences for others.

But I moved around in my research quite a bit and I think that avoiding too much trauma might be part of the reason too, that I just don't want to be constantly in that world of sexual and gender based violence. But in reality, it is inescapable—wherever I go, violence against women raises its ugly head. When I moved into the construction project, I hadn't really given much thought to the prevalence of violence against women in that industry, but of course, it's a massive issue there too and it jumped out at us very quickly.

What Strategies Have You Put in Place for When You Are Dealing with Heavier Texts or What Specific Things Did You Wish You Had Set Up with Your PhD Student?

This is something I've got better at over time. I'm now a big fan of debriefing sessions. For instance, in the construction project we debriefed after every field visit. I've done this less consistently with other projects too, around the ICC, with a colleague who just absolutely gets it. So when it gets too much, I sit down and have a coffee with her just sort of protect each other a bit that way, but I suppose with that particular PhD student and students since then I've been really careful to raise the issue with them right up front, bring it up in our supervisory meetings to make sure they're doing ok, and get access to any counselling and support if they need it. To also make it clear that you know if there's a point where they need to shift their focus of their research, then you know we can find ways around it. And indeed, in the last 12 months that has happened because a student has had her own trauma triggered by her violence against women topic. That's been very confronting for all of us to see how damaging it has been to her mental health as well as her project, but we've worked on resolving it collectively, and think we've found a good solution.

Can You Talk Us Through the Mechanics of a Debrief Session?

I was a joint researcher on the construction project with my PhD student. She was the one to do the majority of the site visits, supported by another team member, who took a turn. We set up a formal system that after every visit the PhD student would debrief with another team member; sometimes it was with the team member who was with her, and so sharing stories from the site visit, and other times it was with someone who hadn't been present, but who asked questions and sometimes just let her talk about her experiences. We recorded all of these and we actually used them as data, which was really interesting. It added to the triangulation, because especially when two of us had been on site, we sometimes had very different experiences, or sometimes saw very similar things. Most debriefings would take an hour or so, but always try to do it straight-away and record it on one of our phones, so that nobody had to take notes, and so there was no burden on us. It also helped us manage any emerging mental health challenges in the group, especially with our PhD student who had herself left the industry because of a whole range of sort of toxic practices that we were witnessing on site, and sometimes that would really trigger some stuff for her. But the debriefing meant she could express how she was feeling, get supportive feedback. It was a very productive process to go through. I'd highly recommend it.

Are There Any Other People Who Are Involved in Your Life That Your Work Might Cause a Risk to, for Some It's Family, Colleagues or Others, Does That Apply to You?

Yeah, I understand what you mean. I don't think my family is at risk as such, but they definitely carry a burden. My field work often takes place overseas or away from home, and it's time consuming, and all that comes with a cost. And you know, that cost varies with shifts in the family, as my kids have gone through different phases, so have these costs and pressures. It's very intense when they're little, and then there's a few years of what I call the 'golden age'—same school pick up, no raging hormones, not too much homework stress—then to my current situation with my boys in Year 12 and Year 8 where I'm confronting an entirely new set of issues, but I've got the huge advantage of a mostly work from home husband who is incredibly hands on with our sons. Also, I've never taken them into the field in a direct sense. We've lived away for my work when I've been doing my fieldwork, or on sabbaticals and so on. We've had the opportunity to live in many wonderful places which has opened the kids' eyes to the world, but it has also been disruptive, uprooting the boys from school and my husband from his job. So, that worked for us as a family, but still, in my drive to do research I disrupt everyone else's life.

In terms of colleagues, I think there is a similar burden, especially in my current role as Director of the Australian Human Rights Institute. Because I want to continue to be an active researcher, I have to push work onto other people when I'm having really intense research times, and that adds stress and the additional responsibilities onto them, which is something that I'm very conscious of. As I get older, I'm increasingly questioning where the limits are. You've got to be very selfish in a way to keep your research going, it means pushing back, batting away other things, because everything else will easily encroach and then you don't do it. You have to keep your eye on the important rather than the urgent, and in our university system that's a really hard thing to do.

What About with Your Media Work, Do You Get Pushback Going Through Some of Your Commentary in the Media?

Oh god yeah! Any work on gender and equality will cause explosions, so will human rights commentary. The former brings out all the misogynists in seconds, the latter descends into a debate about Israel and Palestine, regardless of the topic, within no time. I've been fortunate, I haven't had any serious trolling or attacks, but I'm very conscious of how toxic social media can be for my feminist colleagues and women politicians and everyone else, so, yeah that's constantly in my mind and I'm always sort of expecting it. I feel like I haven't quite been found yet by those who want to really get stuck in, so I'm waiting for that to happen.

Are You Ready?

I'm not sure. I'm watching how others manage to block it—literally and psychologically—but I feel like I don't want to walk away from that public space, I think it's terrible just to be pushed out, leaving a nasty vortex of negativity and toxicity. I've got a fabulous communications manager who gives me great guidance on when to enter into debates, so I'm learning a lot from her. More often than not, she advises me not to engage. This goes against the grain a little, as we are constantly driven by the university system to gain more clicks, likes, retweets, whatever, so stepping back also means recognising that there's no point engaging unless you can bring something specific, new or interesting to the debate. Adding a voice just for the sake of it is not really valuable. That's been a great lesson.

If things get tough for me, I'm fortunate to have some wise people around me who have experienced this sort of thing and could give me advice. For instance, the great people at Human Rights Watch, where they are outspoken and fearless, but committed to facts and the protection of everyone's human rights, have to manage constant trolling on a daily basis, but they do it so well, without 'getting down in the mud' so to speak.

Could You Reflect on the Younger You, or Think About Giving Advice to a PhD Student, Someone Who's Not Really That Used to Fieldwork, What's the Thing You Wish You Knew When You Were Getting Started?

What I wish I knew back then is how valuable ethnographic approaches are to the type of research questions I want to ask. I really would have taken a very different methodological career path had I known this earlier. For studying gender power relations, these methods enhance the richness of the data and insights. I'd also say, be prepared to be constantly learning: don't be afraid to keep pushing at your own boundaries, whether across fields of research, theories or across methodologies. I didn't understand this when I was getting started, I thought you had to be an expert in one area and that was that. It didn't help that early on I was going to the big mainstream North American conference where everyone identified themselves via their theoretical/methodological and subdiscipline areas: "Hi, I'm Max, a constructivist IR scholar," or "I'm Angela, a quantitative US comparativist". What is that? Aside from saying I was a feminist scholar, I really had no idea how to respond to these people. In my view, to be 'locked' in to a field and method for life strips away all the joy that comes with exploring new approaches and fields—which is for me the real pleasure of an academic life. That probably sounds very indulgent, but it's true (and after all, we are incredibly fortunate to be able to do what we do).

What I know now is that it is possible to travel across different research domains, collecting different theories and methods on your travels. When I've had to sit down to write a narrative of my career for one of those awful applications for a promotion or something, I've realised that it's been my willingness to try new things that have given me such a satisfying career, including connecting me with really incredible people. I'd also say, don't be afraid to drop things if they no longer interest you. I've dabbled in a few areas of research, then decided it's not for me, or I might grab hold of it and spend a full ten years on it like I did with the ICC project. And you know I've got to say it's the PhD students and the Early

Career Researchers (ECR) that help me to constantly evolve and learn new things and I've learnt to be open to the wisdom that's come from below, you know, that's where the mighty work is going on and they constantly demonstrate to you that there's always more than one way of doing things.

The other thing is that I used to get very nervous doing those interviews. Even writing the message to ask for the interview I'd be feeling sick. I sympathise with my PhD students now when they are feeling very nervous approaching their interviewees. But like many things, it's practice, practice, practice. Also, with time it's become easier—I'm now a grey-headed woman, and I'm at a point now where those people are at the elite level, they're my peers so they are nowhere as intimidating as they once seemed, no matter their position. There's a sense of confidence in knowing I was born around the same time as they were, that we're equal on some level because of what we share—growing up listening to the same music, watching The Brady Bunch or Lost in Space after school, that sort of thing. I don't feel ill now, instead I feel like it's almost my duty to call things as I see them, because if I don't do it now, I never will, and the world is in one hell of a mess, and we cannot maintain the status quo, whether in relation to climate, gender relations, Indigenous rights or any other social justice issue.

I've also now had enough of those Wizard of Oz moments where I've pulled the curtain back and seen what's happening inside, and realise that nothing is perfect and that everyone is performing their roles, including me. Being conscious of the performativity of what we're doing really makes it easier in some ways. Also reminding myself that as a professor I don't have anything to lose, that I need to use my voice to express my concern about the issues I care about. I do recognise my privilege, and take it seriously, and constantly try to use if for the good.

Postscript Since the transcription of this interview, and after some discussions with the editors, it's dawned on me that in some senses this piece, like all my work, is more restrained than it could be. Especially when reflecting on my most difficult experiences, I've pulled my punches. To say what I really want to say would raise the risk that those who I've been discussing could be identified. Without an opportunity to give their side of the story, it would be wrong to say more than I have. It feels like, to quote Elvis, I'm 'caught in a trap', but it's one that comes with the territory of qualitative research with marginalised communities, and one which I am willing to bear to be able to try and identify the power relationships underlying our society.

References

Chappell, L., & Mackay, F. (2020). Feminist Critical Friends and De(con)structive Critics: Dilemmas of Feminist Engagement with Governance and Gender Reform Agendas. *European Journal of Politics and Gender*. https://doi.org/10.1332/251510820X15922354996155

Mackay, F., & Rhodes, R. A. W. (2013). Gender, Greedy Institutions and the Departmental Court. *Public Administration, 91*(3), 582–598.

8

Risking the Self: Vulnerability and Its Uses in Research

Tanya Jakimow

When we aim to reduce risk in research, we are, in part, seeking to reduce our vulnerability. We are, as human beings, innately vulnerable, dependent upon 'Others' for our social existence and bodily integrity. This vulnerability is often seen as negative. Masculinity requires a disavowal of vulnerability and vulnerability is seen as diminishing agency (Butler 2016). Our vulnerability—and therefore the need to reduce risks to ourselves and others—can limit research, where we can go, who we can talk to, what we can talk about. I am not suggesting that these limitations in themselves are always positive, but I nonetheless want to espouse vulnerability as a practice to both enhance the quality of our research, as well as make it more ethical. I am in conversation with scholars such as Judith Butler who argues that a "deliberate exposure to power" (2016, p. 22) lies at the heart of political resistance, and feminist approaches to a 'Politics of Care' as an alternative ethic to justice (Held 2006; Tronto 1995). Vulnerability as an ethical practice means being purposefully open to

T. Jakimow (✉)
Australian National University, Canberra, ACT, Australia
e-mail: tanya.jakimow@anu.edu.au

© The Author(s) 2020
P. Wadds et al. (eds.), *Navigating Fieldwork in the Social Sciences*,
https://doi.org/10.1007/978-3-030-46855-2_8

being affected by the other, to have one's very core sense of who one is and is becoming challenged in our encounters with others (Jakimow 2020). Vulnerability in this sense increases risk, but I propose that the benefits of becoming *more not less* vulnerable outweigh the costs.

Vulnerability is particularly important for the kinds of research that I do. My research biography can be roughly split into four main projects. My PhD research was an ethnography of how small local non-government organisations (NGOs) in Uttarakhand, India, produce and circulate knowledge and information. It consisted of participant observation and interviews. As a postdoctoral fellow at the Commonwealth Science and Industrial Research Organisation (CSIRO), I was part of an interdisciplinary research project examining the ways agrarian livelihoods were changing in the face of climate variability in Telangana, India, and Nusa Tenggara Barat, Indonesia. My role was to lead the qualitative research on livelihood pathways, generating life-history narratives with a cross-section of rural households. It was at this point that I became very interested in personhood, or ongoing becoming, arguing that we need to centre the self-in-process to understand agrarian change (Jakimow 2015). This interest in personhood persisted in my next project, which was a comparative ethnography of local development agents in Medan, North Sumatera, Indonesia, and Dehradun, Uttarakhand, India. Although these were two distinct types of development agents (community volunteers and women municipal councillors respectively) I found a common experience of 'susceptibility'—that is, the threat of having one's sense of self threatened in an encounter—to be pivotal to the way power operates in urban development.

I fell in love with the women municipal councillors in Dehradun, or more specifically, about doing research about/with women in politics. I returned to Dehradun in 2018 for the next round of municipal elections, in which many of my friends were contesting seats. My previous research had revealed the importance of the affective dimensions of the women's experiences, and I focused on the affect and emotions of these elections. I am extending this research focus in my current project (2020–2024): a four year comparative ethnography of women political actors, again in Medan, Indonesia, and Dehradun, India. The focus is women's political labour (much of which is emotional and affective labour) and the political capital that they generate (including the affective, the generation of sentiments, fear, gratitude, outrage and loyalty). Personhood is again central as I seek to also understand why women become political actors, and the mechanisms of their exploitation.

This research is risky but not in a conventional sense. There are emotional risks that come from empathising with an other, by becoming a raw nerve. There is a risk that in my involvement in the research I have my sense of self threatened, or the sense of self of the people whom I work with. I expose them and me to moral risks, the danger of doing something we later consider wrong or feel uneasy about. There is also a risk that the data that I generate, the knowledge that I produce, is either not credible, or lacks veracity as I examine the hidden, the unspoken, the subjective. Or as a consequence of the perception of my research in that way, there is a risk to my career. I nonetheless think these risks are necessary, and I aim to show why heightening my vulnerability is necessary to the research I do.

Emotional Risk and Risking Self/What Do We Risk?

The week after the Dehradun municipal elections was really difficult. We had followed eight women candidates during the campaign, out of which seven lost. A couple of the losses were close, and visiting losing candidates afterwards in their home we encountered disappointment, anger and emptiness. Homes that had been bustling with activity only a few days early were deep with silence. Even the light seemed subdued, and the bright sunshine outside refused to penetrate the dark guest rooms. Many of the losses were large. A sitting municipal councillor came a distant fourth, other candidates received barely a couple of hundred of votes (out of an electorate of 5000). One candidate, the youngest and perhaps most emotionally vulnerable, received only 26 votes: this after having invested the equivalent of five month's salary into the campaign. We, my research assistant (RA) and I, had spent the better part of three weeks campaigning with these women, knocking on doors, attending rallies, putting up posters. Some of the women I had known four years. We were emotionally invested in their campaigns. Now, we shared in their devastation.

Such research is emotionally risky. For reasons that I outline below, in order to produce rich empirical material on emotions, I needed to empathise, to try to feel as the women candidates felt. I needed to become a raw nerve, to heighten my senses, become more susceptible to being affected, in order to have access to the emotional and affective dimensions of the campaign. The election research was for this reason the most emotionally exhausting research that I have done. But all social research is emotionally exhausting. It is fraught with uncertainties and anxieties. How will people react to me? Will I get access? What do they think about me, really? Am I asking the right questions? Am I speaking to the right people? What am I missing by attending this event and not others? These are indicative of the multiple questions we ask of ourselves each day, trying to predict how things will pan out when humans and societies are highly contingent and unpredictable. For me, as I do research in India and Indonesia, most often being the only white person in the room, I am also hyper-visible, which brings certain privileges but also means that I need to be on my best behaviour all the time. I go a bit loopy while on fieldwork, and there is always the risk that the emotions will become overwhelming, that something will break inside.

As social researchers, particularly anthropologists, we also *risk ourselves* in our encounters with others. And here I am talking about 'self', as in who we believe ourselves to be. Anthropologists necessarily undergo a transformation in the 'field' (as problematic as that term is). I agree with Ingold (2018) that anthropologists do not, or should not seek to catalogue difference, but rather to engage curiously with the world to reveal different ways of living, different human potentialities. To understand those potentialities, to learn *with* not *from* people from other societies and cultures, we dwell in the unfamiliar. Throop (2018) argues that ethnography is about disorientation, inhabiting a different world in which expectations are unknown, or unfamiliar. In the process of orientating oneself, one's attention becomes drawn to things that might otherwise go unnoticed. This responsiveness, to being open to the world, to becoming with and in relation to the world, is a basic human condition. We are attuned not only to the world as it is, but also as it unfolds and as we encounter it (Throop 2018). We are also relational beings, and the relations we form through our research is part of our ongoing becoming. In forming a new relation, a new moral relation, the former self is put at risk (Zigon and Throop 2014). That is, quite simply, we change, and in the almost inevitability of this process, we are susceptible to have our more durable sense of who we are threatened.

Again, susceptibility or risk need not have a negative connotation in this case. Of course we want to change, we are not static constant beings, a singular unitary self, but rather always in a state of becoming (Biehl and Locke 2017), inhabiting multiple selves. I was asked in the interview how much of the selves we inhabit while on fieldwork is a performance, and whether we are consistent while we are doing research compared to 'back home'. My response is that the performance and the being are not two separate things: we become what we perform in iterative acts of power. For example, I drink alcohol maybe three or four times a week in Australia, where it is acceptable for women to do so, and it has no negative connotations. Secretly, I sometimes also visit the upmarket liquor store in Dehradun when on fieldwork, ensuring that I take the empty bottles to a different rubbish tip so the people in the hostel do not know I drink. This is because it is not really acceptable, or seen as usual, that a woman of my age and class would drink. Stigma and stereotypes mean that when a woman drinks, she is 'loose', or perhaps poor and crass. But in the act of me 'performing' that I don't drink, I am reiterating the norm, I am living the norm. So that when election time comes around, and the women are complaining that the men are drinking and that as they are women they do not serve alcohol and serve only vegetarian food, my feeling of disgust and virtuousness respectively is genuine. I would not dream of having a couple of drinks with my friends after a hard day of campaigning. Maybe this is a transformation in my being, or my inhabiting multiple selves. But it is 100% important for me to understand, to change in this way. If I *feel* disgusted, I have insight into what it is to inhabit those norms. If I only *intellectually understand* that they are disgusted, I merely identify the norm.

But I appreciate that change, or becoming, is different to *risking a sense of self*. The risk comes in the uncertainty as to how we will be accepted, what relations we are able to form, how people respond to us. We are impressed upon in our encounters with others in ways that are radically involuntary (Butler 2015). So I may be meeting someone, and I have this durable self-image that I carry around with me, not a consistent unitary self, but a narrative about who I am. This sense of who I am is reaffirmed by an 'Other', in fact I need this reaffirmation for my ongoing sense of self, to sustain the narrative. But the 'Other' may respond in ways that challenge this sense of self, make it unsustainable, that demand a modification in my relationship to myself. For example, I think I am a competent researcher with a good sense of morals and ethics, and then I encounter a woman activist who questions my motivations, my actions, who treats me as part of the problem of white feminism, who questions whether I can be part of the solution. This has not happened, but I am waiting for it to happen. In this scenario I am impressed upon, my self-narrative is threatened. I personally find the research encounter particularly fraught due to the anxieties mentioned above. I am meeting new people, I have attuned myself to be hyper-responsive to cues, and I am uncertain. In research, I am constantly risking my sense of who I am.

So there are two risks here. First, there are the emotional risks that arise as I purposefully open myself up to 'feeling', as I become a raw nerve. Second, there is the risk to my self-narrative, the durable self that is the core to my being. To reiterate, both these risks are necessary. I need to feel in order to understand and capture the affective dimensions of life. And I need to be open to and responsive to others, attuned to how they see me, open to change. But it is really hard, and exhausting. And so we need, or I need, to manage the toll of this risky environment. I have already mentioned one strategy, and that is furtive visits to the liquor store. I also join a gym. I need the release of physical exercise; exercise has always been a part of my routine since childhood, and it provides a constant. Running, even on a treadmill, is my time, when whatever mask I have put on for the day is taken off, I am myself. Gyms are also where I feel most at home. I (usually) speak in English, and meet people like me. I also watch a lot of crap TV in the evenings, to the detriment of my language (Hindi or Indonesian), such as Grey's Anatomy during my PhD, America's Next Top Model during my postdoc and most recently Survivor. This routine in the evening returns me to the more durable sense of who I think I am. I think we all need to find ways to survive the assault on our being, particularly as the risks are actually an important part of the process.

Risking Others/Who Bears the Risk?

It is one thing to risk one's own sense of self, or our durable narrative, and quite another to risk the self-perceptions of others. When we are thinking about the risks for our research respondents, or our research assistants, we are usually thinking in terms of physical threats, or the risk of inducing emotional trauma, or their social standing. But in inviting their participation in ethnographic research, we are often also asking them to be susceptible to having their sense of self challenged. To give an example, I invited community volunteer organisations in Medan to a workshop to discuss research findings. The aim was to spark a reflexive dialogue about the practices of community-based development, prompting them to critically reflect on what they do and why, so that they think anew and modify their practices (see Mauksch and Rao 2014). Four organisations had been invited, three of which brought between five and ten members. But one of the coordinators came by himself, unable to convince his fellow volunteers. Even worse, one volunteer actually came, but acted in the capacity of a community member, rather than volunteer. The reasons why the volunteers did not come or chose not to associate with the organisation is an interesting question. It could be a prompt for the coordinator to reflect on his leadership practices, and the actual success of the organisation. But who can ask that question? The coordinator had invested his whole sense of being into the organisation and volunteer activities. He told us that he had 'found himself' in the program. To get him to critically reflect on, to find fault in his leadership is far too painful, it would risk the sense of pride he has as a coordinator. So instead I was complicit in papering over the absence of the other volunteers, finding ways to reaffirm to him that I thought he was doing a marvellous job as leader.

The research also has unrecognised risks for research assistants. Some of these are mundane, but nonetheless important. So for example, needing to ensure that my RAs can fulfil their social and familial responsibilities, so that they do not risk their social standing, casual employment or domestic harmony. Managing this risk impacts the research process, so, for example, I can't often take them to events that occur outside of regular working hours, such as campaign rallies. Other risks are more obvious, and inherently uneven. I have a layer of protection due to my being an international researcher, someone with presumed backing from the Australian government. If I were to be kidnapped or raped, it would be a news story. At the same time, if something goes wrong, if I end up spending a night in the police cell, or get caught up in a scandal, I (mostly) leave the stigma and shame behind once I get on the plane. None of this has happened to me, so maybe these are assumptions; let's hope they are never tested.

But for my research assistants, the gravity of such events is greater, and the protections are lower. So, for example, one night we were staying in a small town in Telangana, when police came and knocked on our door at about 3 am. The hotel is on a highway, and is frequented by prostitutes. My RAs were assumed to be prostitutes, or at least threatened with that accusation, perhaps to extract a bribe. I was untouched by the stigma, and when I eventually opened the door, they did not pester me. I also had my husband on the phone, who, had I been arrested, would have called the embassy to arrange help. Few of my research assistants would have such power on their side. Further, if the research did go really badly, if through my fault we ruined relationships with, say, a municipal government, I return home, I build another 'field-site', I recover. But for my research assistants, who live and work in that locality, they depend on these relationships far in the future. There is, I think, therefore a greater risk for people doing research closer to home.

I also implicate my Research Assistants into all that is morally or ethically fraught in the research. Building relationships with respondents is an important element of the research process, to gain the trust and openness required. I am not always able to stay in the 'field' for more than a couple of months at a time, and it is often my RAs that sustain the relationships in my absence. I hope that these are not purely extractive relationships, in that they don't exist solely for the purpose of generating data, but are reciprocal, or at the least, involve genuine care. And I do care deeply for the people who I do research with, but the reality is I am often far away. WhatsApp has changed this a bit, but particularly at the time of doing research on community development in Medan, I was back in Australia and unreachable for months at a time. There are also unequal relationships, in the sense that I, and my research assistants, have access to more resources—economic, cultural and social—than most of our respondents. So sometimes a respondent would reach out to an RA and ask for help—a loan, a contact for a job—or ask them to take part in social obligations, such as attending a wedding, or grieving a family loss. So the costs of maintaining a relationship can be great, and it is one that is borne by my research assistants, more so than me. I also consider this a moral risk. We enter into relationships in which we may inadvertently do something wrong, that again threatens our sense of self. I benefit from the relationships, without bearing the risks associated with it.

We are also susceptible to have ourselves threatened in these relationships. I start my most recent book with an incident with a so-called beneficiary of the community development program I have mentioned earlier. We had known Pak Alex (a pseudonym) for two years by that stage. He was a 'key respondent', meaning that we had co-constructed a profile with him, entailing at least four formal interviews and many informal conversations. When we set up the relationship, we were careful to outline the benefits and risks of his participation, as per the formal ethics requirement. As we came to interact with him, it became clear that he had other expectations on us. He was someone who used to ring up my RAs and ask for a loan, or for contacts to help him sell his goods, for example. We continued to remind him that the project was a research project, with indirect benefits, and to say he can withdraw at any time he wanted to. But it was only after the profile was completed and we came back to share what we had done with it, that he told us how disappointed he was. He said that research is good if the information it produces helps the people who give it, but this research has only helped the researchers. "You have come back after some time, and I am still living in the same conditions. You will come back in a year, and things will still be the same. Research should be mutually beneficial".

This interaction hurt at the very core of my being; it highlights my susceptibility to be affected, to be impressed upon in ways that challenge my core sense of who I am and what I am doing: the risk to self that I mentioned earlier. But I have also implicated my Research Assistants. They too were with me during the research process. They guided me in what was appropriate, they dealt with his claims, they were responsible for 'my' emotional wellbeing. Following the encounter we reassured each other, said things to alleviate our collective hurt. We referred to other respondents who had no complaints and welcomed us as friends, and spoke about the official ethics process and ongoing process of consent. We overcame the threat to our sense of self, we reduced the risk through mutual assurances.

If I had been a better researcher, I would have opened up this wound, interrogated what we did individually and collectively that could have been better. I would have allowed the encounter to transform our relationship with Pak Alex, to be more responsive to his demands, to actually challenge the power relations between us. This is what I describe as vulnerability as an ethical practice (Jakimow 2020). By vulnerability I mean a purposeful openness to allow oneself to be impressed upon in ways that challenge a sense of self. It means a purposeful practice of being more susceptible to being affected by people who are less powerful, or with whom I am in an unequal relationship; or in other words, enhancing their capacity to affect in the relation (Anderson 2014). But I did not. Instead I made my own excuses, and I continued to abuse my power to set the terms of the relationship. Vulnerability as an ethical practice means heightening the risk to self, for me, and the people who do research with me. This risk is, I suggest, critical for ethical research, particularly in scenarios of unequal power. It nonetheless needs to be managed carefully.

How Do We Reduce the Risk of Getting It Wrong?

Probably by this stage there are at least a couple of readers who are thinking that with research on personhood, subjectivities, emotions and affect, surely the greatest risk is that the data generated is neither 'objective' nor verifiable. As noted earlier, we over-identified with the respondents, allowed our own emotions to shape our interpretations, our 'subjective' interpretations. One's inner being, the 'self', is impenetrable even to our own full comprehension; we can only describe the self through the subject positions available to us (Butler 2005). So how do we do research on personhood? How can we even suggest that we can give an account of others (to paraphrase Butler 2005). Affects are arguably even more difficult to capture. Affects are invisible, they are intensities, circulating energies between bodies but made manifest through bodies. We cannot record the affects circulating in a rally, or the energy circulating among a crowd. So how can we speak of any certainty about the affective dimensions of elections? Even emotions are fraught objects of research. When feelings are articulated and translated into language, they are positioned within discursive regimes (Anderson 2014; Pedwell and Whitehead 2012). That is, I cannot simply ask candidates, "so how did it feel to only get 26 votes?" and then transcribe the response as the emotions of the elections. To describe an emotion and put them into words is to lose the immediacy of the feeling, to subject these feelings to power, to bring in their own intellectual interpretation of the feeling in order to put it into words. Such accounts are useful, as they reveal (gendered) emotional repertoires and discursive regimes, but they do not always get at the heart of feeling.

Instead, as noted earlier, I need to feel the devastation of loss, the joy of election, the anger at betrayal myself. One cannot do research on emotions and affect by refusing to be moved, refusing to feel. I did not need to understand their experiences intellectually, or this was a small part, rather I needed to understand it emotionally and affectively. I needed to get under their skin, to try to feel what they are feeling, to empathise with them. In addition to the emotional risks this entails, there is, admittedly, a huge risk that I will get it wrong. Often I am overwhelmed with doubt, thinking that what I am writing is baseless, or I am transposing what I feel onto others who have altogether different affective experiences.

There are two main ways that I seek to minimise these risks. First, we generate data about the biographical details of the people whose affective experiences we are trying to understand (see also Beatty 2014). How a person feels depends upon who they are as a person, the experiences they have had, what they wish for in the future. So in addition to participant observation that captures the immediacy of the event, we also co-construct profiles to gain a deep understanding of the person. I will understand the effect and affect of an insult better if I know whether it touches a nerve in a particular individual. Second, I work with research assistants with whom I check my interpretations. I have found wonderful research assistants in both Medan and Dehradun, who understand conceptually what I am seeking to do, and who are able to share their own feelings and interpretations of the feelings of others. We are from different cultural and social backgrounds, and therefore have different affective pedagogies and emotional repertoires. Theirs are more similar to the research participants. Just as I must learn social norms and practices, I must also learn these repertoires. My RAs are critical to this education, and to making our collective interpretations as robust as possible (see Jakimow and Yumasdaleni 2016 for an account of this method).

There is still a degree of speculation. We aim to achieve verisimilitude in our research: that is, the sense that this is true, rather than merely plausible. But we do not claim certainty, replicability or verifiability. There is a difference between empathetic knowledge and claiming a truth about how another feels (Pedwell and Whitehead 2012). It is interpretive research that does not accord well with a positivist epistemology. But just because the findings are uncertain, does not mean that the research is not worth doing. To ignore emotions and affect is to leave out that which "constitutes the very fabric of our being" (Hemmings 2005, p. 549), the texture of life, and to overlook important ways that power works (Wetherell 2012). Nobody says to a quantum physicist, "the research you do has too many uncertainties, is probabilistic so we should not seek to illuminate our understanding of the micro world", instead they say "here, have 100 million dollars for an experiment that may work", or at least that is what I, as a somewhat bitter social scientist thinks happens. But emotions and affect and interpretive social sciences are 'soft', feminine and devalued. It is therefore no surprise that the biggest leaps in understanding emotion and affect have been from feminist scholars. But then this research gets pigeonholed, I use the word devalued again, marginalised in academia.

And so the final risk is the risk to our careers when we chose research subjects that are fundamentally interesting and important, yet lie outside mainstream academia. I have a double whammy, as I do research on emotions and affect, and also on women politicians. In part the latter focus is due to necessity. Male politicians often do not see me as credible, are less interested in having me follow them around, and I work with an NGO known for women's empowerment. Further, it is not really safe for me to go out campaigning with men, drinking alcohol and partying, for example, at least not in India. I also have a deeper empathy with women. So I am restricted by my gender, but happily restricted, as I believe not only are women politicians important as a subject, it is through looking at politics through the eyes of women and their experiences that we can advance our understanding of politics writ large. But articles on women in politics are relegated to 'Gender and Politics', cited in research that is about other women in politics. Articles about male politicians are about politics in general, cited in political science much more broadly. There are exceptions, such as Björkman's (2014) article on money in elections in India that is based on ethnographic research with women, but they are exceptions. I actually do not know how to mitigate this risk, other than to continue to produce scholarship that is so illuminating it cannot be ignored.

How Do We Do Research Better, Even If It Is Also Riskier?

We do not, however, do research only in order to further our career and build upon our already massive egos. We do research because we are very much interested and curious about the world. We are drawn to research subjects that sustain that interest and curiosity. We also want to do research that has an impact, where a difference can be made. My research with women political actors is very satisfying because I am seeking not only to understand politics, but to also increase the number of women elected. At least this is the narrative that I tell myself. This is my sense of who I am as a researcher, my account of my motivations, whether or not I have actually penetrated the depths of my actual drives. What I have suggested in this chapter is that we may at times need to put at risk this sense of self, or at least not be afraid to open it up for contradiction and challenge.

This vulnerability has, I suggest, important uses. First, when we become open to being affected by the other, when we become susceptible to being impressed upon, we gain access to news ways of understanding: particularly the affective dimensions of life. Second, we change the terms of our relations with our research respondents. By enhancing our susceptibility to be affected, we increase their relative capacity to affect, to make demands on us, to seek new forms of relating, thereby creating stronger ties. I suggest that vulnerability in this way can lead to more ethical research, particularly in scenarios with vast power differentials between researcher and researched. Finally, being open to change is part of what is attractive about anthropology. Seeking not only potentialities in other cultures and societies, but potentialities of the self. I don't want to use the word personal growth, as there is nothing inevitably progressive about change. The ability to be exposed in ways that spark new self-imaginaries is, however, a privilege of my work. But the risks to self are considerable, and require self-care and care for others.

References

Anderson, B. (2014). *Encountering Affect: Capacities, Apparatuses, Conditions.* Farnham: Ashgate.

Beatty, A. (2014). Anthropology and Emotion. *Journal of the Royal Anthropological Institute, 20,* 545–563.

Biehl, J., & Locke, P. (2017). Introduction: Ethnographic Sensorium. In J. Biehl & P. Locke (Eds.), *Unfinished: The Anthropology of Becoming* (pp. 1–40). Durham: Duke University Press.

Björkman, L. (2014). "You Can't Buy a Vote": Meanings of Money in a Mumbai Election. *American Ethnologist, 41*(4), 617–634.

Butler, J. (2005). *Giving an Account of Oneself.* New York: Fordham University Press.

Butler, J. (2015). *Senses of the Subject.* New York: Fordham University Press.

Butler, J. (2016). Rethinking Vulnerability and Resistance. In J. Butler, Z. Gambetti, & L. Sabsay (Eds.), *Vulnerability in Resistance* (pp. 12–27). Durham: Duke University Press.

Held, V. (2006). *The Ethics of Care: Personal, Political, and Global.* Oxford: Oxford University Press.

Hemmings, C. (2005). Invoking Affect: Cultural Theory and the Ontological Turn. *Cultural Studies, 19*(5), 548–567.

Ingold, T. (2018). *Anthropology: Why It Matters*. Cambridge: Polity Press.

Jakimow, T. (2015). *Decentring Development: Understanding Change in Agrarian Societies*. Houndmills: Palgrave Macmillan.

Jakimow, T. (2020). *Susceptibility in Development: Micro-Politics of Urban Development in India and Indonesia*. Oxford: Oxford University Press.

Jakimow, T., & Yumasdaleni. (2016). Affective Registers in Qualitative Team Research: Interpreting the Self in Encounters with the State. *Qualitative Research Journal, 16*(2), 169–180.

Mauksch, S., & Rao, U. (2014). Fieldwork as Dialogue: Reflections on Alternative Forms of Engagement. *Zeitschrift für Ethnologie, 139*, 23–38.

Pedwell, C., & Whitehead, A. (2012). Affecting Feminism: Questions of Feeling in Feminist Theory. *Feminist Theory, 13*(2), 115–129.

Throop, J. (2018). Being Open to the World. *HAU, 8*(1/2), 197–210.

Tronto, J. C. (1995). Care as a Basis for Radical Political Judgements. *Hypatia, 10*(2), 141–149.

Wetherell, M. (2012). *Affect and Emotion: A New Social Science Understanding*. London: Sage.

Zigon, J., & Throop, J. C. (2014). Moral Experience: Introduction. *Ethos, 42*(1), 1–15.

9

Enter the Dragon: Coming of Age as Blond, White, Female Researcher in Fragile Contexts

Susanne Schmeidl

My research career started over three decades ago and I've used a variety of methodologies over that time. What has not changed to date, however, are two guiding principles of sorts. First, my strongest driver for doing research is a wish to change the world for the better, very common among peace scholars (Barash and Webel 2017). This perhaps is at least in part due to guilt, wanting to make-up for Germany's war-mongering past and Nazi holocaust. To me research needs to have a social justice purpose and produce change, inform something or influence somebody.

Secondly, rather than treating other human beings as 'data', I strongly believe in engaging closely with the people and persons living in the contexts I research, and thus in co-constructing knowledge. To me this is common sense, after all, researchers come and go and communities are there to stay and must deal with both positive and negative consequences of our research intervention.

S. Schmeidl (✉)
School of Social Sciences, University of New South Wales,
Sydney, NSW, Australia
e-mail: s.schmeidl@unsw.edu.au

My first research project was during my undergraduate studies (1985–1986) when, as part of my social work placement, I was asked by my host organisation to interview around 300 women living in a slum at the outskirts of Mexico City. At the time, I had limited training in research methodologies, so I had to learn a lot on the go. The women were very gracious with their time and me. I spent about six months speaking to three to four women per day. It gave me a rich understanding of life in Mexican slums, especially as experienced by women. I am still very grateful for the time these women gave me, they helped me to understand poverty, the oppressive role of the Catholic church, gender relations—their stories shaped the feminist that I am today. It is there I fell in love with field research and I owe it to these women.

My PhD research took me away from the field, it was highly quantitative (Schmeidl 1997). I constructed my own dataset through archival research with the UN Refugee Agency. When I finished, I was itching to go back to the 'real' field. This happened after I joined the Swiss Peace Foundation in 1998.

My first major collaborative research project was to develop a Conflict Early Warning Mechanism for the Intergovernmental Authority on Development in the Horn of Africa. Here I started honing my approach to co-researching with people from my research sites, focussing on partnerships and reciprocity. I'm still proud of that project and edited book, which was truly co-produced with my Kenyan colleague Cirû (Mwaûra and Schmeidl 2002). She taught me a lot about East African politics, society and culture. She added rich nuance to our work.

Around the same time, I also started conducting research in South Asia: Pakistan, India and Afghanistan. Being new to the region, I had to start from scratch—speaking to as many people I could during field visits: journalists, researchers, human rights activists, politicians, whoever gave me time; it was a constant snowballing of contacts, constant learning, lots of listening. I am still humbled at how much time people gave me during my two field visits.

After my first visit to Afghanistan in 2000, then under Taliban control, I fell in love with the country and people and found my longer-term 'research home'. Between 2002 and 2014, I lived and collaborated there with two civil society organisations and continue research on the country to date. I've never thought of myself as an ethnographer—perhaps because I was not trained as such—but if you live and work in the area you also research, your entire life becomes one long ethnographic encounter. It is hard to say at times where research starts and ends.

Tell Us More About Your Research. What Was It About and Who Did You Interview?

I already spoke about Mexico and East Africa. In Afghanistan I was involved in over 30 research projects, either directly or as a project manager, always with Afghan colleagues. This is why I will speak of 'we' and 'us' from here on, as my research projects in Afghanistan were all collaborative endeavours. A lot were context-assessments following the 'Do No Harm' (conflict-sensitive) approach by Mary Anderson (1999) which is meant to help development actors avoid unintentional negative consequences of their work; basically, socio-anthropological/socio-political assessments of an area. Others were research on subject-specific social justice issues, such as internal displacement, state legitimacy, customary justice, Taliban justice, private security companies, local politics and insurgency dynamics, US military kill and capture missions, youth activism and elections.

We mostly worked with qualitative methods, such as participant observations, semi-structured interviews and focus group discussions with a wide range of stakeholders: civil society, government, NGOs, journalists, human rights, youth and women activists, traditional elders, strongmen, security providers, military and of course community members (men, women, youth).

It was our research projects and research questions that influenced who we needed to speak to, not the other way around. This meant also interviewing people you didn't particularly like, such as the odd commander, governor or police chief who you knew had killed or tortured people. You want to call them out for it, but that is not really your job—so you just focus on the interview and move on. This really comes down to your personal professional ethics and whether you see yourself as somebody using research to produce change or advocate for change while researching.

How Did You Cope with Challenging Interviews/Interviewing Difficult People?

Sometimes you want to shake the male community elder who keeps telling you women's rights are limited by the lack of paved streets. Especially if you have interviewed them over a decade and they still sell you the same BS. You just can't insult such people; it would be rude, it's not the purpose of research. I want to emphasise that sometimes I also wanted to shake international actors (military, civilian) about things they said, but again, you listen and move on. The goal was for our research to influence projects that could produce some positive change. How one would assess our research impact would be a great research project.

In a series of interviews with the Ex-Taliban Minister for Religious affairs in 2012, for example, it took me four hours over three sittings to get past the formalities about religion and good governance until he finished the interview by saying, "It is war, when we come to power all these things [human rights violations] will change". Sometimes you need stamina. Stay polite and slowly peel back the layers. That is why I prefer to speak to communities about how they experience Taliban justice, government action, or private security contractors. I find that more honest.

The toughest gig perhaps was my research with private security companies, as I basically had to enter the world of mercenaries. They were cashed up guys with little regulation, guns and a lot of issues. They behaved as if they were the law (above it actually). In many ways, they behaved like cowboys in the wild west. I had to go to Kandahar for interviews and one guest house my Afghan colleagues had arranged fell through, and the UN guest house was booked. The only other guest house was run by a private security company. I had not really considered getting such a close-up experience, but I needed a room. It felt like entering the lion's den. That night in the guesthouse is still one of the more confronting experiences I've had. I was surrounded by hypermasculine men, who drank, swore, and talked derogatory about the country (Afghanistan) and people I loved. It was such a boy's club, they were the saviours of the war, I should be grateful for the work they did, ideally by going to bed with them. I went to my room, alone, and I triple-locked my door and just got the hell out of there the next day.

I still feel dirty about these interviews. I just wanted that report written so I could move on. I never followed up on the research; I had exposed the damaging impact of the industry and contributed to a conversation about poor regulation (Schmeidl 2008). As far as I was concerned, my job was done. I handed some loose ends to an investigative journalist who wrote a great expose about one of the more notorious firms (Schulman 2009). I did that more than once, when there were parts of a story I could not or did not want to tell, then I tried to find somebody else who could. In Afghanistan you were as much a researcher as the subject of research. I was interviewed countless times about my research and accumulated knowledge.

What Was Collaboration with Local Partners Like?

When working with local partners, there is often a division of labour dictated by logistics and access. Research projects were collaborative, and everybody was interviewing their own 'tribe'. This was partly influenced by language (to my regret I never spoke Dari and Pashto fluent enough to do my own interviews as I did in Mexico) and security context. In the organisation I worked with, we developed a methodology where we involved people from the affected areas in research, both for access and security, but also so we could give something back to communities by paying researchers and training them on how to conduct research. We would like to think this made our research less extractive.

My role was often to conduct the elite-level interviews especially when my Afghan colleagues became increasingly uncomfortable to be seen entering foreign compounds, let alone a military base. They did not want to be thought of as spying or collaborating with the enemy, the people in power.

My Afghan colleagues also felt that they would not be taken as seriously by international actors, so I interviewed the UN, NGOs, Embassies; more or less my 'own tribe'. This is really depressing in so many ways as it has strong colonial overtones and my Afghan colleagues hated that there was a double-standard, how they were treated and that they were considered less objective because they were local. International researchers instead were objective. Really?

I also got to speak to Police Chiefs and Governors, and here it was more about the access a white woman might have with Afghan men of power. I was exotic. I always joked that my Afghan colleagues knew when to send in 'the Blonde'. How do I best explain this? In Afghanistan a lot is by association—who you are seen with or considered allied with. When you come as an outsider, and perhaps especially as a foreign woman, you have a bit more leeway. You don't yet fit into any domestic power-structures, which is helpful in a highly competitive political marketplace.

I tried to minimise the risk for my colleagues by always taking a different person to translate for me. That way it was clear who was leading the interview and asking the questions and none of my Afghan colleagues would be seen as too associated with the individual we interviewed. In the end they could feign innocence as a hired hand, just trying to put food on the table by working with this foreign lady.

Women are also not taken as seriously as a man. While I could have gotten offended (and it did irritate me at times), I ended up using it to my advantage. I sometimes could ask questions to domestic strongmen and government officials that perhaps a man could not have asked as easily. Sometimes my Afghan colleagues were surprised what I learned when I interviewed, for example, a Provincial Chief of Police. They would have never gotten that kind of information, mostly because the police chief would have been guarded, wondering why my colleagues wanted to know about the security situation. But, what on earth could a woman possibly do with such information? This was not my first experience of such sexism. I learned from Mexican women how to use stereotypical views of femininity to my advantage. This is not to say that I flirted during interviews, I did not—I simply got away with asking "naive" questions. I got very good at having men explain things to me, even if I knew a thing or two about them.

Reflecting on this, being taken seriously has pros and cons. My Afghan colleagues did not want to interview international actors out of fear of not being taken seriously (or to become guilty by association), and I could interview male elites, because they did not take me as seriously. I know it sounds paradoxical, but it worked somehow.

Can You Say a Bit More About Your Experience as a Female Researcher in Such Contexts?

In my case it was about being a white and blond female. In Germany that is a dime a dozen, but in many of the places where I researched that combination put you on some strange pedestal of desirability. It made me frequently uncomfortable, especially in the early days. Until I arrived in Mexico, I never knew how 'desirable' it was to be white and blonde. Naive, I know. This colonial legacy that made for white blond privilege was a hard pill to swallow.

This light skinned privilege comes with a double-edged sword for a woman, however, as you are hypersexualised. And because Western women are assumed to be promiscuous, it can lead to frequent harassment, although this also happens to Mexican or Afghan women operating in public spheres. Being a foreigner, a *kharegee*, simply dialled things up a notch. Getting cat called, groped on the street, on the bus, anywhere men think they can get away with it. There is even a joke about Mexican buses being an all-inclusive spa—you get to sweat, and you get a massage. This is also why the Mexican subway is segregated, into a part that only women and children can access, enforced by police.

South Asia and especially Afghanistan is an entirely different story; very conservative Muslim countries, where women were less visible in public life and those who were are thought of as 'less honourable'. I learned from Afghan women what mattered when dressing, such as covering your 'assets': boobs and butt. Covering your head with a scarf was important, but secondary—after all you are not Muslim. When you sat down on the ground, you had to ensure that you cover your crotch—I always had an extra scarf with me for that purpose. That rule also applies to men; don't man-spread. It was all about modesty.

You could rage against this or just remember that in Western culture over the years there have been heated debates over women's dress, so who are we to judge? The notion that women should dress down as not to tempt men is not uniquely Muslim, it's men not taking responsibility for their own desires.

I dressed conservatively, in local clothing, especially when I went to rural areas. This was sometimes commented on positively by Afghans and mocked by foreigners. But I was not in Afghanistan to start a revolution; I was here to work and research. How you dress can send subtle signals about your cultural understanding. For me it was simply about wanting to be able to interview a man without him unnecessarily distracted by how I was dressed.

Did it always work? No. I also got groped in Afghanistan when I walked in crowded places and a couple of times when I went alone for interviews, I got propositioned—a minister tried to kiss me and so did a Pakistani ambassador. So, it was always best to take a colleague along, not just for translation but as male guardian (*mahram*).

For the record, it's not just about Afghan men, Western men can be just as sexist and appalling. I don't know what it is about (post) conflict environments—but I feel some basic social norms just go out of the window.

So How Risky Was Research in Afghanistan, More Generally and for a Woman?

I never thought of my work as 'risky'. But I know how it looks when conducting research in a conflict country: dangerous and edgy. Perhaps part of it was that I had normalised militarisation before I arrived in Afghanistan. I grew up in 'occupied' Germany in the 1970s/80s, in a village with about 30,000 inhabitants and 10,000 American soldiers, I saw military vehicles, tanks and soldiers on the street and sometimes woke up to manoeuvres in the pastures close to where I lived. This perhaps made seeing military and tanks on a daily basis less confronting until it started to proliferate.

Some of the normalisation might have also come from the slow security deterioration, from the initial years when things were still more or less OK, the times I could walk to work, the times my parents visited me, the times I could drive relatively safely to most parts of Afghanistan, to when I no longer could do any of this.

I made a deal with myself early on, that the moment I got scared, I would leave. But I understand now that fear is quite a relative concept, and that sometimes we repress fear to cope. I experienced this detachment first when I was caught in the first big earthquake in Mexico in 1985 (8.0 magnitude), and I was watching things unfold around me like a movie, with limited emotions. Those came when I watched the news about the earthquake in the evening. Perhaps in Afghanistan, I also managed a certain detachment, where things were less real if you were not 'in the thick' of it (e.g., caught in a skirmish or suicide attack).

I was never kidnapped, for example. I was not shot at, though at one time when we came back by road to Kabul from Jalalabad, the Taliban had attacked some trucks in front of us, and the Afghan military was returning fire overhead—heavy machine gun fire over the top of our car and other cars. My husband who was visiting me at the time, was in the car and claims I slept through most of the fire exchange, he calls me 'hardened'.

Thankfully, I have never been struck by improvised explosive device (IED) or suicide bomb. Yes, we heard them, and when the first truck bomb exploded in 2004, it was not too far from our office, and I thought the house would come down. I could feel this invisible push, and we had some debris land in our yard. I was startled and remember our guards shrugging their shoulders, they had lived through a war, and this was minor. It shook me a bit, also because one of my academic mentors was caught in a truck bomb in Iraq at the same time, he was the sole survivor, which was a miracle, but he lost both of his legs. That showed you what could happen—and what you usually push to the very back of your mind.

What you usually did when there was an explosion, you called around, figured out if anybody you knew was hurt—and then, moved on, sometimes you even went straight back to sleep. You also text your family that you are OK (thank god for cell phones). I might have a thicker skin than others. One night there was a sustained attack on the Afghan parliament, and the fighting went on all night. My flatmate was super worried, while I was only worried about losing sleep due to the noise. It was a long night.

I realise this means that I've normalised insecurity and as long things didn't get personal, I was able to compartmentalise associated emotions somehow, or bury them somewhere deep.

One summer things got very personal.

First an Afghan journalist I knew was shot by US soldiers during a Taliban suicide attack and shortly after two Germans I knew well were killed in a botched kidnapping event while hiking. That was traumatic, they were all such lovely people and I always had planned to come along hiking with them one day. I remember I cried a lot. In times like this, war becomes real, and compartmentalisation becomes harder. You wonder when your number is up. I wonder how all of these emotions influence the knowledge production, they must.

Otherwise, it's mostly about health issues, stomach bugs, carbon-monoxide poisoning from mal-functioning heaters (people have died from this). I've pretty much had most digestive bugs you can think of. We all were walking pharmacies and got good at identifying symptoms and self-medication. It was a simple rule: feeling funny, have a coke, if that doesn't help, drink some vodka (internal disinfection), three days in, take medication.

Until a German health clinic opened, there were limited options of where you could go. A friend once had an appendix crisis, and I had to negotiate with the German military to get him into the army hospital.

Worst was when I contracted viral pneumonia while doing a field trip to Deh Rawud in Uruzgan. I was in this mud house with an outdoor toilet when a heavy fever came on. I knew this was not good. I had some broad-spectrum antibiotics with me, so I took them. I also took some paracetamol tablets. I was falling in and out of consciousness, lying on a *toshak* (futon) on the floor. My male colleagues kept coming in and asking if I was ready to do my interviews. Eventually they packed me into the car and we drove back to the capital Tirin Kot. I could barely stand up. It was one miserable trip on an unpaved road. In Tirin Kot, they got elders out of a room where they were doing interviews, just so I could lie down, there were no bedrooms. I was vomiting at the time. With the help of a Western intern, I finally got the fever under control and managed to take the next flight out of Uruzgan. Back in Kabul, my housemate who had worked with Doctors without Borders suggested pneumonia, so I went to the German clinic and got penicillin. I waited until I felt well enough to take the 20-hour journey home to Australia. That was no fun.

Did You Do Anything Special to Mitigate These Personal Risks?

A lot is about being prepared, and a lot is about learning on the go. It's a steep learning curve and you need to be able to adapt and learn from those local to a context. You need to understand culture, gender roles, where it's safe to go and perhaps where not and what not to do. You need to be able to read your surroundings, which comes with experience. I do that a lot by observation, try to pick up context-based clues and see what locals are doing. And above all listen to colleagues and friends and learn who you can trust.

I was never part of the UN/diplomacy security structure. I was always protected through my local support structure, the Afghan organisations and colleagues I worked with. I knew all our drivers, and I would never go somewhere or be picked up from somewhere without knowing the driver they would send for me. I also had their phone number. If I knew the driver, then the risk of kidnapping was minimised. I still believe that some of the higher-profile kidnappings in Afghanistan were to some degree insider jobs, where the security apparatus of an organisation got somehow compromised. The organisation I worked with used drivers that were vetted through personal channels, many were ex-mujahedeen—they might not speak English well, were a bit rough around the edges, but they would not sell you out. It was about honour for them.

Sometimes you need to be able to take calculated risks. One day our car broke down in the Salang tunnel (a northern pass road). There was no place to stay the night for a Western woman. I was with two Afghan colleagues, and we found a car to take us back to Kabul, essentially hitchhiking, while our driver sorted the car out. That might sound risky, and I suppose it was, but I felt the only risk was getting in an accident given the way those guys were driving. Insane.

Otherwise, risk mitigation was always about low profile. This means, you don't drive around in a very visible vehicle associated with foreigners (mostly big SUVs, later armoured cars). You go in a beat-up Toyota Corolla, the vehicle of choice. Of course, as the security deteriorated and the use of IEDs and suicide bomber proliferated, low profile alone was no longer good enough. In my most recent trip to Afghanistan, my Afghan colleagues put me into an armoured car, which while more visible ensured you survived the first explosion. It's about trade-offs and what is best at the time.

As a woman you always sit in the back of the car and you always wear a headscarf when you leave the office. Although I can never pass for an Afghan woman (too tall, wrong features), it was always about ensuring you are not recognised at first sight. This means that when you are in rural areas, you might even have to cover part of your face. Sometimes my colleagues might cover the window—which is culturally appropriate when travelling with women. You just don't do anything that would be a dead give-away that a foreign woman was in the car.

Yes, I could have worn a *burqa* (full body cover with only a grill for vision), and we always had an emergency burqa in the car when we travelled (just in case), but it's better not to push that envelope too much, as Afghans can get quite angry if you sell them for stupid. Hiding under a burqa is hard to pull off; for starters, it needs the attention to detail such as your pose, and the shoes you wear, what you do with your hands and so forth. Details matter. As I was tall, I would look like a man hiding in a burqa and only suicide bombers did that, so better not to go there.

Over time, Kabul became bunkerised, more roads blocked, fortified embassies and office. At times it felt quite surreal, like being caught in a video game where you had to avoid obstacles and risks. Our drivers were instructed to try to change route when encountering a military convoy, or just not drive through parts of the town if it could be avoided. The drivers themselves don't want to get killed, so they would also just get away from roads they did not feel comfortable on.

In the end it also comes down to luck. There is only so much you can prepare for. It comes down to not being in the wrong place at the wrong time. You can mitigate and plan, but not for everything (e.g., that earthquake in Mexico). In Afghanistan, I did start asking myself when my luck would run out. That is partially why I left at the end of 2014. I needed a break, I needed to get back to some form of normality. When I travel now to Afghanistan, I prefer winter (less fighting) and shorter stays. My last visit was ten days, which is not enough time for people to know you are there and plan a kidnapping.

Can You Say a Bit More About the Role of Your Local Colleagues?

They are essential. Frankly, anybody who tells you they can do research on their own in fragile contexts are lying. I know very few researchers who know the Afghan context and languages well enough that they can do it all on their own; and even then, I'm sure they get some help. Recently I came across a special journal edition of *Civil Wars* that introduced the notion of a 'research broker' and their importance in helping with research in insecure context (see Baaz and Utas 2019). I had not thought of this term, but it is accurate.

For me this includes local colleagues and translators (often the same), but also local drivers and guards (both perhaps least acknowledged). Sometimes they are co-researchers, and sometimes they just help you do research. I never liked the word 'fixer'—perhaps because it is used by journalists, but also because I don't feel it gives enough credit to what they actually do for you. An Afghan colleague early on said that he would prefer to be called a consultant—and I agree, they are in more than one way your risk consultant, context consultant and often protection. Without them I would have been lost.

You need to listen to your colleagues, even if you professionally outrank them somehow. This of course necessitates trust, and you need to develop this trust relationship. I am not saying follow blindly everybody who is local, as that can also be dangerous. I was lucky again, I developed a trust relationship with a couple of local colleagues, and they selected drivers, translators and guards for me. As one of my Afghan colleagues came from a prominent domestic family, those chosen by him to work with us were bound by honour—they could not let anything happen to me, it would mean dishonour for them.

One trip we were coming back from Bamiyan via Wardak at a time the insurgency had started to infiltrate the province, and my colleague at one point asked me: "Do you mind lying in the back and we'll put some blankets on top of you?" Perhaps I minded, but I took the clue. They judged that stretch of the road to be insecure, and what if they were stopped by insurgents, a foreign woman in the car could be a liability, perhaps even get them killed. I did what I was asked until they told me to come out.

In 2011 during a visit to Uruzgan, riots broke out in neighbouring Kandahar about a pastor in Florida (US) burning a Koran. My colleagues feared the riots might spill-over and were nervous in case our office would be looted and a foreigner would be found. I could see they were torn, they wanted to get rid of me somehow, but they also wanted me to be safe. One colleague ended up taking me to his house to hide me in the women's compound. Pretty much the safest place, as the Taliban respected the privacy of the women's quarter. I sat with the women, chit-chatting about mundane things, marriage, kids, getting perms and so on. Later I went into the military base for a meeting with Australian aid workers. They had totally forgotten about me and were about to boot me out, when the sole female Dutch development worker on the team intervened and said: "You can't just send her back out there, she'd be the only international left; we don't know what might happen". Thanks to her I spent the night in the compound in a container and flew out the next morning. My colleagues were relieved.

Can You Say a Bit More About Becoming a Risk for Your Colleagues?

When security deteriorated, it eventually meant I had to stop walking, driving on my own, being driven by others. Later it meant limited travel outside Kabul—and if we travelled, then by plane. Roads were too dangerous, at least for me—so often I flew, and my Afghan colleagues drove. As my research radius increasingly became limited, my Afghan colleagues had to take on the risk of field research. I am grateful to date that none of them got killed for doing so.

There was a big debate at the time that a lot of foreigners took jobs from Afghans when security was good and later Afghans had to pick up the pieces when it got dangerous. There were also discussions around double standards in security protocols for Afghans and internationals. At least as I worked with a local organisation, they made those decisions, but yes, my presence could expose my colleagues and put them at risk.

After an Afghan journalist friend got killed by US soldiers for being mistaken for an insurgent (Schmeidl 2011a), I urged my Afghan colleagues to be careful. I told them when they encountered the US military, to just ensure their hands were visible and away from their body. Ideally, just lie on the ground spread-eagle. I worried a lot.

As the war progressed, more foreigners became part of the conflict and perceived by many as the 'enemy', so being seen with a foreigner could get an Afghan killed. It was common knowledge at the time that when foreigners and Afghans went somewhere and were both kidnapped, the Afghan would be at a disadvantage. There was a very prominent case at the time with an Italian journalist who was kidnapped with his translator. The journalist got released after ransom was paid, but the Afghan translator was beheaded (AP 2007). Internationals are assets in these contexts, your governments may pay money for you or do a prisoner swap; and so there is higher likelihood for you to make it out alive. Although I would not bank on your government bailing you out, some kidnap victims were in limbo for years.

Still, your colleagues might not even be as lucky.

That's why you have to listen to your local colleagues and don't actually push them to do something that can get them killed. This is why I let my Afghan colleagues make the judgements about my mobility, where I could and could not go. I often gauged the security situation by where I was allowed to go and whether I was invited into shops or peoples' houses. The less secure, I would get a lot: "I'd love to invite you to my house, but I'd rather speak to you in the office"—or "When you come to my house (or office), please don't leave the car until it has entered the compound" (which is then out of people's view). You can't question your colleagues unnecessarily, even if sometimes it might piss you off when you are told you can't do something.

I don't have a death wish, and I don't want to get my colleagues killed for being seen with a foreigner that stands out as much as me. Sometimes you just have to suck it up and err on the side of security and understand that you've become a liability for your colleagues.

How Did You Adjust Your Research Because of Insecurity?

We had to continuously adjust how we did research, you had to be flexible and adaptive to your environment. For example, I only took notes and never recorded interviews. Written documents are dangerous enough but a voice on a tape could identify a research participant far more easily. I never taped a single interview.

Sometimes my colleagues even stopped taking notes, at least during interviews. Nobody would talk to you in insecure environments if you were seen taking notes. Thus our analysis relied on what researchers might memorise from interviews and their participant observation, with note-taking happening at the end of the day. This of course has an impact on knowledge production, as memory is fallible, even in an oral culture. In the end, we hired people from the areas we researched, simply because they fitted in. Being 'foreign' at times of conflict can mean being not from the same village. Trust breaks down during times of war.

My Afghan colleagues ended up burning interview notes and smashing thumb drives whenever a research project was finished. I kept electronic transcripts, often in obscure places on my laptop or in the cloud.

My colleagues said: "If you get caught by the Taliban with a flash disk, they will assume you are spying". They also cleared their phones before travelling into Taliban territory. Anything that could be traced back to your international contacts became a kiss of death. While there might have been theoretical and practical differences to what military vs. civilian actors were doing, it was all lumped together and you were guilty by association, even if your work and research was strictly with civilian actors only. Technicalities would not save your life if the Taliban thought you were collaborating with the enemy. This is one reason why I despise using the word 'informant' for research participants—just too close to spying.

Sometimes we invited people to come to us for interviews, rather than us going into insecure areas. But of course this could also be risky for community members, especially if they were seen speaking to internationals and or going into areas frequently by internationals, which the capital Kabul pretty much was. This could be construed as spying—which meant you might be beheaded or have your throat slashed. These things happened. At the time you had to justify travel if stopped at a Taliban check-post, so a lot of research participants made up visiting a sick relative in hospital.

We were very transparent about these adjustments to our research methodology and the bias this might introduce. Our methods sections were quite long, and somebody once told us that we were putting our research into question, when I felt it was the ethical thing to do to be honest about how data was collected.

Of course, you would never name anybody; you always had to de-identify your sources. You never shared details that could identify.

A donor once questioned our research and demanded to see the entire interview transcripts. They argued that, as they paid for the research, it was theirs. I argued confidentiality. They persisted. It got nasty and I had to consult a lawyer. After I sent an email noting that the interview material was the intellectual property of the interview partner who had not given consent for the material to be shared with third parties, the donor finally backed off. But we also lost that contract, it was terminated. It was nasty.

What Were the Risks to Knowledge Production in Such a Militarised and Polarised Context?

There are many. It boiled down to who you did the research for (who funded it), who ended up reading it, and increasingly what kind of information (especially details) you included in your research. Later it was also about what kind of research you did.

In Afghanistan there was a mad blurring of lines between civilians and military because of the attempt to build peace while continuing to fight a war. The Afghan context was militarised and politicised from day one, and rather than getting better, the security situation deteriorated over time. This schizophrenic dual mission meant that many international missions were split, having both civilian personnel (providing development and humanitarian assistance and) and soldiers living in the same spaces. The situation became super distorted with the creation of Provincial Reconstructions Teams (PRTs), a US invention of combined teams of military, political officers and development workers (see Maley and Schmeidl 2015). So even if you were a civilian worker, you were associated with a party to a conflict. What Afghans saw was military, increasingly fortified embassies, lots of guns.

Enter Human Terrain Teams (HTT), embedded anthropologists helping soldiers read the "terrain" and ostensibly do less harm, another crazy idea by the US military. The American Anthropological Association was swift to condemn this as an unethical use of anthropological research (AAA 2007). Things got worse when the US started its 'Hearts and Minds' campaign in 2010, among other based on the notion of the '10-dollar Taliban' driven to fight by poverty, with economic incentives aimed at buying support for the government (Fishstein and Wilder 2011). This was aid on steroids, aid as bribes, with money thrown at 'quick impact projects'. Afghanistan was such a testing ground for dangerous concepts with lasting impact. This made the work of civilian actors more dangerous. Communities started asking about the reward for insecurity and if they should invite the Taliban in so they could get some projects.

In that environment we wrote our Do No Harm assessments aimed at development actors so they would know how to manoeuvre a political and social competitive environment and ensure aid did not exacerbate conflict. If you think about it, that same information could be used for the opposite purpose and all of sudden the military started to get interested in our reports written for civilian actors. Most of our work was not even public, internal white papers to inform international development and peacebuilding policy and practice. What we made public were synopses, very general and had rich layers taken away. It was safer that way until, of course, the military got a hold of them.

We found out the hard way that some of our reports were shared with the military; sometimes even when the front-line development workers never got them. We found out that we had no control over what happened to our reports. This freaked us out.

One day a Norwegian researcher interviewed us for her research and asked: "How we felt about being funded by donors who are party to the conflict"? She had told us she was funded by the Norwegian government, so I simply responded: "Well, how does it feel?" Switzerland aside, there was really no donor country that did not also have military in the country. I don't know where this arrogance comes from, but I found it irritating.

It is hard to mitigate a situation like this—especially with on-going contracts, so we started being more careful what went into the reports and ended up taking some sections out entirely where we felt that information might just be too sensitive at the time. You had to keep asking yourself, what might be used to harm communities? Even when I was not the primary drafter, I reviewed our reports before they went out and ensured things were deleted that could do harm—such as a general statement that all nomads smuggle weapons for the Taliban. I had to argue sometimes with other international researchers who felt they were reporting the truth, but in a context such as Afghanistan, what really is the truth, and what is what people want you to know? And even if it was the truth, is it worth it to taint an entire community because some smuggle weapons? It is just too dangerous.

In the end, you have to remember who you are doing the research for. Yes, you get funded by donors or foundations—but our main purpose was to raise awareness about the situation in Afghanistan. Our primary commitment was to communities. You have to mitigate any risk to them. It is their stories you are telling, after all.

It was an intense period. We grappled with all these questions. Were we going to continue doing context-assessments? If yes, what would we include and what did we think was too dangerous to include? Who could we do research for? I eventually walked away from doing these assessments, with the exception of the Swiss government, who was not militarily involved and embraced Do No Harm for what it was.

This is also why we began to focus more on peacebuilding and development projects. We had always tried to reciprocate with communities giving us their time by participating in research, as research is an extractive exercise. But often it takes too long for your research to lead to projects, so we started giving directly back to communities where we could. Our research then became about evidence-based programming or advocating for change.

We also increased our social justice research to hold international actors accountable, such as research collaborations on "kill and capture" missions by the military (Gaston et al. 2010, 2011). This was about bearing witness, getting the story out about what was happening, and how human rights violations were committed also by international actors.

I once got so angry about human rights abuses by the US military; I wrote a satirical blog called "The Dummies' Guide to the Geneva Convention" (Schmeidl 2011b). I suppose this did not endear me to them, but then why should it? These days I always get pulled into secondary questioning when I go to the US. One time one of the border protection officers asked if I ever wrote anything that could have pissed anybody off. I told him to Google me.

While a lot of our context assessments were not public, our social justice research was and was the most scrutinised. We have been told off more than once by a UN agency that we were exaggerating the situation on the ground. But mostly it was just about pointing out protection gaps (see e.g., Schmeidl et al. 2010; Schmeidl and Tyler 2015). Nobody wants to look like they are doing a bad job. And we certainly did not do research to protect the reputation of international organisations. You can't cave in to criticism that wants you to align with dominant political narratives, you have to stand by your research. It was about allowing communities to tell their stories, as subjective as these might be. Of course, we triangulated, but we did not allow powerful agencies to tell us that we were wrong—or that communities were wrong. Their experiences matter.

If anything really traumatised me in Afghanistan, it was the push-back from some donors and international organisations when our research did not match their own understanding of a situation, to the point of insult. It showed me how political research can be and that even if you try your best to do it ethically, if your findings go contrary to dominant narratives, your research gets questioned. If you don't budge, it might get personal. I was once called the 'Dutch Bitch', though not to my face. That still hurts.

What Did You Do to Take Care of Yourself in Such a Stressful Context?

There were various ways. Key was to have your own place, shared or by yourself, that you make into a personal space, and exercise. In my first bungalow, I had a walking machine and importantly a punch bag. I miss that punch bag. I swam in the UN guest house pool as often as I could—I learned freestyle there. Later I had an exercise bike. Sometimes we would go out on weekends for picnics, always with Afghan colleagues, and sometimes went on hikes. Towards the end, I did a lot of yoga—and helped set up a yoga network. Mostly to build community, a community outside the heavy drinking, crazy party-as-if-you-die-tomorrow culture that existed and made me uncomfortable. The movie 'Whiskey, Tango, Foxtrot' was spot on. I felt if you had to drink to that extent in order to escape reality and cope, why come to Afghanistan? At least I had fallen in love with the country and people.

I preferred the quieter get-togethers, having dinner and watching a movie or playing cards with friends, ideally with Afghan friends. I wanted some sense of normalcy, so I liked visiting Afghan families, going on picnics with them, playing with their kids. I was living in Afghanistan after all; foreigners came at an increasingly rapid pace. Friendships with Afghans provided continuity and a sense of normalcy.

I did enjoy a drink sometimes, I'm not a saint. I did go to restaurants, but I didn't go to bars. There were very few bars anyhow, that there were any is somewhat absurd in a Muslim country where drinking is illegal. I did go to embassy receptions, but often did not stay that long. At one embassy party, when I was about to leave, somebody said to me, "Why are you leaving, the close protection team of the ambassador is about to strip". I responded: "That's exactly why I'm leaving".

Afghanistan is a country with extremely high social control. We all had drivers, guards and cleaners. They all know what you are doing and who you were with. As a western woman you were already thought of as promiscuous, no need to confirm their prejudice and sleep around. I knew that the moment my personal reputation goes so does my professional reputation.

Based on Your Experience, What Would You Advise Future Researchers?

I think that preparation beforehand cannot be underestimated. I learned this the hard way; I went to Mexico a bit naive. Yes, I learned the language, but I did not research the context enough, certainly not the gender relations; a must for all researchers.

After that I prepared a lot before going overseas. In addition to understanding the culture, you must understand the risks and prepare mitigation strategies. It is not good to leave things to luck. Have a good plan, and ideally have a Plan B, maybe even C. But also know who you could call on when things go pear shaped and be able to adapt locally and make new plans. Build research mentorships before you go.

There are two pieces of very useful advice I got before I went to Afghanistan. One was that I would be considered the 'third sex',[1] a sociocultural gender construct that gave me different access and privilege than an Afghan woman, but less than a Western or Afghan man (see Partis-Jennings 2019). For example, I could walk around without a *mahram* (male guardian, usually a family member) and engage with Afghan men.

---

[1] Thank you Barnett Rubin. This was one of the best pieces of advice I ever got.

The other was to tell people that I was married and had two children.[2] As I'm a terrible liar, the latter was harder for me. While I wore a wedding band, I never could lie about it—too much to remember when you create 'alternative facts'. I went for being engaged.

And, of course, if you can, find a local partner organisation. It is just more ethical when you do this. Good research is about relationships and reciprocity. Try to give something back, either by building capacity or ensuring the research benefits your local colleagues and the communities they work with. Research for the sake of knowledge is important, but it should not be too extractive. Best to build these relationships before you go and give yourself time to continue to build them while you are there.

Develop your personal research ethos. We should not just be guided by formal ethics processes; we need to develop our own standards. My research did not have to go through an official ethics process, but we still deliberated over how to do the research ethically. I was strongly guided by the 'Do No Harm' approach that Mary Anderson (1999) developed. It's underused for research. And it is best to sit down and talk through some of these possible dilemmas one might encounter when doing field research.

It takes time to figure out any context, and who you are as a researcher. I tend to advise against going to too dangerous contexts in the beginning. Go somewhere relatively safe and make the time to get to know the place and the people. I know we are all pressed for time and money, but I would not recommend flying in and out for research when you are just starting out. I would recommend at least a month in a country or setting before you start research, ideally longer. I was able to manoeuvre Afghanistan because I got to know it well. But if you dropped me now into Iraq or Syria, I wouldn't know what to do or how to act. I would need to learn about the context and build up my local networks.

Learn the language. I spoke Spanish relatively well when I went to Mexico, it gave me great access and I could do all interviews on my own. I never learned to speak Dari (or Pashto) well enough in Afghanistan. It is a major regret. It limits who you can speak to, and you may miss specific verbal clues. I got very good at developing contextual

---

[2] Thank you Ahmed Rashid.

understanding, and that is always good to have. But it does not trump being fluent in the language you are researching in.

If you do use translators, ensure you spend time with them. They need to understand the questions and the research you are doing. So much can get lost in translation. Again, it helps to have at least some notion of the language. I knew most of the time when the translator skipped over material or struggled to translate something.

Finally, observation is key, don't forget participant observation as an important part of research, it helps you learn faster about your context and gauge your research participants beyond the verbal clues they give. I think active observation is sometimes undervalued and underused by researchers.

References

AAA. (2007, October 31). *Executive Board Statement on the Human Terrain System Project.* American Anthropological Association. https://www.americananthro.org/ConnectWithAAA/Content.aspx?ItemNumber=1952

Anderson, M. (1999). *Do No Harm: How Aid Can Support Peace – Or War.* Boulder/London: Lynne Rienner Publishers.

AP. (2007, April 8). Journalist's Afghan Translator Beheaded. *Associated Press.* https://www.cbsnews.com/news/journalists-afghan-translator-beheaded/

Baaz, M. E., & Utas, M. (2019). Exploring the Backstage: Methodological and Ethical Issues Surrounding the Role of Research Brokers in Insecure Zones. *Civil Wars, 21*(2), 157–178.

Barash, D. P., & Webel, C. P. (2017). *Peace and Conflict Studies* (4th ed.). Thousand Oaks: Sage Publications Inc.

Fishstein, P., & Wilder, A. (2011). *Winning Hearts and Minds? Examining the Relationship Between Aid and Security in Afghanistan.* Boston: Feinstein International Centre, Tufts University. https://fic.tufts.edu/wp-content/uploads/WinningHearts-Final.pdf

Gaston, E., Horowitz, J., & Schmeidl, S. (2010). *Strangers at the Door: Night Raids by International Forces Lose Hearts and Minds of Afghans.* Kabul: Open Society Foundation/The Liaison Office. https://www.opensocietyfoundations.org/publications/strangers-door-night-raids-international-forces-lose-hearts-and-minds-afghans

Gaston, E., Reid, R., & Schmeidl, S. (2011). *The Cost of Kill/Capture: Impact of the Night Raid Surge on Afghan Civilians*. Kabul: Open Society Foundation/ The Liaison Office. http://www.opensocietyfoundations.org/sites/default/ files/Night-Raids-Report-FINAL-092011.pdf

Maley, W., & Schmeidl, S. (Eds.). (2015). *Reconstructing Afghanistan: Civil-Military Experiences in Comparative Perspective*. New York: Routledge.

Mwaûra, C., & Schmeidl, S. (Eds.). (2002). *Early Warning and Conflict Management in the Horn of Africa*. Lawrenceville/Asmara: Red Sea Press.

Partis-Jennings, H. (2019). The 'Third Gender' in Afghanistan: A Feminist Account of Hybridity as a Gendered Experience. *Peacebuilding, 7*(2), 178–193.

Schmeidl, S. (1997). Exploring the Causes of Forced Migration: A Pooled Time-Series Analysis, 1971–1990. *Social Science Quarterly, 78*(2), 284–308.

Schmeidl, S. (2008). Case Study Afghanistan in Joras, U. & Schuster, A. (Eds.). Private Security Companies and Local Populations: An Exploratory Study of Afghanistan and Angola, Bern: swisspeace, 9–37; https://www.swisspeace.ch/ assets/publications/downloads/Working-Papers/6e03da2e1f/Private-Security-Companies-and-Local-Populations-An-Exploratory-Study-of-Afghanistan-and-Angola-Working-Paperswisspeace.pdf.

Schmeidl, S. (2011a, September 9). *The Death of an Uruzgan Journalist: Omaid Never Stood a Chance*. Kabul: Afghanistan Analysts Network. http://afghanistan-analysts.net/index.asp?id=2062

Schmeidl, S. (2011b, December 31). *A Year-Ender: The Dummies' Guide to the Geneva Conventions*. Kabul: Afghanistan Analysts Network. http://aan-afghanistan.com/index.asp?id=2396

Schmeidl, S., & Tyler, D. (2015). *Listen to Women and Girls Displaced to Urban Afghanistan*. Oslo: Norwegian Refugee Council. http://www.nrc. no/?did=9194479#.VWZqJtLLc1l

Schmeidl, S., Mundt, A., & Miszak, N. (2010). *Beyond the Blanket: Towards More Effective Protection for Internally Displaced Persons in Southern Afghanistan*. Washington, DC: The Brookings Institution. http://www. brookings.edu/reports/05_idp_protection_afghanistan.aspx

Schulman, D. (2009, July 7). The Cowboys of Kabul. *Mother Jones*. https:// www.motherjones.com/politics/2009/07/cowboys-of-kabul/

10

'If You Want to Know About Evil, Ask the Devil': Research in Post-conflict Countries

Kim Spurway

Can You Give Us Some Background to Your Research?

I was a professional researcher for 13 years before I started my PhD in Australia. So, much of what I am going to discuss relates to the period before I joined a university—when I worked for large international non-governmental organisations (INGOs) doing research in post-conflict countries. During that period, I worked outside of Australia in the humanitarian mine action sector as well as the primary health care and HIV/AIDS prevention sectors. I started out as a volunteer, working with the Lao national HIV/AIDS prevention programme, then worked with CARE Laos and a local Non-Government Organisation (NGO) called CHAMPA.

K. Spurway (✉)
Institute for Culture and Society, Western Sydney University, Sydney, NSW, Australia
e-mail: k.spurway@westernsydney.edu.au

CHAMPA was the first place I went out into the 'field', travelling out to villages with Lao medical teams to train District Health staff in primary health care (PHC). This was based on the Chinese idea of the 'barefoot doctor', where a village health volunteer was trained to meet the basic health needs of remote communities. After this, I almost exclusively worked in the management of surveys on the impact of landmines and unexploded ordnance (UXO, also called explosive remnants of war). I worked on everything from project setup and closure, logistics, operations, data management, quality control, data entry, questionnaire design, planning, security protocols, data analysis and writing up the final report. Despite being managed from inside the country, the field teams had limited control over some aspects of the survey since this had been decided at meetings by the international community reps. We often engaged in spirited discussions with our HQs and international 'consultants' when we wanted to make local adaptations.

These surveys came out of the 'Ottawa process', the 1999 Ottawa Mine Ban Treaty.[1] After the treaty, donor countries, like the United Kingdom, the United States, Canada, Australia and the European Union, wanted to compare affected countries. They wanted to know which country to give money to, who to prioritise. The survey was supposed to give them this kind of information. It was also supposed to be for national governments and local organisations, so that they could plan. I worked in several countries, each with their own challenges and risks, including Northern Iraq, Lebanon, Chad, the Democratic Republic of the Congo (DRC) Laos and Vietnam.

Were There Common Experiences Across Settings?

These surveys were quite homogenous in many ways. All the surveys were all run by externally funded INGOs with a mostly expat management team, usually composed of two to three people. The process started with

---

[1] See: http://www.icbl.org/en-gb/home.aspx

the managers (like me) being recruited by the INGO running that survey. We'd be briefed at the INGO HQ in Manchester, Washington, Brussels or Lyon, put on a plane and sent off to start work on the survey. We'd arrive in-country and, if the INGO had a country office, the local team would introduce us to our designated government counterparts. If we did not have an in-country presence, such as in Chad, then we started from scratch, usually with the help of the United Nations.

Setting up the project involved weeks, sometimes months of discussions and meetings, negotiating the finer details of how the project would work with government counterparts. We often worked with the Ministry of Defence (MOD) but it also could be other government agencies such as the Ministry of Labour and Social Welfare in Laos.

All this taught me that good research involves a lot of hard work to set up, to make everything work in practice. This was not always clear to our field teams. In Lebanon, we lost a lot of local researchers because they told us, "research is not what we thought it was". There was too much admin, quality controls and other things they were not interested in. We had two levels of quality control, for example, one managed in the field and the other when the questionnaires arrived back at HQ. Our university-trained fieldworkers just wanted to get to the nitty gritty of doing interviews and analysis without all that administrative stuff and nonsense.

Once we knew about affected provinces, field teams were sent out to meet with local leaders to introduce and discuss the survey (with all the necessary paperwork from the central government, of course!). Then, we would visit villages in affected areas to ask about contamination and to set up community interviews.

Communities were all very different, some open and friendly, some not interested, many had bigger problems than landmines or UXO. This was one of the main problems with the survey, it came from the international community and was set up to meet the needs of donors and national governments. It did not always meet the needs of the communities themselves.

What Did You Learn from This Work?

One thing was that things that were important for the international community were not necessarily important for local people. Many communities had lived with UXO and landmines for years and had gotten used to their presence. Not using certain agricultural fields or walking kilometres out of the way to get to markets was common in many countries. In Chad, although communities were willing to talk to us, many villages were in drought and had water stress, they needed wells and clean water, not surveys. On several instances, our field teams gave their water to villages because they had no potable water to drink. This was part of the survey logistics in countries like Chad, where we carried potable water, drums of diesel and food along with the teams since we often worked in remote villages sometimes a long way away from petrol stations and functioning markets.

You also have to meet and work with people and organisations you would never think you could have worked with. In Lebanon, we met with the civilian wing of Hezbollah, the local NGOs who worked in disability and mine action mostly. Contrary to what some of the expats in Beirut and the media were saying, we were always treated with respect, unlike some of the other political parties I could mention. They would always put on a small feast for these meetings, lots of Lebanese coffee, pastries of all kinds, including croissants and long discussions. It was the same with the Lebanese Communist Party, they were so happy to meet with us and always greeted us with big hugs and kisses on each cheek. A lot of the more traditional Muslim men, of course, do not even shake hands with women, you both touch your hand to your heart when you meet. Food and coffee were part of any meeting, and by the end of a day meeting with people, I could literally smell the coffee coming out of my pores.

I learnt it is important to listen, to take your time and let people talk about what their concerns are, not to impose yourself on them too much. Trying to control the flow of the conversation and put in your two cents worth is rude, disrespectful and stops you learning things you never expected. Lebanese people love to talk about politics, for example, and I had lots of conversations about the war and the state of the nation as well as talking about the survey. I learnt so much about Lebanon this way, the politics, the sectarian violence, the ways people coped, their incredible ability to get on with their lives while bombs were falling, and people were shooting at each other. This was something I could not get from the books and newspapers I read before going to a country.

The time we went to meet with members of Hezbollah's military wing, however, was an eye opener. We put on scarves and dressed in long flowing clothes to be respectful. In this instance, there was another expat woman who was the deputy manager of the project, who had worked in Lebanon before. It was one of the only times there was another woman in the management team. We always carried scarves with us and dressed conservatively. Carefully covered up. Once we arrived at this meeting, we were told immediately that this was not necessary as Western women and we could remove our scarves. The meeting showed us that this wing of Hezbollah was really only concerned about security, about Israel and about military issues. Once you factored that into your work, they were, strangely enough, the easiest to work with.

Respecting the concerns of local players was always important. One day we travelled close to the Israeli border with a couple of Lebanese Army colleagues, we had picked up a local guide who was walking with us and talking about the war. We started approaching a wooded area, but the guide said that this was a Hezbollah military position and we should stop. One of the army guys loudly proclaimed that Hezbollah did not control Lebanon and proceeded to storm up the hill. He was met by about ten Hezbollah members armed with AK-47 s, pointed directly at him. We then had to have a long conversation where we apologised, assured them we were leaving, that we were naïve Westerners. Fortunately, they let us go and the army guy had the good sense to shut up while we were talking, although he harrumphed a few times. This is why it is so important to be aware of your surroundings, to respect other people and groups (even if you don't agree with their politics!) and have the good sense to back down when you need to.

I Imagine Knowledge of Language Was Very Important in All This? Did You Use Translators?

I tried to learn several languages, French, Arabic, Lao, Chinese, and could speak two colloquially. I could understand many of the informal conversations but needed translation when you needed to have formal discussions with village leaders or government officials. When we were in communities, we did several things and most of them involved using translators to some degree. All of the interviews were done by local researchers trained in survey methods and the use of the survey questionnaire. In some countries such as Chad, we used a lingua franca such as Arabic or French for the questionnaire and meetings since there were so many local languages. In the DRC, we switched between Swahili and French. All of our fieldworkers had to be literate in the lingua franca to be able to read the questionnaire and sometimes they also spoke English.

Although essential, a lingua franca led to issues in fieldwork where the only literate person in a village, usually the local teacher or health worker, would translate from our French questionnaire, let's say, into a local language and back into French for the survey teams to transcribe onto the questionnaire. This certainly created problems with consistency but when you are in situ, it is not possible to stop the interview to interrogate the translator. I cannot think of any way around this given the circumstances we faced in these countries.

The survey package also included a database with GIS (geographic information system) functionality that had to be translated into the local language. But we were not supposed to change it significantly. In Chad, the project coordinator changed the whole thing to fit with local conditions. I found out later that the IT guys in Washington were really pissed off about this and they reconfigured the database back to standard.

I knew there were potential translation issues from working in countries where I had a reasonable level of language such as Laos and French speaking countries. Once I was interviewing a high-ranking Lao army officer about his experiences in the war and post-conflict clearance activities in Xieng Khouang province. This interview aimed to identify areas affected by war for survey, so having accurate information was important.

My translator decided I would be offended by some of what he was saying and decided to protect me from what he was saying about 'falang' (foreigners).

My translator said that the officer was saying something like, "during the war there was a lot of bombing in the province and that the war was terrible for Lao people living in the area". But I could see he was visibly angry, his actions did not match what she said he was saying, he was clearly upset to the point of crying and started hitting his desk with his fist. I understood enough Lao to know that what he actually said was something like, "I understand the Thai, they have been our enemies for a long time and we have always had wars with them, so I understand why they were involved in the 'American War'" (the Vietnam War as it is called in Indochina). "But the Americans", he said, "what have we ever done to them? I don't even know who they are. Why did they come here to bomb us and kill us?"

We tried to reduce some of the issues with translation by doing reverse translations on all questionnaires to check for errors. This means translating into Arabic, for example, then taking that translation and putting it back into English to see if there were problems. We often found issues with translation and had to have long discussions about how to translate English words into other languages. The main thing was that the field teams understood the concepts, so we also spent a lot of time discussing the meaning of the words in the trainings. This was so they were aware of the meaning behind the questions and could present the meaning, not necessarily the exact question.

This Sounds Complicated, What Other Issues Affected Your Work?

One issue was the amount of time allocated in our budget and timelines to implementing the survey. Our US-based consultants believed we could churn through two communities in a day and that was how it was planned. We weren't working in downtown Washington, we were in countries recovering from war. In countries such as Chad (no paved roads, poor infrastructure, long distances) or even Lebanon in winter (snow, road closures, blizzards), it was not possible to do the survey as planned. We often were behind in our timeline and went over budget because of this disconnect.

It wasn't only the infrastructure, terrain and weather conditions that made this difficult, it also took time to set up relationships. Some communities took longer for various reasons. People had to come to the interviews after working in the fields (e.g. Chad, Laos and DRC) or come after work (Lebanon), for example. This meant we were often waiting for community members to show, which could take hours. And this did not account for the complexities and discussions required that necessitated several visits to communities to negotiate access. It was often impossible to do two surveys in one day and this always put us under incredible pressure.

This survey was a long, complex process with a very complicated questionnaire with a lot of other activities. The standardised questionnaire was designed at international meetings of explosive ordnance disposal (EOD) experts, deminers and 'yoghurt knitters' like me (a term used for us by ex-military guys). These took place in cities like Oslo and Washington, then had to be translated from English and applied to all countries, which was sometimes a nightmare to implement with all the in-country variabilities.

So, we would arrange a meeting with community members to conduct a group interview. The first part of this was a participatory mapping exercise where we asked the group to draw their community with key landmarks (temples, mosques, churches, bridges, markets). Then we used this to talk to the community through our questionnaire which covered demographics, injuries/deaths from UXO or landmines. We then asked them about the impact on the social and economic life of the community: what farmland, ricefields or grazing land they couldn't use, for example. Once the questionnaire was completed, the field teams would take a global positioning system (GPS) reading of the designated village centre. They would then go to the edge of the contaminated area (sometimes more than one) and take another GPS reading and photos, being careful to keep their distance, of course. We needed the GPS readings to locate contaminated areas and photos so that our survey users knew what the terrain looked like for clearance. You could not rush this, it was important to maintain trust with communities, not to treat them as if we were just there to take information and walk away even though the original survey plans did not allow for the niceties of buidling relationships and trust.

How Did You Find the Right Teams to Do the Work?

Finding the right people to work with was hard. We had about 50–70 people working in the organisation's head office usually based in the country capital to be deployed as either as field teams or work as data entry staff. The use of a lingua franca and the complexity of the questionnaire and the survey methodology meant we had to recruit educated people who could read, write and had been exposed to research to some degree. But they also had to be able to travel away from their families, go out into the field, work in often harsh conditions for long hours. Countries like Chad and the DRC had a very small pool of people. Lebanon had a lot more because the country had a better education system. And it was a hard mix to find in many countries: educated but able to endure long, hard working conditions away from family. Given women's gendered roles in the family, finding a good mix of women and men was always a problem.

Once we recruited people, we would train them in surveys and participatory research methods. They were then sent out into the field as part of a team with team leaders. The teams would interview a group of community members, supposedly representative of the community but usually selected by the village chief. Although necessary as we were outsiders, using the village leaders always had a downside. They were usually men, so we sometimes just did not get the experiences of women. Our village interviews were usually dominated by one or other political or ethnic group, so we also missed out on minorities and marginalised voices in communities. Although we were supposed to have separate meetings with these groups if possible, the tight time and budget limitations prohibited this in most cases.

In smaller, remote villages it was easier as the whole community would know about our visit. Some villages had never encountered white people, and we arrived in big white cars with lots of equipment, and gadgets. In some countries like Chad and the DRC where people had so little, we were the best show in town! In some countries such as Chad, we supplied villages with 'treats' such as bottles of coke to thank them for their time as there was no payment given to communities.

The field teams had a tough job, they had to collect high quality information to 'international standards' and often travelled into remote regions with little infrastructure, poor roads and sometimes limited water supplies. In addition, these were all countries undergoing a post-conflict transition, some more advanced in this than others with some slipping regularly back into conflict. Many of these places had ongoing security issues. So, part of the survey protocols included security, protection against armed groups, sometimes against rogue army elements. We had to manage security risk, we'd pull teams in if we thought their lives were potentially at risk.

In the field, there were field supervisors who managed field teams of ten or so people and went out to communities met with the head of the village to introduce and plan the survey with the community. The supervisors would set up a time for a community meeting where the data collectors would ask questions from the questionnaire. The data collectors did the community surveys, using the questionnaires and then geo-referencing the village. Teams included data editors who checked in the field for inconsistencies in information and that data collectors were completing the questionnaires correctly. In addition to the field teams, we also had support teams working in the country capital, providing logistical support, making sure that teams had all the materials they needed and that the vehicles and equipment (GPS, cameras) were maintained and operational. It was a lot of hard work for everyone, and intense! So, finding the right people to do this kind of work was always very challenging.

How Did You Recruit People for the Community Interviews?

In theory, community members were invited to the meeting by the community leadership and we tried to make it as representative as possible, a mix of women, men, ethnicities and religions, if necessary. In Lebanon, this would mean in a mixed community our projects could include any combination of Shiite, Sunni, Maronite, Eastern Orthodox, Armenian Orthodox and so forth. It also meant ensuring we had a good mix of different political parties such as the Future Movement, Free Patriotic Movement, Hezbollah, Amal, Lebanese Forces, Lebanese Communist Party or Progressive Socialist Party to name a few. In many cases this went surprisingly well considering the history of war in some of these countries, and the community meetings were surprisingly harmonious and effective. In Laos, which is very ethnically diverse, this would mean trying to make sure that ethnic minorities were included such as Hmong-Mien, Tai Dam or Khammu as much as possible.

The real problem did not always lie with communities. The problem we had was with local politics and local politicians. In Lebanon, for example, a lot of political parties offered benefits to membership, one of which was the party would find jobs for them. We had a couple of parties that really pressured us all the time to recruit their members and not others. We had so many meetings to discuss this, but we stubbornly wanted to overcome sectarianism with mixed teams who could travel into any community. A local academic at Beirut university actually wrote a paper about our survey, she thought it was wonderful. After recruitment had ended, one of our military counterparts told us we had successfully recruited our teams on a par with Lebanon's sectarian mix. The percentage of staff affiliations matched almost perfectly the number of people affiliated with each sect and political party.

Despite attempts to get a mix of participants, there were definitely dominant groups in these interviews (men, political parties, ethnicities). They tended to turn up to interviews and some groups were excluded. Some of my photos show that the majority of community members were men and/or from the main ethnic or religious group. In some countries, men thought that landmines and UXO were "men's business", that women did not know enough about them. However, we really wanted women's perspectives, they did different things to men, collected water and wood, for example, that took them to different locations and exposed them to different risks.

In Laos, we were speaking with a group of men about how many children were killed and injured by UXO. They confidently said "nah, no kids killed here", then a woman appeared and started shouting in Lao to let us know that her child had been killed playing with a bombie (cluster bomb unit from the American bombing). She also knew of other children who had also been injured or killed in the village. We quickly took down the information, but this is the kind of detail that these surveys most likely missed.

Women in some countries were very difficult to interview or include in group meetings. In some parts of Chad, it was not possible to have male researchers interview women for cultural reasons, and special meetings had to take place. In one village, I was the only woman in the team. We conducted the interview with the women, with the survey team on the other side of a wall while my male colleagues shouted questions across to the women. The men were not allowed to enter the women's compound on the other side of the wall, but I was able to go in and introduce myself in French while my colleagues shouted my words back in Arabic over the compound wall.

Nomads were also one of the groups hardest to interview. In Chad, we spoke with anthropologists and tracked seasonal nomadic movements from North to South to try to meet with them when they stopped to pasture their herds. In Lebanon, we tried to interview Bedouin groups as they passed through various parts of the country. However, often we just did not have the time or budget to chase down different groups to get a representative sample. So many of the surveys had a distinctly masculine bias and captured the ideas of a given dominant group.

Were There Times Where All This Went Astray? What Did You Try? Did It Work?

Definitely, oh yeah, quite a few times. I was put at risk, my colleagues were put at risk and so were participants. We were working in insecure, post-conflict countries travelling a long way from hospitals or medical help in many instances. These risks to life and person also 'threatened' the way knowledge was collected and used.

When you're embedded in a situation, you just seem to keep plodding along, and constantly trying to get things to work. And there was a lot of pressure on you to do that. There were lots of little things that make up a daily routine that are hard to explain to someone who has not lived in an insecure environment.

In Kurdistan (northern Iraq), the capital city, Erbil, was our operating base. I did not sleep in the same location as my Kurdish colleagues but was placed in another location so that I did not draw any unwanted attention to the Kurdish survey teams. Out in the field, I usually slept in a demining INGO house, with high walls, armed guards and mega security. In Erbil, I stayed in the "international compound", which was a walled section of the Christian sector taken over by the international community. This compound had high walls, 24/7 armed guards and a checkpoint to enter and leave. Everyone was armed, everyone seemed to have war junk, mostly small arms that had been pilfered dropped by the Iraqi Army as they fled. As lots of people did not know how to use guns, some of the risk came from the expats inside the compound. There were signs all around the compound that said, "In case of an attack, please do not shoot the guards". We had regular radio checks and could call for help if someone came over the wall. Fortunately, I never had to call for help while I was staying in Erbil compound.

These kinds of security protocols were also common in countries such as Chad and the DRC. There was a lot of debate in Iraq about security, some organisations followed mainstream security protocols: travel in convoys, maintain a distance of 30 metres between cars, wear flak jackets and helmets, travel with armed guards. Many INGOs thought this just drew a big target on you, they travelled under the radar, drove local rented cars and dressed like locals (no quasi military outfits or journalist vests). I did this most of the time as I could 'pass' as a Kurdish woman (if I kept my mouth shut): green eyes, short, lots of clothing, sat in the back with the other women. I did get into trouble, not from insurgents, but from USAID (our donors!) because I 'disappeared' without telling them where I was. I had travelled under the radar, going to visit another INGO working in humanitarian mine action. There were urgent radio messages demanding where I was and what I was doing.

After that, they demanded I follow their security protocols if I was working on the project, but I still used to sneak out and visit my Kurdish colleagues' homes for dinner and meet their families. Best experience ever! And I believe this built relationships with the teams that could not be achieved sitting at home by myself safely walled off in a compound. It was relationships like that that would save your life, not all the armed guards and high walls. It was local people who would protect you, warn you of an attack if you had built that connection of course. I also always made sure I ate with the teams in the field. Kurds are really generous people, I never paid for one single meal in Kurdistan, so I always bought sodas for them at night to have with dinner. They really appreciated this. Fortunately, nothing really bad happened to me in northern Iraq although we did have some close calls and potentially bad moments.

In Lebanon, so many things kept sending the project astray. First, there was so much politicking involved in the set up and running of the survey, I considered closing the whole thing down. Politically motivated local NGOs were constantly trying to influence the way the survey was being run so that it suited their interests, tell us who to recruit (their political affiliates) and what villages we would survey (their villages). In addition, there was also a low-level risk being in a country that vacillated between sociable and friendly to sudden (or so they seemed to people like me) acts of intermittent violence. Being an expat means you don't have the local knowledge to know when things are simmering away and then ready to explode. There were several car bombs (targeted assassinations really) that took place while I was in-country, for example. Both times I worked there, Israel had just withdrawn troops, the country, its physical infrastructure, its people and its social contract were all shattered. We had to be aware of security, not to the same degree as Iraq, but still needed to be aware.

It was in Lebanon that I was detained by one of the local political groups who wanted to convince me of the need to do as they said.

Can You Tell Us About That?

So, I walked into what I thought was an ordinary meeting with local political actors, I was doing these kinds of meetings on a daily basis. It was in the South of the country, the room was an average office space for Lebanon: large ornate desk with a bright red vinyl lounge, armchairs and coffee table in front of it for meetings. I was seated on the lounge, my two 'abductors' sat opposite me. They had pushed my colleagues outside and locked the doors. I could hear my co-workers banging on the door and shouting in Arabic to be let in. They then started to harangue me about the greatness of their political party and the glories of their leader (it was not Hezbollah, by the way). They also told me I had to recruit the people they sent me, that they had a kind of deal with their followers that they would find work for them.

This went on for 15 minutes, maybe half an hour, they kept repeating the same information. I would respond with things such as, "I want to include as many people from as many communities as possible, we are working so that we can have mixed teams so that we can work in different communities, we have an agreement with the army that our project would work with all communities and include all political parties, etc., etc." Eventually, somehow, my colleagues burst through the door, shouting and arguing with the two men. My colleagues grabbed me and bustled me out of the room, with a lot of Arabic expletives and fist shaking. We found out later that these two men were called up in front of the party leader and given a thorough dressing down for doing this.

The other thing about this incident was how strangely calm I was, emotionless even, during this whole incident. It was like everything became very clear and sharp. I can distinctly remember the look and feel of that sofa, the feel of the vinyl, how firm it was to sit on and the shape of those red buttons. Even now, talking about it makes my heart beat faster thinking about how easily this situation, given the history of the conflict in Lebanon, could have turned bad for me if my colleagues had not managed to break into the room.

We did not have many problems with this group after this. The time we had spent building a relationship with the defence ministry paid off, although we were also lucky because we were working with a really amenable and smart counterpart. He did not take sides but tried to work things out in a fair and reasonable way.

I also experienced bad things happening to other people, not really terrible, but outside my experience anyway. On the border between the Congo and Zambia to the South-east of Pweto, I was waiting with the two Zimbabwean medics working on our team. We had medics because there was little medical support in the area where we were working. There was a small team from Médecins Sans Frontiéres working at the very run-down district hospital in Pweto, but this was a day's travel from the clearance teams. Anyway, I was waiting to get across the border, and our car had broken down. The driver had gone off to get help back at our compound.

We were standing there next to the car, waiting when we heard the sound of a baton being used to beat someone in the customs office. We could hear several 'whap' sounds followed by screams. So, we debated what to do. If we went in, we were putting ourselves at risk. If we didn't go in, he could be beaten to death or seriously injured. We decided not to go in, and just waited to see what happened next with the thought that since they were medics, we might be able to help if he made it out alive. Eventually, he did come out—he was stumbling along, and you could see he was in a lot of pain, but he was able to walk away. We watched him walk off, it was good to see he would survive at least. But there was nothing we could do about it as it would have put our lives at risk also. It wasn't always the insurgents who were the problem, the military in some countries could be particularly nasty.

What About Risk to Your Colleagues?

There were also real risks for our local colleagues. I consider myself a very risk averse person, especially compared with some of my co-workers overseas. I'm very big on duty of care to staff. Some people were not. Expats also seemed to think that shouting at people made them work harder, go faster or take more risks. I can remember one time one expat shouting at our local colleagues that they were "a bunch of girls' blouses" because they were completely confused by his instructions. The translator actually looked at me and shrugged to say, what does that mean? I had to explain it to him but in much politer terms and he was able to tell the team what to do. I also tried to pull people in from the field as soon as I thought they might be in danger. In northern Iraq, there was a bombardment of a US army base, which was right near our field office. I pulled the field teams back to our compound in Erbil. I was already a little paranoid since we were working for an American INGO and were considered a potential target for insurgents.

Anyway, I shut down fieldwork for a few days, insisting the field teams stay in Erbil until it was safe to return. The country director was unavailable when I tried to call him, so I did this through our office in Washington who agreed that the teams be pulled out. The country director was not of the same opinion and I received a bit of a rebuke for doing this. The field teams were very happy and thanked me for taking care of them and thinking of their safety.

We had similar issues in Chad around security, in the North of Chad especially, around the Tibesti region. All that northern area was unstable because there were lots of rebel groups still operating up there as well as in the east of the country. We had a radio system in Chad, each car fitted with radios and a full-time radio operator in N'djamena who did twice daily radio checks. In Chad, our radio code for a security issue was to say, 'it's snowing'. The team in the North had to leave areas quite a few times because of 'snow falling', the team evacuating to the district capital.

There was also the issue of different perceptions between expats and local colleagues. I usually relied very much on the field teams' judgement, but a few times I overrode them and said, "you're not doing it, I can't let you – I'm the manager – I just can't. If you walk into that minefield, which in Lebanon they wanted to do, and you blow yourself up – I know you think you think it's okay, but nope we're not doing it". Of course, the team later went back and walked through the minefield without my permission. Fortunately, they didn't blow themselves up. My sense at the time was that we were following a dodgy local informant who is saying "yeah, don't worry – there used to be a minefield here, but we can walk through it – it's not a problem I've done it many times" and my Lebanese colleagues were going, "yeah, yeah".

People became used to the risk, they were used to moving about in spaces polluted by landmines or bombs. I was not. A lot of my colleagues had grown up with war, some even told me they had played with small bombs as kids, were used to picking them up and moving them. So, we also had to deal with these differences as well. This can be hard since you want to get the job done and trust your colleagues but as a manager you had to have a strong sense of duty of care for your staff, even if they didn't always have it for themselves. It was my responsibility and if anything went wrong, it would be me who was primarily at fault.

All this affected our ability to get information and the way we gathered it. In every country, there were zones too dangerous to enter (usually because of security or military operations) and these communities were not surveyed. But there were other risks to knowledge creation such as the instances I knew about where data collectors were completing questionnaires at the base camp rather than in the community interview. This was more common in those cases where they had missed some information on the questionnaire and did not want to travel back to the village to get the answers to just one or two questions.

When a village leader called a meeting with his mates, many data collectors could not challenge the community leadership about this. This is understandable as village leaders were quite powerful in their own right and it would have been difficult for our data collectors to say something to them. Even when we sent our field supervisors back in to set up a meeting with women, say, this was not always successful especially since in many countries landmines and UXO were not considered 'women's business'. The example I gave before about the children in Laos was because the men did not even think of asking a woman to join the meeting as they would not know about bombs or the war, that was 'men's business'.

Another consideration was that communities did not always agree with each other on issues raised in interviews. In one community in Lebanon, the different political factions in attendance at a community meeting started arguing about what happened during the war. Some of the men started to push and punch each other and we had to stop the interview. You must remember this was a country that had had one of the most vicious civil wars of the twentieth century. People were shot when stopped at roadblocks, for example, just for having an identity card from the 'wrong' sect or political group. We really wanted some information from this village, so we returned to the interview with a couple of army officers in tow who were there to moderate. The meeting went much more smoothly but this, of course, most likely skewed the interview process with community members now not as able to freely speak and express their opinions. We would not have been able to collect any information if we had let the first interview continue as it was, and we would also have placed our field teams in danger if we had let it continue as it was.

This Must Have Been Really Stressful. What Strategies Did You Develop Day to Day to Take Care of Yourself, to Reduce That Stress?

The job was pretty stressful, we worked most weekends and late into the evening to get things done. In some countries, we were on call to deal with emergencies or issues in the field that needed a decision. This obviously spilt over into our personal lives. People coped with this stress in several ways. My most healthy option was exercise but in countries like Chad, Iraq or the DRC, I could not even go outside for a walk. Laps of the compound were one option. I also took along a suspension trainer, yoga and exercise DVDs for countries where I could not go outside to walk or ride a bike because of security concerns. I would do yoga in my living room or use my suspension trainer or one of the exercise DVDs to try to stop myself going crazy. I also took along a portable hard drive with movies to entertain myself.

A lot of us coped, of course, by socialising, drinking and having lots of random sex. The social life was strangely intense overseas, and I really miss it in some ways. Of course, it was easier for men to go out, drink and meet women, or men even. Much harder if you were a woman, you had to be especially careful because even in relatively 'open' countries like Vietnam or Laos. Social morés for women were much more restrictive in every country I worked in. It was a bit different for white foreign women, of course. One of the expat Red Cross women working in Laos said, and I agree, that expat women were treated like "token men". My social scene was usually a bunch of single people working on aid projects, with INGOs, at the UN or embassies. Although places like Laos and Vietnam, being relatively secure, had some families, they tended to hang out together. But having a social life, not just working, slogging away in the office, was very important to destress. I must say I had a great time drinking and dancing in the gay bars of Vientiane and Hanoi.

In general, though, I think the most important is to be what they call 'situationally aware', be aware of your surroundings, be cautious when travelling, know what's 'normal' in your neighbourhood and what's not, know where you'll go to, if there's a problem. Err on the side of caution.

I worked in a highly militarised sector, and there was a lot of bravado and a masculinised ethic of downplaying risk. In Iraq, some of the expats were armed, there was quite a gun culture prevalent there, which I had not seen in other countries. Having a different perception of risk was also very gendered. In the DRC, my male expat colleagues were convinced there were no problems with security. I tried to walk home from town one day by myself and immediately had local people staring, commenting loudly, laughing and making aggressive gestures at me. I started to freak out a bit but my male colleagues, who I had left drinking in the local bar, the only one in town, had felt guilty and drove up and took me back to the compound. I had asked about security when I arrived and was laughed at, "the only thing the locals would want to do with a white person would be to eat them". A bit of racism thrown in there for good measure.

You got paid-out about being too cautious, most of my expat colleagues were ex-military and those that weren't had a 'wannabe' attitude of trying to out tough the tough guys. But no-one died or was seriously injured on any of my surveys. We had some stupid accidents like the time a field team that did not secure their machete properly, then rolled the car, and the machete flew through the air slicing into them, but they weren't seriously injured. Alway secure the machete.

I maintained standard security stuff even if the rest of the team did not. In some countries, I varied my route to and from work, changed my routines, so it is more difficult to predict where I'd be the next day at the same time. I kept up to date with security alerts and incidents. In countries like Iraq there were multiple incidents on a daily basis and warnings out about avoiding things like parked cars or suspicious items next to the road in case they were hiding improvised explosive devices (IEDs). One thing we were also supposed to do was avoid US military convoys since they were known to shoot at cars that got too close. But if you got tangled up in a traffic jam with one, it was almost impossible to get away from them. One of my strongest memories from Iraq, was being trapped in a traffic jam, only several metres from armoured vehicles with scared looking young soldiers sweating away under helmets, flak jackets and aiming mounted machine guns at the crowd.

I also asked colleagues about what was happening and what to do. My colleagues were always ready to give tips on how to deal with snipers and other things. In Lebanon, they were the ones who suggested I stop taking my usual short cut from work to my apartment as it was down a narrow lane and it was too easy for me to be ambushed.

A lot of these strategies also depended on the country. I travelled with my car doors locked in countries like Chad or the Congo, where people were dragged out of their cars, mugged and their cars stolen, especially in the Kinshasa and Lubumbashi. The idea was that you did not stop for anything especially in the evenings when there were very few people around. You drove straight through red lights if possible, slowing down for things like people or goats but never stop. In insecure countries, I tried to be home before dark, which was very hard, because we always worked long hours and were under incredible pressure to stick to timelines and budgets. So, working until 10 o'clock at night wasn't unusual for us, so we worked a lot from home. Working on weekends also wasn't unusual. All offices and homes had guards, often armed, and in some countries twice daily radio checks. If you didn't respond, the UN or your organisation would send someone around to see where you were. So, if you forgot your radio or had it turned off, you were possibly putting someone from your team at risk.

You Mentioned You Worked Without Ethical Approval of Any Kind? How Did This Work and What Do You Think of the Transition to University Ethical Processes?

INGOs at the time often did not have written ethics for data collection. Even so, I always tried to be ethical in my approach to research, most importantly protecting the people giving us information in the surveys, but also protecting my team. In the field, I would emphasise respect for our survey participants, that people could decide not to talk to us and that you could not bully people to participate. Information in these contexts was not seen as neutral, information was highly prized during war time and knowing about what your enemy was doing was very important. That meant that people could be hostile and suspicious of us especially as we worked for organisations that local people associated with their enemies or with a government that they distrusted or feared. If I'd lived through these wars, I wouldn't want to give information to my kind of people either.

Having ethics was difficult at times as none of the INGOs at the time had ethics as part of their survey protocols. When I could, I put these into the survey methods, but I could not always do this because there was resistance from other staff members, both expat and local. Most expats seemed to arrogantly think that communities had to talk to us, the project was supposed to help these people after all!

For local staff, it was different, most of them had not thought about ethics. In Lebanon, we had a discussion with the field teams who wanted to interview former members of the Israeli-allied militia, the South

Lebanon Army (SLA), who were seen as collaborators and widely hated. My Lebanese colleagues argued that ex-SLA would have information about the location of landmines and UXO that no-one else did and that we should find them and get them to talk to us. I decided that we needed to talk this through, so I called a meeting of all project staff and we discussed and debated for more than an hour. Eventually, most of them could see that we would be endangering these people by identifying them although I don't think I convinced everyone. I think it was easier because a lot of our staff were university trained, so arguing for ethics was easy in this environment. In other countries, where I wasn't the head honcha, we did not really have this kind of principle and there was little discussion of the ethics of what we were doing. It was assumed that people should and would participate and that we did not have to obtain permission, imposing ourselves on them really.

By contrast, I just completed a National Health and Medical Research Council (NHMRC) ethics application and it is long, repetitive, and has so much detail that it took me weeks to complete. After I completed the first draft, it went for review and we went through four iterations of the application, each time something different was demanded of us from the ethics committee. It was an incredibly tedious and time consuming process and quite incredible compared to what I was doing before. We spent the first six months of our current project getting the ethics right, which had such big implications for our research budget and timeline.

This could not happen in international development or humanitarian action, there was no allowance in our budgets for a six month ethics process. I do know that some INGO staff did pretty dodgy things in the field. Their need for information was more important than the person that they're talking to and whose information they are taking and using. I remember interviewing a former soldier in Laos, who talked about the intensity of aerial bombardment over Xieng Khouang, how the ground shook from the bombs, how planes came over the mountains in formations drop bomb after bomb, how people fled and hid in caves up in the mountains. When I mentioned this to one of my expat colleagues, he scoffed at what this man said, "Ah, you can't believe these people, these old soldiers like to exaggerate, this was the best time of their lives. I know for a fact that the US did not do that kind of intensive bombing in Laos".

The foreign expert always knew more than the person who had lived through the war.

The least sensitive method of information gathering I encountered overseas was that done by US teams in Laos trying to find the bodies of missing soldiers from the war. They literally flew into villages in helicopters, then they would jump out and start to interrogate anyone who would speak to them. One of the village chiefs who had suffered through one of these fly-in, fly-out visits told us that not one villager told them anything. And the villagers knew of the location of at least one downed US plane, which they had stripped for metal and which had had some remains in it. There was no way they would tell these Americans, the visit brought up too many bad memories from the war. They felt very disrespected by these guys. They made us promise never to say which village they were or where it was in Laos, they didn't want the Americans to know. And I never have.

What Would You Tell People Going into These Places, What Would a Key Lesson Be?

I suggest that people working in other countries start somewhere where you don't have to worry about roadblocks, violence, or security. That is, places where you do not have to continually worry about risks to yourself, your colleagues or the people you are interviewing. Start somewhere where you're not faced with having to tie up your research with concerns about anyone's security. Somewhere you learn the basics without having to worry about things like, well, people shooting at you, IEDs or landmines.

Start somewhere where the context and the culture are friendly, especially for women. I think as a woman it is very important to choose a country where you can work and live without too much hassle. And if you are gender and sexuality diverse, also take a lot of care which country you go to. Again, I found that some countries people do not care. In Vietnam, for example, my government counterparts knew that I shared a house with two women, one expat one Vietnamese, who were in a relationship. They even mentioned it in a meeting but were not concerned. So, think about that.

This also raises the issue of surveillance—be prepared for your host government to follow you around, to check you out and know details of what you are doing, even during your free time. In Beirut, the expat team decided to go out one night to a famous gay bar that was supposed to be hip and happening. We drove there in our work car, parking out front. It turned out to be a dud because we were there too early and too tired to wait around. The Lebanese don't start to party until at least 10pm. I was called into the ministry office the next day to say that the registration plate on our car had been written down as being at the bar and that we were never to go there again. If we wanted to go out, go somewhere respectable like the Beirut casino! I never went to the casino, but we were all more careful about what we did and where we went. And Lebanon is considered one of the more liberal, open-minded countries in the middle east.

Choose your first country carefully. Laos was a great place, I was very lucky I started in Laos. People in Laos were really open to women working in professional roles (or at least white expat women). I think it taught me so many things, especially in terms of how people see the world differently from me. It was really life changing. As my first country, I often laughed at my own misconceptions and the way people challenged my presumptions about everything. They'd say something and I'd be like "Oh wow", I'd think, "Of course, you don't see it my way, why should you?"

Don't accept things at face value. Don't just listen only to expats because they have a very distorted, narrow point of view. Talk to lots of different local and international people and hang out with local people just as much as possible. Talk to as many people as possible because everyone has a different experience and take on things. Talk to your co-workers, respect your colleagues and their lived experiences, they are certainly different from yours, but this doesn't mean they are lesser. Talk to women, both expat and local women, not just men as I have found that men do not get how different it is to be a woman in any given country. They miss the subtle cultural mores and differences that can have a real impact on what and how you do things. I think be polite and respectful but keep a certain distance, be strong on certain issues that could compromise you. My favourite comeback when a married man asked me out was, "That would be wonderful, I would love to meet your wife and children".

Be person centred, not always task oriented. Be prepared to work 10 and 12 hour a day. Working with difficult people, even people you do not like is very common, whose politics and philosophies are so different from yours. Our main counterpart in the Congo, for example, I called him the 'genocidal general', was the head of the armed forces in the region. He came to dinner once at our compound and I actually sat opposite him and two of his wives. I was politely distant, made small talk but was fortunately rescued by a colleague asking me to dance. That was a good save! I think that these people, even as much as we dislike them and their actions, are interesting to talk to because we rarely get to meet people like this.

Essentially, play the role of the naïve but interested outsider, try not to let your preconceptions limit your work too much. Get the information because you just don't often get many chances to talk to someone accused of genocide. As one of my Lebanese colleagues said during our meeting about interviewing the South Lebanese Army: 'if you want to know about evil you don't ask a saint, you ask the devil'.

11

Sharing Stories

Phillip Wadds, Nicholas Apoifis, Susanne Schmeidl, and Kim Spurway

To finish this collection, we want to pull back the curtain on this whole process, the journey of this book. We want to tell you what *we* have learnt in producing this book about 'risk' in the social sciences. The chapters are there for all of us to access as we see fit, to filter through our own realities, and to mine for wisdoms that are relevant to our research and work. And so, here, we want to talk about what happened 'behind the scenes'; the chats before and after the interviews, the frantic emails in post-production concerning redaction of sensitive information, and the many discussions of ethics, all of which arose *around* the book's creation.

P. Wadds (✉) • N. Apoifis • S. Schmeidl
School of Social Sciences, University of New South Wales,
Sydney, NSW, Australia
e-mail: p.wadds@unsw.edu.au; n.apoifis@unsw.edu.au;
s.schmeidl@unsw.edu.au

K. Spurway
Institute for Culture and Society, Western Sydney University,
Sydney, NSW, Australia
e-mail: k.spurway@westernsydney.edu.au

For one, some of our contributors struggled to write these stories colloquially and with emotion, as we had asked them to. It's not easy. We have been disciplined by our disciplines. The way we write is usually constrained by academic formality and convention. The form and function of our stories are often homogenised and sanitised to conform to the requirements of publication. We have to follow rules: the methods section here, the limitations section there. And we are coached to follow these rules. The systems we work in revere and reward this, the neo-liberal university machine demands it. We are paid to publish in prescribed lists of journals, ranked not by their creativity or innovation, but for their *prestige* and impact factor.

But what are we producing? Our work can be inaccessible, hidden behind dense language and prose. Our participants can be reduced to single, 'punchy', quoted lines. Our emotions and our experiences are routinely sidelined altogether: they don't belong in these expected forms of academic communication.

And when we are asked to produce research differently, it's hard. We saw this. Some of our contributors needed constant encouragement to let go, to produce writing that was candid, raw and vulnerable. But when they did let go, we received written work that was lucid, enticing and inviting, which spoke to nuanced human encounters.

As interviewers, we also found it tough to get our colleagues to speak freely during our recorded exchanges. This was surprising. We suspected our familiarity with them and their work would lead to *easier* conversations. Perhaps part of this difficulty related to workplace power relationships—we were junior to some contributors, and more senior to others—but we aren't so sure about that. We actually think it is that we are not encouraged to speak like this about risk and the difficulties of fieldwork, and certainly not for the purposes of publication.

We had to push for the intimate details, to hear of the lived encounters and emotional reactions to risk and the field. Our contributors initially had stock responses: intellectual for sure, theoretically complex, but mechanical, learnt through years of crafting formal academic responses. But once they overcame these blocks, the stories were amazing. It was in these moments that we were excited about the potential of this book. It's not that we thought our colleagues were being deliberately defensive, we instead believe they had normalised their behaviours regarding risk. It needed seasoned fieldworkers to help draw these stories out.

It was in these moments that we also learnt of the emotional toll of doing fieldwork. It was evident that we all took these stories home with us. One of our contributors broke down during the interview, and many were left emotionally drained by the process. You could see the physical effect that recounting stories of risk had. Some needed debriefing, while others wanted a stiff drink.

And then there was *all* the talk about ethics and the university. So much talk about protocols, bureaucracy and the institutional struggles of doing engaged (risky) fieldwork.

Either before, during or after every interview, we shared frustrations about ethics approval processes. We heard about absurd rejections and onerous expectations. We shared stories about ridiculous rejoinders from committees, like being requested to wear high-visibility university badged t-shirts during 'covert' observations, or demanding a foreign government's written letter of support for research that was to be conducted alongside hostile dissident groups within their borders. Across our disciplines and field locations, a pervasive sentiment was shared: that embodied field research coming out of universities is under threat.

A common concern was that institutional ethics processes seem to be dominated by people from the medical or natural sciences, people who do not seem to understand what we as social scientists are doing. They seek a level of certainty that can never be fully known in the context of the field. They regularly assume a set of linear and fixed futures, viewing social research settings as akin to laboratories where 'control' rests at the very core of research validity and value (Halse and Honey 2007). They demand we individualise research subjects, expecting consent or endorsement from every person involved in a fieldwork space—a near impossibility in ethnographic and field encounters where we observe group culture and interactions (Delamont and Atkinson 2018). This biomedical model is almost always incapable of dealing with the iterative, emergent and complex nature of field research.

It's hard to get through these formal ethics procedures. Often we fight, rarely we win, and sometimes we are forced to concede. It can be physically and emotionally exhausting. But it's always trying.

And when we do get ethics approval, there are other barriers. Universities have multiple layers of red tape that constrain and even prohibit the kind of fieldwork described in this book. We heard stories about colleagues having ethics approved only for university risk assessors to deny travel based on their (mis)understandings of 'danger'. The frustration is that many of us have been in these settings before and are far more competent to make that call. When it comes to *these* decisions, the contemporary neo-liberal university is, at its core, risk averse.

But our research is important to us, it is a key part of what inspires us to go to work every day, so we battle on.

This discussion is not seeking to downplay the importance of ethics. Quite the opposite. For those who contributed to this book, an ethics of practice is indispensable. We all believe in taking a strong, ethical approach to research. The experience of writing and editing this collection illustrates perfectly how seriously we take this commitment. Almost every author censored, edited or withdrew text from their chapters after the interview and before publication. Our contributors agonised over the details of their stories. Because we all care about the impact of our words.

We received emails from our contributors expressing their unease. We spoke at length about the continuing emotional labour of disseminating work and publishing fieldwork. Again, an almost universal concern highlighted the anxiety this can produce. We worry. We worry about who will read our work and who might take exception to it, even years or decades after the research is done. Is everything and everyone de-identified? It's these questions and thoughts that keep many of us up at night and demonstrate the level of dedication that good ethical practice in field research requires. To do anything less would be to totally disrespect our collaborators, participants and interviewees. Clearly, risk and ethics are deeply intertwined. And that's one of the many reasons we think this book is so important.

It is part of a collective effort to reconceive how we view research and storytelling. Our stories are frank. They speak of mistakes, danger, risks and rewards. Importantly, they speak of learning. They show that constant reflection and refinement is part of a commitment to good research. Our research settings change all the time, and so we need to adapt our thinking. We need to be honest about the vulnerabilities that come with research, vulnerabilities that make fieldwork an exciting endeavour, but also an inherently risky one.

We need to do this because we need fieldwork. We need it more than ever. In an age increasingly dominated by hard science and big data, field research is more important than ever. The vivid and powerful accounts captured through field and ethnographic research are vital to academic enquiry. Sharing these stories is part of a commitment to effect change on the world, to ameliorate hardships, and to increase our understanding of the lives of our participants. They provide a facility through which observation can move beyond superficial or distanced accounts of human behaviours and interactions and explore elements that can often be neglected in less intensive analyses. Fieldwork helps to critically balance and juxtapose rival claims, giving voice to the lived experience of complex social and cultural systems. It illuminates power, it highlights disadvantage, and provides checks on official claims regarding a range of social issues.

It is our hope that this collection of stories enables students and researchers at all stages of their careers to better navigate the risky, dangerous, but ultimately rewarding journey of researching in the field.

References

Delamont, S., & Atkinson, P. (2018). The Ethics of Ethnography. In R. Iphofen & M. Tolich (Eds.), *The Sage Handbook of Qualitative Research Ethics* (pp. 119–132). London: Sage.

Halse, C., & Honey, A. (2007). Rethinking Ethics Review as Institutional Discourse. *Qualitative Inquiry, 13*(3), 336–352.

Index

A

Access, 2, 15, 16, 18–20, 25–27, 33, 52, 63, 64, 66–74, 97, 98, 108–112, 124, 139, 150, 155, 160, 167–169, 184, 185, 196, 215

C

Consent, 13, 20, 29, 46, 77, 78, 109–111, 131, 156, 179, 217
Co-production, 8
Culture, 5, 16, 32, 54, 62, 66, 67, 73, 74, 83, 88, 92, 108, 150, 160, 164, 170, 173, 178, 183, 184, 208, 212, 217
Customs, ix, 5, 83

D

Danger, 3, 4, 20, 41, 63, 87–89, 95, 113, 122, 123, 149, 205, 207, 218
Dissemination, 5, 8, 31, 58, 108, 121, 127, 134, 138–139

E

Ethics
  ethics committees, ix, 4, 30, 44, 56, 57, 77, 82, 98, 103, 131, 211
  ethics of practice, 77, 185, 218
  institutional/university, ix, 4, 30, 43, 56–57, 75, 77, 82, 98, 116, 117, 210–212, 217

F

Familiarity, 5, 69, 79, 216
Family, 3, 25, 39, 41, 46, 47, 49, 64, 81, 89, 94, 103, 105, 140–141, 155, 172, 176, 183, 184, 197, 202, 208
Fear, 1, 23, 51, 59, 61–83, 88–90, 117, 122, 123, 149, 169, 171
Field notes, 44, 64, 115, 116, 119

G

Gender, vi, 6, 8, 13, 14, 34, 41, 47, 52, 53, 123, 124, 129–131, 133, 135, 136, 141, 143, 144, 159, 164, 173, 184, 212

I

Interview(s), 5–7, 9, 18–20, 22, 25–27, 39, 42, 53, 55–59, 62–64, 68, 72, 74–78, 80–82, 90, 92, 94–98, 100–103, 107, 111, 114–117, 123, 129–145, 148, 151, 155, 164–170, 172, 173, 178, 179, 185, 191, 194, 196, 197, 199–200, 206, 207, 210, 215, 217, 218

L

Language, 5, 6, 27, 28, 42, 43, 45, 46, 69, 74, 83, 101, 102, 112, 136, 152, 157, 167, 175, 184–186, 194–195, 216

M

Masculinity, 103, 124, 147
Mitigation, 127

N

Naïvety, 75
Narrative, v, ix, 2–4, 6, 7, 26, 43, 48–51, 82, 89, 116, 121, 123, 124, 127, 143, 148, 152, 153, 159, 182, 183

O

Observations, 61, 62, 64, 68–70, 72, 80, 123, 129, 130, 135, 148, 157, 165, 173, 178, 186, 217, 219

P

Preparation, 79, 184
Privilege, v, vi, 2, 6, 27, 32, 35, 50, 144, 150, 160, 169, 184

R

Rapport, 5, 63, 64, 66
Risk, 112–114, 122, 123, 125–127
  mitigation, 173, 174, 176, 181, 184
  physical, ix, 3, 63, 74, 75, 87, 90, 94, 171, 201
  psychological, 3
  risk to knowledge, 105, 122, 149, 156, 179–183, 206

risk to others, 5, 58, 79–81, 88, 91, 99, 110, 112, 153, 177–179, 198, 201, 205, 210

risk to self, 88, 91, 110, 120, 149, 151, 155, 156, 160, 172, 176, 201, 204

S

Security, 9, 62–74, 66n2, 76–79, 81, 94, 95, 114, 117, 118, 165–168, 171, 173, 174, 177, 178, 180, 190, 193, 198, 201–203, 205–209, 212

Sexuality, 6, 13, 16, 30, 35, 212

Stories, vii, ix, x, 1–9, 13, 16, 32, 42–44, 46–54, 56, 64, 69, 72, 73, 81, 82, 91, 92, 96, 101, 104, 105, 108, 111–113, 115, 116, 119–127, 133, 136, 140, 145, 154, 164, 167, 169, 182, 183, 215–219

Storytelling, 15, 39, 72, 218

Strain
  moral, 5, 74, 183
  physical, 5
  psychological, 5, 101, 171, 172

T

Travel, 143, 175, 177, 179, 197, 199, 201, 204, 206, 218

U

Unpredictability, 63, 78, 80, 82

V

Vulnerability, viii, 9, 103, 147–160, 219

Printed by Printforce, United Kingdom